TECHNIQUES OF
FINANCIAL ANALYSIS

TECHNIQUES OF FINANCIAL ANALYSIS

ERICH A. HELFERT, D.B.A.

Assistant to the President
Crown Zellerbach Corporation
San Francisco, California

 1972

DOW JONES-IRWIN, INC.
Homewood, Illinois   60430

First Printing, March 1972

Library of Congress Catalog Card No. 72–77480

Printed in the United States of America

PREFACE

The purpose of this book is to provide the businessman, analyst, student, or other interested person with a concise reference collection of the more important tools and techniques of financial analysis, without delving into their broad theoretical and institutional backgrounds. In this sense the book is self-contained—an application-oriented survey of key concepts, with enough perspective to assist in understanding the setting and the reasons for use of the analytical techniques.

The book has evolved from a collection of what are known as "technical notes" on basic tools, concepts, and techniques made available to students in the MBA program at the Harvard Graduate School of Business Administration. These notes are designed as short briefings in financial analysis, supplementary to the broad reading matter assigned in the finance area. They equip the reader with the basic skills and knowledge required to analyze case problems and guide him toward more specialized sources of information should he desire to do further research on any topic.

Techniques of Financial Analysis places emphasis on viewing financial analysis as part of a system of management decisions, with stress on an integrated concept of investment, operations, and financing. Much of this emphasis is due to the rapid increase of financial modeling in the business world and the need to tailor the book to both the practitioner and the participant in management development programs.

The book maintains a straightforward and relatively uncomplicated approach to a basically complex subject. The key thrust is toward understanding the doable and practical—in a sense an "executive briefing"—and toward the building of a basic ability to grasp financial relationships. The book presupposes some familiarity with fundamental accounting and financial statement preparation.

I would like to express my appreciation to my former colleagues in the finance teaching group at the Harvard Business School, and to the administration of that institution—both under former Dean George P. Baker and under Dean Lawrence E. Fouraker—for the opportunity to develop and publish the original materials and for the suggestions and encouragement given me. My thanks also go to my colleagues, too numerous to mention, at universities here and abroad for their extensive application of the book and its concept, and for their many expressions of interest.

Finally, I would like to express my particular appreciation to the President and Chief Executive of Crown Zellerbach, Mr. C. R. Dahl, and to the former President, the late F. O. Boylon, for the opportunity to teach in the management development programs at this company, to which many of the materials and concepts have been applied.

February 1972   ERICH A. HELFERT

CONTENTS

INTRODUCTION

The financial manager, analyst, or student must, in his analytical efforts for planning or problem solving, rely on a variety of financial analysis techniques which help him answer questions of significance. This book provides such tools for use in understanding problems and opportunities of a financial nature, and contains practical examples on which to exercise the application of these skills.

A critical point should be made here: While the tools and concepts exposed in the ensuing chapters are explained and discussed in detail, they must not be viewed as ends in themselves. It is not enough to master the techniques! Financial analysis is a process which helps to answer questions properly posed; it is a *means* to an end. We cannot overemphasize the need to view financial analysis only as an aid in the process of planning for investment, operations, and financing by the manager, and in the process of valuation and projection by the prospective investor. In each situation an objective must be clearly stated before putting pencil to paper—otherwise, the exercise becomes idle "number-crunching." Some have referred to effective management as the "art of asking significant questions"; this is no less true of proper financial analysis, which, after all, is one aspect of corporate and financial management.

Perspective is also required in choosing the degree of refinement to which any financial (or other) analysis should be carried. The chapters in this book often present refinements of the methods of analysis, which should, however, be sparingly applied to areas of real significance only. Otherwise, the effort far outweighs the results in belaboring obvious answers or foregone conclusions.

In applying the tools presented, one should therefore consider the following points, before starting any analysis:

1. What precisely is the issue to be analyzed and resolved? Has the problem been clearly spelled out?
2. Which factors, relationships, and trends will likely be helpful in analyzing the problem at hand?
3. What ways can be found to get a quick "ball-park" estimate of a possible result?
4. How exact does the answer have to be, and how much effort should be expended in refining results?
5. How reliable are the data available to work with, and how is this likely to affect results?
6. What are the limitations of the tools themselves, and how is this likely to affect results?

Only after consideration of these issues should work proceed on the analysis and the tools be applied. We are here talking not only about good financial analysis, but about a rational approach to problem solving. And in the end, this is what management, research, and financial decisions are about.

CHAPTER

1

BUSINESS AS A SYSTEM
OF FUNDS FLOWS

The starting point of this chapter, and indeed the focus of the whole book, is the concept of a business operation as a series of resource deployments for profit, based on management decisions. Viewed in their broadest sense, these decisions involve the *investment* of resources, the *operation* of the business with the help of these resources, and the proper mix of *financing* to provide the resources. While business has infinite variety—manufacturing, trading, financial, and service institutions of large or small proportions and with different legal structures —there is the common theme of management: directed commitments of resources for the purpose of creating, over time, sufficient economic value to recover the resources and a margin of profit beyond. Over the long run, the result of this resource deployment should be a net improvement in the economic position of the owners—including the ability to make further resource commitments. If this is not the case, the economic viability of the business is in question.

The techniques developed in this chapter are designed to assist the student and practitioner in analyzing the pattern of resource deployments in a business over a given time period. The concept employed for the purpose is funds flow analysis, which is a way of expressing and displaying resource movements in monetary terms, based on the periodic accounting statements of financial condition and profit and loss. Along with other techniques developed later in this book, this analytical process will provide a basis for judging management effectiveness.

We are interested in funds flow analysis because it allows us to reconstruct from accounting statements—which are summaries of the transactions of the period—many important resource decisions made regarding investments, operations, and financing. It is a *comparative* process which identifies shifts in financial condition and the impact of operations, and sorts these into a framework of resource (funds) *uses* or applications, and resource (funds) *sources* or provisions. This decisional view of business operations provides additional insights beyond the mere balance sheet, which is a static "snapshot" of financial condition at a point in time, and the standard operating statement, which is a summary of revenue and expenses applicable to the period. For this reason the inclusion of a funds flow analysis statement has, in recent years, been made mandatory for the accounting reports of publicly traded companies to obtain a more dynamic picture of the basic decision process.

Funds flow analysis techniques rest heavily on an understanding of commonly accepted accounting methods, since accounting statements generally have to serve as the raw material for analysis. A thorough funds flow analysis can involve a variety of fairly complex adjustments, as the effect of accounting conventions is translated into funds movements. Once the basic concepts have been mastered, however, the complexities become only variations of the resource deployment theme. In fact, funds flow analysis is a more natural way of characterizing business operations and conditions than the standard accounting statements.

The chapter will contain a gradual buildup of complexities in funds flow analysis. We shall demonstrate the simple, generally applicable notions first and then develop complications which have to be considered largely because of the *timing* of funds decisions. Moreover, accounting conventions must be analyzed as to their effect on funds movements, since the objective of accounting reports is to achieve first and foremost the reporting of financial condition on a *given date,* and operating profits for a *period.* Finally, we shall discuss the interpretation of the results of funds flow analysis in an attempt to understand and judge the nature of the decisions made by management.

WHAT ARE FUNDS?

In the most basic sense, we think of funds as cash, since cash is the easiest form of expressing economic value and is readily convertible into good and services. A business operation normally involves a great number of cash transactions over a period of time, as wages are paid, machinery acquired, sales and revenues collected, etc. If a business were operated strictly on a cash basis, and some simple businesses are, it would be very easy to trace the key commitments and recoveries of cash over a time period. This cash flow pattern would present a picture of economic resource deployment.

Not all resources, however, are committed or obtained on the basis of cash transactions. This introduces a degree of complexity into our analysis. Management has the discretion to grant or obtain credit, and every time this discretion is exercised, an economic resource has been committed. Eventually, such transactions will result in cash changing hands, but in the meantime we cannot ignore the resource commitment. If a business grants trade credit to its customers, for example, its funds or resources are in effect used by someone else until repayment. If a business obtains trade credit from a supplier, someone else's funds or resources will in effect be employed in the company until repayment is required.

Furthermore, an imprudent management can overcommit an enterprise by taking on too many credit obligations, which represent other people's money, with no cash having changed hands. Examples would be obtaining merchandise on account, acquiring machinery on loans and notes, or trading a piece of land as part payment for a larger property with the difference due some period hence. It would be hard to deny that economic values have been shifted by these management decisions.

The concept of funds, therefore, should be broadly interpreted to cover all measurable resources including cash, and we shall use the term in this wider sense throughout the book. The point of view of the person analyzing funds will to some extent influence the precise meaning of the concept. The financial officer worrying about repayments of obligations will have a concept of funds very close to cash and current credit, while the operating executive being judged on return on investment will define as funds all the resources under his command. It should be clear, however, that cash is only one form of funds, and when referring to cash or cash items in their specific definitions, we shall employ the concept of "cash" or "liquid funds" throughout the book.

SIMPLIFIED VIEW OF A BUSINESS OPERATION

It may be best to illustrate the analysis by taking a very simplified example of a business and adding realism step by step. We shall employ the example of a man operating as a news vendor for the purpose. Our vendor initially is selling papers on the street corner, without a booth or any equipment. He has invested some of his savings in a working cash fund, which is the only investment required to operate.

Figure 1–1 shows the operation of this very simple business. Financing is provided by the owner in the form of $150 (A), shown as owner's equity and a working cash balance. During the day, $80 (B) of this working cash is spent to pay for newspapers, while revenues of $100 (C) are received. The profit or earnings from operations, $20 (Egs), in effect increases the working cash balance to a net of $170, and this increase is also reflected in owner's equity as earnings.

We have drawn a simple balance sheet at the beginning and at the end of the day, showing the effect of these transactions.

Figure 1–1

FUNDS FLOW DIAGRAM I

Cash Transactions Only

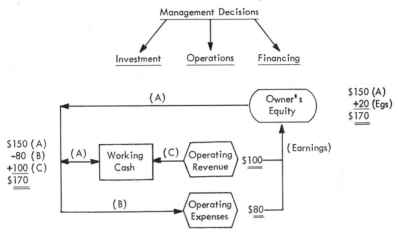

Balance Sheets

Assets	Beginning of Period	End of Period	Differences
Cash	$150	$170	+$20
Liabilities			
Owner's equity	$150	$150	–0–
Retained earnings	–0–	20	+$20
Total Liabilities	$150	$170	+$20

Operating Statement

	Period
Operating revenue	$100
Operating expenses	80
Earnings for Period	$ 20

Funds Flow Analysis

a) To start up the business:

    Use of Funds
        Cash balance established $150

    Source of Funds
        Owner's investment $150

Figure 1–1   (continued)

b) To operate the business for one period:

> *Use of Funds*
>   Increase in cash balance $20
> *Source of Funds*
>   Profit from operation (retained earnings) $20

It is clear that the day's operations have provided a $20 in-
crease in cash, and an offsetting increase of $20 in owner's
equity. This is the only difference between the two balance
sheets. The operating statement for the period reflects the
profit of $20.

We can now turn to funds flow analysis, but not before
defining our ground. In this instance it is possible to analyze
two distinct phases, the establishment of the business and the
operation of the business. This distinction does not have to be
made, but since we are interested in the effects of major decisions, it may be useful to establish the separation. The first
analysis, the establishment of the business, shows that our man
used $150 worth of cash to establish his working cash balance.
The *source* of these funds was his own private savings. The
second analysis spanning the day's operations shows that the
changes in the funds picture are a use of funds of $20, which
increased the working cash, and a source of funds of $20, which
is the profit from operations. As we shall see in later sections of
this chapter, the selection of time periods is a critical aspect of
funds flow analysis, since the impact of decisions we are trying
to picture may be obscured if too long a time period is chosen.

Several things become apparent from this simple illustration.
First of all, we find that funds flow analysis is very closely related to the normal decision-making process of the business.
In fact, one could carry the funds flow analysis to the extreme
and arrange every single transaction which took place during
the period in terms of sources and uses. This is unnecessary and
impractical for most purposes, since we should be satisfied to
reconstruct only the major resource decisions of the period.

Second, we find that funds flow analysis is very closely related to the accounting statements, the balance sheet and the income statement. As pointed out before, funds flow analysis focuses on the differences between periodic statements. While oversimplified here, the process is apparent.

Third, as already pointed out, it is important to recognize that funds flow analysis is related to a time span. We must choose the period over which funds movements are to be observed, and the analysis and judgments must be related to those time periods. In this simple case, the only question that comes to mind is the fact that $20 of funds has been committed to an increase in the cash balance. One might ask if it was reasonable to let this cash accumulate, or whether a different use for these funds might have been found by the owner.

Let us now introduce some complications in the form of delayed transactions. Figure 1–2 shows the operations of our news vendor on the following day, when he decided to sell some news magazines along with his papers. Since the magazines selected are weeklies, he can maintain an inventory for several days. Our vendor decided to invest an additional $250

Figure 1–2

FUNDS FLOW DIAGRAM II
Some Delayed Transactions

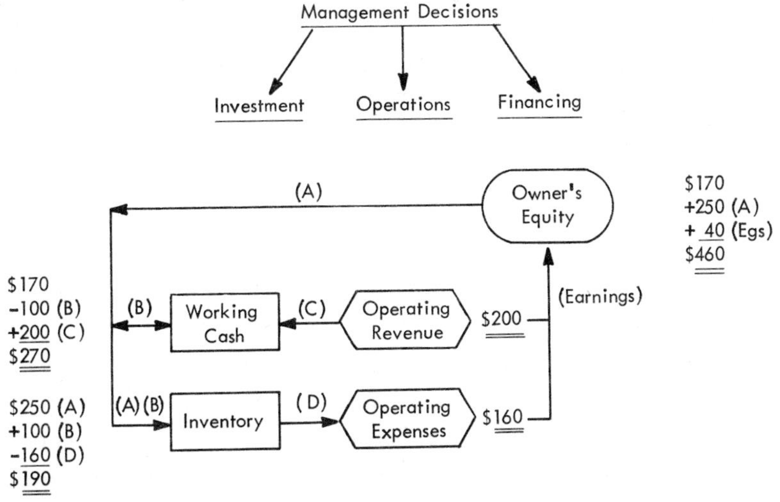

Figure 1–2   (continued)

Balance Sheets

Assets	Beginning of Period	End of Period	Differences
Cash	$170	$270	+$100
Inventory	–0–	190	+ 190
Total Assets	$170	$460	+$290

Liabilities			
Owner's equity	$150	$400	+$250
Retained earnings	20	60	+ 40
Total Liabilities	$170	$460	+$290

Operating Statement

	Period
Operating revenue	$200
Operating expense	160
Earnings for Period	$ 40

Funds Flow Analysis

Uses of Funds

Increase in cash balance	$100
Increase in inventory	190
Total Uses of Funds	$290

Sources of Funds

Additional owner's investment (increase)	$250
Profit from operations (retained earnings)	40
Total Sources of Funds	$290

(A) from his own savings to purchase a quantity of these magazines. He also buys the day's supply of newspapers of $100 (B) from his working cash, and the papers become part of his inventory. Sales for the day are $160 (D) worth (at cost) of magazines and papers, against which operating revenues of $200 (C) are taken in. The profit for the day is the difference of $40 (Egs), which shows up as earnings in owner's equity.

Balance sheets at the beginning and the end of the period show the differences in the accounts, while the income statement reflects the earnings of $40 for the period. Our funds flow analysis sorts out these differences: an increase in the cash balance of $100 and an increase in inventory of $190 are *uses* of the funds, while the *sources* are the additional owner's investment of $250 and the profit from operations. The main question which arises here is about the wisdom of the decision to provide additional ownership capital to increase both the cash balance and the inventory, and the potential risk of doing so.

Some long-term perspective is added in Figure 1–3, which reflects the operations of the ensuing period. Our vendor now invests an additional $450 (A) of his own savings to increase his inventory by an additional $400 and to prepay required licenses and taxes of $50 for his operation. Furthermore, he

Figure 1–3

FUNDS FLOW DIAGRAM III

Some Long-Term Perspective

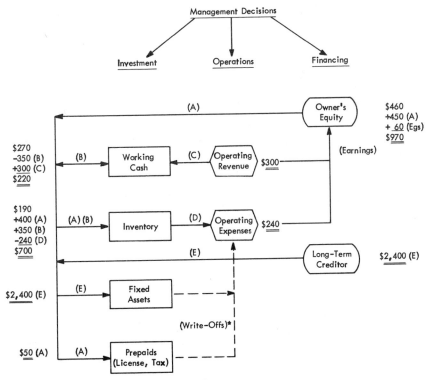

° Omitted for purposes of funds flow analysis.

Figure 1–3   (continued)

Balance Sheets

Assets	Beginning of Period	End of Period	Differences
Cash	$270	$ 220	−$ 50
Inventory	190	700	+ 510
Fixed assets	–0–	2,400	+ 2,400
Prepaids	–0–	50	+ 50
Total Assets	$460	$3,370	+$2,910
Liabilities			
Long-term liabilities	–0–	$2,400	+$2,400
Owner's equity	$400	850	+ 450
Retained earnings	60	120	+ 60
Total Liabilities	$460	$3,370	+$2,910

Operating Statement

	Period
Operating revenue	$300
Operating expense*	240
Earnings for Period	$ 60

* To be increased by amount of write-offs for *accounting* purposes.

Funds Flow Analysis

Uses of Funds

Increase in inventory	$ 510
Increase in fixed assets	2,400
Increase in prepaid expenses	50
Total Uses of Funds	$2,960

Sources of Funds

Deacrease in cash	$ 50
Increase in long-term debt	2,400
Additional owner's investment (increase)	450
Profit from operations (increase in retained earnings) ...	60
Total Sources of Funds	$2,960

decides to have a sheltered newsstand, and a friend and long-term creditor is providing him with the $2,400 (E) to elevate his operations to a more dignified level. Purchases of papers and magazines for the day amount to $350 (B) for inventory, while the value of the items sold is $240 (D). Due to higher sales of \$300 (C) the profit for the day rises to \$60 (Egs), reflected as earnings in owner's equity.

Our balance sheets and operating statements are becoming slightly more complicated, and the differences in balance sheets at the beginning and end of the period highlight the major funds decisions. The key funds use was, of course, the increase in fixed assets, which has come totally from debt sources. The additional owner's investment provided an increase in inventory, and the cash account has been reduced by \$50 for the first time. As we have more transactions and details to work with, our funds flow analysis begins to provide a basis for asking questions about the size and nature of the resource commitments, the sources which have provided them, and the wisdom of doing so in relation to risk, profitability, and business objectives.

One additional element has been introduced to this picture, the *write-offs* necessary to amortize the fixed assets and prepaid investments over time. From a resource deployment standpoint, the funds commitment was made when the fixed assets and prepaids were acquired. Accounting procedures require, however, that book entries be made to show the declining value over time. From a funds standpoint, these write-offs are not relevant, however, and we have therefore not introduced specifics at this time. The earnings of \$60 for the period are overstated from the accounting standpoint to the extent of any write-offs, but from a funds standpoint (cash flow) the \$60 is the appropriate figure. We shall have more to say on this point later.

The diagram of Figure 1–4 shows the introduction of *accounts receivable* and *trade creditors* in addition to the elements shown in the earlier examples. Our news vendor's business has now grown to such a size that it reflects the most common transactions we expect of the normal business operation. No additional ownership investments have been made in this period. In contrast, \$50 (A) of dividends was paid to our owner for the first time, a use shown as a reduction both in owner's equity and in

Figure 1–4

FUNDS FLOW DIAGRAM IV

Most Common Transactions

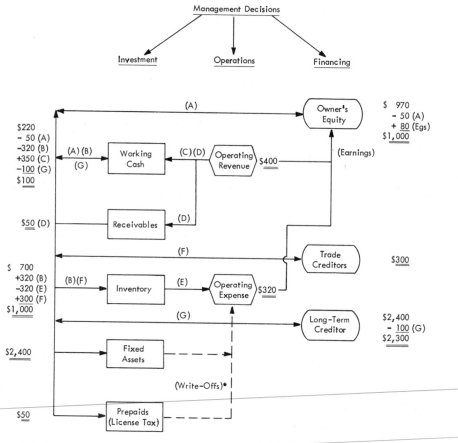

* Omitted for purposes of funds flow analysis.

Balance Sheets

Assets	Beginning of Period	End of Period	Differences
Cash	$ 220	100	−$120
Receivables	–0–	50	+ 50
Inventory	700	1,000	+ 300
Fixed assets	2,400	2,400	–0–
Prepaids	50	50	–0–
Total Assets	$3,370	$3,600	+$230

Figure 1–4 (continued)

Liabilities	Beginning of Period	End of Period	Differences
Accounts payable	$ –	$ 300	+$300
Long-term liabilities	2,400	2,300	– 100
Owner's equity	850	850	–
Retained earnings	120	150	+ 30
Total Liabilities	$3,370	$3,600	+$230

Operating Statement

	Period
Operating revenue	$400
Operating expense*	320
Earnings for Period	$ 80

* To be increased by amount of write-offs for *accounting* purposes.

Funds Flow Analysis

Uses of Funds

Increase in receivables	$ 50
Increase in inventory	300
Decrease in long term debt (repayment)	100
Total Uses of Funds	$450

Sources of Funds

Decrease in cash	$120
Increase in accounts payable	300
Increase in retained earnings*	30
Total Sources of Funds	$450

* This could be separated into its components: (a) use—dividend to owner, —$50, and (b) source—profit from operations, +$80.

working cash. Also, $100 (G) was used to begin repaying the long-term creditor. Some of the operating revenue of $400 was not received in cash, and is reflected as accounts receivable of $50 (D). The other $350 (C) has found its way into working cash. In the attempt to provide a wider assortment of magazines, our vendor has incurred trade credit of $300 (F), reflected as an increase in inventory of the same amount. The daily operating expense (cost of goods sold) has now risen to $320 (E), which leaves our vendor with a profit of $80 (Egs) for the day before any accounting write-offs.

From a funds standpoint, the picture is clear and fairly complete when we compare the balance sheets at the beginning and the end of the period. We find that most funds were used in this period for a further increase in receivables and inventory, a reflection of the growth of the business. Furthermore, funds of $100 were applied to reduce a long-term obligation. The sources for these activities were a sizable decrease in the cash account and a relatively minor increase in the owner's equity, since more than half of the profit of $80 (before write-offs) was paid out as a dividend to the owner. Trade credit of $300 was required to help support the increase in inventories.

By now it should be obvious that the process of funds flow analysis is nothing more than a sorting out, in resource terms, of the key decisions over a given period—as we said at the start of the chapter. With a little thought given to the differences in financial condition and the results of operations, a great number of significant questions can be asked about the nature of the management decisions and strategies observed. This will be discussed in more detail in later phases of this chapter, but the reader should recognize that the type of question analyzed is a *matching* of funds use and source decisions to see if these agree with the risks involved and the long-term character and plans of the business.

Having dealt with the very simple conditions of our news vendor, we can now turn to a generalized funds flow model, which shows the interrelationships of the key elements of corporate balance sheets and income statements and views them in terms of the investment, operations, and financing framework shown in the earlier illustrations. Figure 1–5 is such a generalized model, which shows current assets, fixed assets, and other assets on the investment side; the operations, separated into revenues and expenses; and the choices of financing represented by owner's equity, short-term creditors, and long-term creditors. The arrows interconnecting all these segments show the possible funds flows which can be brought about by management decisions. Also shown is the effect of accounting write-offs which are dictated by accounting decisions but are irrelevant for funds flow purposes.

Figure 1–5

GENERALIZED FUNDS FLOW MODEL

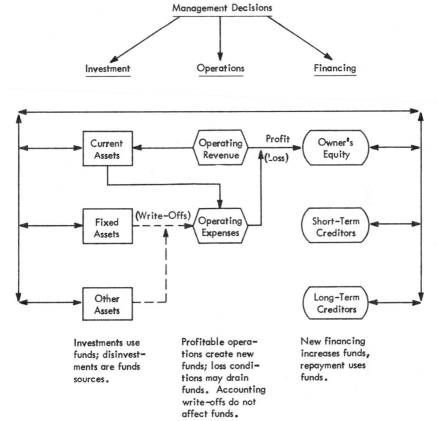

Rules for Funds Flow Analysis

Uses of Funds	*Sources of Funds*
Increase in asset	Increase in liability
Decrease in liability	Decrease in asset
Decrease in equity	Increase in equity
Loss from operations*	Profit from operations*

* Before accounting write-offs.

For a quick summary we have provided the general rules for funds flow analysis, which were used in the simple illustrations of this part of the chapter. Since we are essentially dealing with changes in balance sheet and profit and loss accounts, the rules for defining uses and sources can be simply broken down into increases and decreases of these accounts. For example, an increase in an asset account means a commitment of resources for that purpose, a use; while an increase in a liability reflects the inflow of "other people's" funds, a source. The opposite will be true in the case of decreases in assets and decreases in liabilities. Again, the question of accounting write-offs appears, but we will defer discussion of these to a later section of this chapter.

COMPLEXITIES OF REAL OPERATIONS

Having provided the basic concepts of funds flow analysis, we are now ready to turn to an example developed from the published statements of a major corporation. It is critical to remember that the process of funds flow analysis begins with accounting statements which already contain a variety of write-offs and other adjustments. These elements did not involve funds movements as we now understand them. While important to the reporting of comparable and consistent results to the financial community, stockholders, and other interested parties, these adjustments are mostly irrelevant for funds flow analysis. Funds movements are related to current decisions, while accounting statements are the combined result of past *and* current decisions. Our approach will be to work back from the published statements and, through a variety of refinements, attempt to approximate the funds movements which took place during the period. Some of these adjustments will be fairly complex and are kept for last in the process.

Figures 1–6 and 1–7 are the condensed operating statement and balance sheets of Crown Zellerbach, one of the world's largest producers of paper, paperboard, packaging, and other forest products, for the calendar year 1970. As experienced by the forest products industry and the U.S. economy in general, 1970 was a year of recession and lower profitability, and this is reflected in the financial statements.

The balance sheets contain a column for changes in each of

Figure 1–6

CROWN ZELLERBACH

Condensed Operating Statement

For the Year Ending December 31, 1970

(millions of dollars)

Net sales	$955.3
Cost of goods sold*	788.0
Gross margin	$167.3
Selling and administrative expense	86.9
Operating profit	$ 80.4
Other operating income	2.8
Miscellaneous (net)	0.7
Earnings before interest and taxes	$ 83.9
Interest on debt	17.6
Earnings before taxes	$ 66.3
Federal and foreign income taxes	24.4
Net income	$ 41.9
Cash dividends	35.7
Retained Income	$ 6.2

* Contains depreciation and amortization of $51.9 million.
SOURCE: Adapted from 1970 annual report.

the accounts shown. These changes will be the basis on which we shall develop a funds flow statement, subsequent to which the actual statement published by the company will be shown. Several items are of significant size, and it will be easiest to sort these, initially without refinement, into a statement of balance sheet changes grouped according to sources and uses (Figure 1–8).

The key sources in this picture are an increase in long-term debt of $46.4 million, a decrease in cash of $9.3 million, an increase in retained income of $6.2 million, and an increase in deferred taxes of $5.1 million. The funds thus provided were used for repayment of notes payable of $29.8 million, for a net increase of $13.6 million in properties, for short-term investments of $13.7 million, and for receivables of $5.3 million. Two observations can be made from this limited analysis: (1) a change in the financial structure of the company apparently took place, because of the sizable changes in long-term debt, short-term notes, and short-term investments; (2) the level of

Figure 1–7

CROWN ZELLERBACH

Condensed Balance Sheets and Changes
December 31, 1969 and 1970
(millions of dollars)

Assets	1970	1969	*Change*
Cash .... $	13.8	$ 23.1	−$ 9.3
Short-term investments	17.4	3.7	+ 13.7
Accounts receivable (net)	116.2	110.9	+ 5.3
Inventories	159.3	162.3	− 3.0
Prepaid expenses	15.6	14.5	+ 1.1
Total Current Assets .... $	322.3	$ 314.5	+$ 7.8
Properties: Timberlands,* buildings, machinery, and equipment	1,109.5	1,059.0	+$50.5
Less accumulated depreciation	445.0	408.1	+ 36.9
Net Properties .... $	664.5	$ 650.9	+$13.6
Investments in affiliated companies	28.0	28.9	− 0.9
Other investments and receivables	6.7	10.3	− 3.6
Deferred charges	9.4	4.4	+ 5.0
Total Assets	$1,030.9	$1,009.0	+$21.9
Liabilities			
Accounts payable .... $	82.5	$ 82.6	−$ 0.1
Dividends payable	7.0	9.3	− 2.3
Notes payable	7.7	37.5	− 29.8
Long-term debt due in one year	5.3	8.0	− 2.7
Accrued U.S. and foreign taxes	8.5	10.7	− 2.2
Total Current Liabilities .... $	111.0	$ 148.1	−$37.1
Long-term debt	266.6	220.2	+ 46.4
Deferred income taxes†	67.0	61.9	+ 5.1
Reserve for self-insurance‡	4.5	4.7	− 0.2
Minority interests—Canadian subs.	12.1	11.0	+ 1.1
Cumulative preferred stock	20.0	20.0	−
Common stock	116.3	116.2	+ 0.1
Other capital	63.5	63.2	+ 0.3
Income retained in business	369.9	363.7	+ 6.2
Total Liabilities and Net Worth	$1,030.9	$1,009.0	+$21.9

* Shown net of depletion allowance.
† Result of using different depreciation methods for reporting and federal income tax purposes.
‡ So-called surplus reserves are not counted as part of the capitalization or net worth of the company. As a general rule only surplus items not specifically set aside for a definite purpose are so counted, which includes most "contingency" reserves.
SOURCE: Adapted from 1970 annual report.

investments in properties and working capital elements was not significantly changed during the year.

Further analysis of the company's reports—not provided here —would reveal that a normal refinancing of some of the company's debt took place, which essentially caused the shifts observed. Also, capital investments had returned to a more

Figure 1–8
CROWN ZELLERBACH
Statement of Balance Sheet Changes
December 31, 1969, to December 31, 1970
(millions of dollars)

Sources of Funds

Decrease in cash	$ 9.3
Decrease in inventories	3.0
Decrease in investments in affiliated companies	0.9
Decrease in other investments and receivables	3.6
Increase in long-term debt	46.4
Increase in deferred income taxes	5.1
Increase in minority interests	1.1
Increase in common stock	0.1
Increase in other capital	0.3
Increase in retained income	6.2
Total Sources	$76.0

Uses of Funds

Increase in short-term investments	$13.7
Increase in accounts receivable	5.3
Increase in prepaid expenses	1.1
Increase in net properties°	13.6
Increase in deferred charges	5.0
Decrease in accounts payable	0.1
Decrease in dividends payable	2.3
Decrease in notes payable	29.8
Decrease in long-term debt due in one year	2.7
Decrease in accrued taxes	2.2
Decrease in reserve for self-insurance	0.2
Total Uses	$76.0

° For a first look, the change in net properties is often sufficient, instead of showing the changes in gross property and accumulated depreciation.

normal level after a major expansion program during the latter half of the 1960s.

The statement of balance sheet changes does not, however, provide us with a complete picture of major funds flows. Three major classes of adjustments are to be made for this purpose, and all of these will be worked through. In each, the analyst has to make a decision as to the level of detail which will be relevant, and common sense will have to prevail in the recognition of individual items. In the extreme case, as we did with our news vendor earlier in the chapter, each transaction might be recognized for its funds implications. This is clearly impossible and really counterproductive, since we should focus our interest on significant elements of the funds picture of a corporation.

The major classes of adjustments are as follows: (1) The change in *retained income* usually contains at least two elements of interest. The first is net income or loss from operations, and the second is dividends paid to the various classes of stockholders. Both normally represent major funds movements, and the picture will be clearer if the net amount is separated into its components, one a source and the other a use. Moreover, additional adjustments may have been made to the retained income account and, if of significant size, they should be highlighted. Examples of this might be changes in balance sheet reserves, or value adjustments in asset accounts. (2) *Net income* usually contains a number of book write-offs, the largest of which is depreciation. Other examples would be amortization of patents, goodwill, etc., as well as unusual write-offs or reserve adjustments reflected on the operating statement. If any of these are significant, they should be recognized and eliminated from the funds flow picture so that the true funds movements can be recognized. (3) The change in *net property* is a result of a variety of funds and nonfunds movements. It consists of changes in the gross fixed property account, changes in accumulated depreciation, and often the effect of nonrecurring asset adjustments from retirements of aged plant and equipment. In most cases, recognition of at least the major elements in this picture will make funds flow analysis more meaningful.

Each of the three classes of adjustments will now be discussed in detail.

Changes in Retained Income

In our Crown Zellerbach example, an examination of the condensed operating statement given earlier will reveal that net income for the period was $41.9 million. Cash dividends paid for the same period were $35.7 million, which left a balance of $6.2 million to be retained. This amount also coincides exactly with the increase in the retained income shown on the statement of balance sheet changes. If this had not been the same, we would have to look for clues in the published information as to the adjustments made. As a consequence, we can here limit ourselves to the two significant elements uncovered, net income for the period and cash dividends paid.

The change in our sources and uses pattern will be as follows. Instead of an increase in retained income, a source for the period, we will reflect *two separate* elements: net income as a source of $41.9 million, and cash dividends as a use of $35.7 million. The net effect will, of course, be the same; but a fuller picture has been gained, as reflected in Figure 1–9.

In case of a stock dividend, which is in essence a book adjustment reducing the retained income and increasing capital stock, we would encounter a special situation. Strictly speaking,

Figure 1–9

CROWN ZELLERBACH

Statement of Sources and Uses of Funds
December 31, 1969, to December 31, 1970
(millions of dollars)

Sources of Funds

Net income	$ 41.9
Depreciation and amortization	51.9
Decrease in cash	9.3
Decrease in inventories	3.0
Decrease in investments in affiliated companies	0.9
Decrease in other investments and receivables	3.6
Increase in long-term debt	46.4
Increase in deferred income taxes	5.1
Increase in minority interests	1.1
Increase in common stock	0.1
Increase in other capital	0.3
Total Sources	$163.6

Uses of Funds

Additions to properties	$ 65.5
Dividends paid	35.7
Increase in short-term investments	13.7
Increase in accounts receivable	5.3
Increase in prepaid expenses	1.1
Increase in deferred charges	5.0
Decrease in accounts payable	0.1
Decrease in dividends payable	2.3
Decrease in notes payable	29.8
Decrease in long-term debt due in one year	2.7
Decrease in accrued taxes	2.2
Decrease in reserve for self-insurance	0.2
Total Uses	$163.6

no economic values have been shifted; but if the amount is significant enough, the analyst is faced with the choice of making a reversing adjustment (as discussed in the ensuing sections of this chapter) or ignoring the matter entirely.

Had an examination of the company's statements revealed a significant adjustment to retained earnings, such as might have been caused by a change in the reserve for self-insurance, further analysis might be useful. Let us assume that Crown Zellerbach's reserve for self-insurance, which represents a provision against possible losses and which contained a balance of $4.5 million in 1970, had been considered too large and was adjusted by $2 million through an accounting entry. Such a reduction would have resulted in a write-off of $2 million affecting *both* the reserve and retained income, reducing the former and increasing the latter. This $2 million item would be reflected on our statement of balance sheet changes as an additional use of funds of $2 million (decrease in reserves) and an additional source of funds of $2 million (increase in retained earnings).

It could be properly argued that such an item does not represent a funds movement in the full sense of our definition (i.e., no economic values were committed), and should therefore be removed during our analysis. This can be done simply by *reversing* the effect of the accounting adjustment, that is, reducing for funds flow purposes both the change in retained income (a source) and the change in the reserve (a use) by $2 million each. A similar decision could be made for other nonfunds adjustments which affected retained earnings, if the amounts were material in the analyst's judgment.

Changes in Net Income

As mentioned before, net income is the combined result of matching current revenue and cost elements. Moreover, it contains a series of accounting write-offs and adjustments intended to reflect the effect on the period of past or anticipated revenue and cost elements. Since funds flow analysis is an attempt to recognize the impact of resource commitments, write-offs such as depreciation or amortization of past expenditures tend to cloud the picture. The true impact of net income on a company's funds is really measured *before* any such write-offs, as we saw earlier in the case of the news vendor. Reported net income, however, is stated *after* write-offs, and must therefore be adjusted through reversals such as shown in the previous section. The amount of depreciation for the period is normally easily identified, and the adjustment simply amounts to adding back the amount of depreciation as a source and showing an offsetting use by increasing the net property account. (The details of this latter element are discussed in the next section.)

In our Crown Zellerbach example, the amount of depreciation for 1970 was $51.9 million, which is shown as a source in the funds flow statement (Figure 1–9), with a like amount added to net properties. From this adjustment arises the often cited misconception of depreciation as a "source of funds." Depreciation as such does *not create any funds,* since it is an accounting entry. To the extent that it has reduced net income, however, it must be recognized and reversed. Common practice has led to labeling the depreciation amount as a source, when in fact net income merely had to be restored to its pre-write-off level.

Other elements in the net income picture will sometimes be amortizations and other adjustments of assets and liabilities on the balance sheet. Normally these amounts will not be significant enough to warrant special attention. If they are of material size, however, some analysts will make reversing adjustments of the kind we observed for depreciation—in effect removing the impact on net income to keep the funds picture "pure." Much discussion has been carried on about the merits of such refinements, and this is not the place to argue to a final answer. The main point is to establish the principle and to let the analyst decide the relevance in a particular case.

A word should be said about deferred income taxes at this point. This item on the balance sheet is assuming sizable proportions in many companies and is often misunderstood. The deferred income tax is simply the accumulated difference in net income reported for tax versus book purposes due to the use of faster depreciation methods for tax purposes alone. Net income reported on the books contains the normal depreciation write-offs, while income taxes were paid based on faster write-offs. The amount of income taxes reported on the operating statement, however, is an assumed higher figure than actually paid, with the difference shown as an accumulating reserve on the balance sheet. This reserve is built up against the day when the fast write-offs used for tax purposes will run out. It is an attempt to average out the tax effect of fast write-offs. Since most companies continue to invest in fixed assets and thus enjoy fresh accelerated depreciation write-offs, the "day of reckoning" is postponed almost indefinitely, and deferred taxes continue to grow.

From a funds standpoint, no adjustments need be made, but the nature of the item should be recognized for what it is— an income reserve set aside against potential higher tax payments in the future. In that sense it is a proper source of funds for the period, just as other operating income was, and it can be shown together with operating income among the sources. In the case of Crown Zellerbach, the net change in deferred income taxes amounted to $5.1 million for 1970, including a variety of adjustments too detailed to be discussed here.

Finally, net income is often affected by gains and losses from sale of capital assets. Since the funds effect is normally tied to a combination of circumstances affecting the components of the net property account, the discussion will be taken up in the next section in detail.

Changes in Net Property

The funds flow pattern behind the change in net property is mostly of significant enough size to warrant some special attention. At the same time, it is also one of the more difficult aspects to understand for most newcomers to financial analysis.

Part of the problem is the fact that the account is the *net* of an asset and a reserve account, and another part of the problem is the mystique surrounding depreciation and asset write-offs.

The easiest approach is to lay out the components of the account and to observe the relevance of the figures. Then we can search for clues in other parts of the published statements and make any necessary assumptions should the clues be missing, since they are often tied to inside information.

In our Crown Zellerbach example, the two balance sheets in Figure 1–7 provide the following information:

	12–31–70	12–31–69	Change
Gross property	$1,109.5	$1,059.0	+$50.5
Less: Accumulated depreciation ...	445.0	408.1	+ 36.9
Net property	$ 664.5	$ 650.9	+$13.6

The task is to identify the relevant funds sources and uses, which in combination amounted to the net use of $13.6 million shown. Quite obviously there was an increase of $50.5 million in gross property, which must have been due to new investments (a use); while accumulated depreciation rose by $36.9 million, which must have been due to current write-offs to begin with (a source, as discussed before). For a first look, this analysis suffices and some analysts will let the matter rest here. Yet we already know, for instance, that depreciation for the period was $51.9 million, which is more than the change in accumulated depreciation. Thus there must have been other elements, the effect of which has been netted out and calls for further analysis.

The following questions of significance arise:

1. What is the relevant pattern of funds flows in the accumulated depreciation account, one of which must be the amount of depreciation taken for the year?
2. What was the total amount of new investment in gross properties—a major element in the management decision process?

3. Were there any disinvestments (i.e., reductions in gross properties) which significantly affected the company's plans?

The questions are intertwined and can be handled at two levels. The simplest approach is to assume that normally the amount of depreciation taken for the year ($51.9 million in our case) will be the amount by which accumulated depreciation has increased. If this in fact is not the case, then there must have been some reduction in the accumulated depreciation account which, for simplicity, we can assume to represent the abandonment of *fully depreciated* assets during the period.[1] This simple, but often sufficiently creditable, approach would lead to the following change in our data:

	(1) 12–31–69	(2) Additions	(3) Deductions	(4) 12–31–70	(5) Change
Gross property ...	$1,059.0	+$65.5°	−$15.0†	$1,109.5	+$50.5
Less: Accumulated depreciation ...	408.1	+ 51.9	− 15.0‡	445.0	+ 36.9
Net property	$ 650.9	+$13.6	–0–	$ 664.5	+$13.6

° Forced figure.
† Must be equivalent to accumulated depreciation if fully depreciated assets were abandoned.
‡ Assumed figure to balance the change in the account.

Since we must stay within the net changes of the accounts in the balance sheet, our simple assumption has given us the necessary clues to complete the analysis: we recognize the actual depreciation write-off of $51.9 million as a source (column 2), and a *derived* $65.5 million as new capital investment, a use (column 2). The process rests on the assumed write-off of $15 million of fully depreciated assets, which under normal accounting practice results in an equal reduction in both asset and accumulated depreciation accounts (column 3). This is reflected in our analysis. We are ignoring possible tax implica-

---

[1] Fully depreciated assets, when scrapped, are removed by an accounting entry which credits assets by the amount of the recorded value, and debits accumulated depreciation by the same amount.

tions which would tend to confuse the issue for little incremental gain.

From a funds standpoint, we now have all the elements to separate the sources and uses behind the change in the net property account:

> Source: Depreciation for period ...$51.9
> Use: New investment 65.5
> Net use $13.6

It is obvious that this relatively simple adjustment of net balances in the accounts has led to an improved display of one of the most important management decisions—the amount of new asset investment, as reflected in Figure 1–9. But we are still short of a fully accurate picture, because of our simplifying assumption regarding the asset write-offs. A check of the company's annual report shows that the actual capital investment for the period was $68.4 million, a difference of $2.9 million from our derived figure of $65.5 million.

This leads us to the more complex level of analysis in which we try to dig even more deeply into the property accounts and the accounting adjustments which probably occurred in them. Our assumption of fully depreciated assets left out the possibility of gains or losses on sale or abandonment of property and other fixed assets. Normally the amounts involved are fairly minor, as in the current example, but it will be useful to have worked through the implications for a fuller understanding.

If in fact there were gains or losses on sale of assets—and this can be found from a closer examination of published income statements and balance sheets—there must have been a two-fold effect on the company's statements. First, the write-off in the gross property account and accumulated depreciation must have been different by the amount of the remaining book value of the assets disposed of. This would tend to complicate our basic data slightly.

Second, a gain or loss on sale of assets would normally be

reflected in net income. Consequently, the same amount by which gross property had to be adjusted will also affect net income, and we have to ponder the effect on funds flows.

It will be helpful to sort out our basic data again, this time showing all the details now known to us:

	12–31–69	Additions	Deductions	12–31–70	Change
Gross property	$1,059.0	+$68.3	−$17.8°	$1,109.5	+$50.5
Less: Accumulated depreciation	408.1	+ 51.9	− 15.0	445.0	+ 36.9
Net property	$ 650.9	+$16.4	−$ 2.8†	$ 664.5	+$13.6

° Forced figure, since both additions are now known.
† Loss on sale of assets, corresponding to the book value.

The funds effect of this refinement is to reflect a slightly higher investment as a use, and to show the offsetting $2.8 million book loss as a source, since in fact net income had been reduced by this amount. In keeping with our discussion of changes in net income, the book loss on sale of assets is one of the accounting entries which should be reversed for funds purposes. This is what we have done here, by both actually increasing the property account (a use) and in effect increasing net income (a source):

Sources: Depreciation	$51.9
Loss from disposal of assets	2.8
	$54.7
Use: Investment in property	68.3
Net change in net property	$13.6

Another complication arises if we recognize that some fixed assets were disposed of *for cash* and a gain or loss resulted. Strictly speaking, the proceeds received for the assets should be reflected as a source, with an offsetting use shown as an increase in the cash account. This would be carrying the details of analysis back to the transaction stage, however, and few will want to push the analysis this far. The best way to handle the situation is to trace through the details as we did in the previous case, and let the best judgment prevail.

KEY POINTS OF FUNDS FLOW ANALYSIS

In summary, the series of adjustments shown have followed the concepts of funds movements discussed at the beginning of the chapter. At all times the attempt should be to isolate, in a funds flow sense, significant elements reflecting management decisions on investments, operations, and financing. The key questions to be asked about these refer to the magnitude and type of commitment in relation to the sources from which they were obtained. Have enough long-term funds (retained earnings, new equity, debt) been raised to support major investments? Do temporary loans or other short-term movements constitute the bulk of sources for long-term use? What do changes in working capital suggest relative to the ability of the business to generate funds? Is growth outstripping funds generation? Many of these questions will reappear in Chapter 6, where we shall discuss the business as a total system.

In the process of identifying and analyzing funds movements and relating them to each other, the selection of periods is often quite important. If a business enterprise has a strongly seasonal character, the funds flow analysis should be carefully timed over a period which permits analyzing the swings in the business pattern. Thus, it may be useful to place the boundaries of the analysis on a seasonal high and a seasonal low, instead of straddling the period of seasonality. Again, imagination and feel for a business come in handy—and the analyst must make choices which cannot always be spelled out beforehand.

PRESENTATION OF FUNDS FLOW ANALYSIS

There are two aspects to the problem of presenting the results of funds flow analysis—the development of an analytical framework for internal needs, and the presentation of the key funds movements to the public as part of the total financial disclosure. While not entirely separable, the two aspects do differ, since there is much more flexibility in displaying the data for internal use than in the slowly evolving general format for external publication. Both methods have in common, of course, the desire to show the effect of key management decisions upon the funds picture of the enterprise.

Internal use of the funds flow analysis can and should be tailored to assist top management in assessing past relationships and in planning for future decisions. The amount of detail can be adjusted at will to fit the areas of particular interest and concern. There is an almost infinite variety of ways in which to present funds flow data, and we shall show just one possibility of analyzing the funds flow impact of the decisions made on the three key areas of a business: operations, financing, and investment. For this purpose we shall employ somewhat more detail than heretofore used in our display of funds flows, but at the same time we shall limit the analysis to the data already available in the statements of Crown Zellerbach shown earlier in the chapter. The result of this effort is shown in Figure 1–10, and the reasoning behind the analysis is described below.

The *operational funds flows* are largely contained in the data of the income statement, from which we so far have employed only the net profit and depreciation amounts. It is often useful, as we have done here, to take the key variables behind profit, namely revenues and major costs, and to separate these for funds flow purposes. To display the size of these amounts flowing through the business helps to provide a perspective for the magnitude of the other flows involved. Furthermore, short-term decisions regarding inventories, receivables, payables, and accrued and deferred income and expense are usually intimately involved with operational concerns such as production schedules, credit policies, and payment practices. Therefore changes in the current balance sheet accounts can normally be considered as operational, and should be reflected as such. In the case of Crown Zellerbach, the *operational* decisions for the year 1970 resulted in a net inflow from operations of $105.8 million, which under this concept is an amount significantly higher than the normal quick rule of adding net income and depreciation to obtain "cash flow from operations" ($41.9 + $51.9 = $93.8 million). Note that our analysis has correctly taken into account

Figure 1–10

CROWN ZELLERBACH

Funds Flow Analysis by Area of Management Attention for the Year 1970
(millions of dollars)

Operating inflows:

Net sales	$955.3	
Other income	3.5	
Increase in deferred income taxes	5.1	
Decrease in inventories	3.0	
Total operating inflows	+$966.9	

Operating outflows:

Cost of goods sold, excluding depreciation	$736.1	
Selling and administrative expense	86.9	
Federal and foreign income taxes	24.4	
Increase in accounts receivable	5.3	
Decrease in accounts payable	0.1	
Changes in prepaid and deferred expenses	6.1	
Decrease in accrued taxes	2.2	
Total operating outflows	−$861.1	
Net operating inflows		+$105.8

Financial inflows:

Additional net long-term borrowing*	$ 43.7	
Reductions in affiliated and other investments	4.5	
Changes in common stock and other capital, reserves	1.3	
Total financial inflows	+$ 49.5	

Financial outflows:

Repayment of notes payable	$ 29.8	
Increase in short-term investments	13.7	
Interest paid	17.6	
Total financial outflows	−$ 61.1	
Net financial outflows		−$ 11.6

Discretionary outflows:

Additions to properties	$ 65.5	
Cash dividends paid†	38.0	
Total discretionary outflows		−$103.5
Net outflow from operations, financing, and investment		−$ 9.3

Analysis of cash impact:

Beginning cash balance		$ 23.1
Ending cash balance		$ 13.8

* Net of increase in long-term debt and reduction in current portion of long-term debt.
† Total of dividends shown on income statement and reduction in dividends payable.

the depreciation figure by reducing cost of goods sold, to re-store essentially a cash cost picture.

The *financial* decisions made resulted in a net outflow of $11.6 million, largely due to an approximate balance between net additional debt and note repayments, with interest expenses of $17.6 million. It would be perhaps more revealing to show the full details behind these net financial movements, and more analysis of readily available data could be used to separate gross borrowings and repayments for display.

Finally, investments in new properties and equipment rep-resented the largest single outflow of a *discretionary* nature, followed closely by dividend payments during the year. Again, if desired, more detail could be shown to management on the investment side. Furthermore, the analyst has the choice of showing in this area other discretionary outlays, such as research and development expenses, advertising programs, or pension contributions, if these are significant. The choices are wide and are governed only by the objective of the analysis.

The *net effect* of funds flows for the year can be brought down to show the ending cash balance, which we expected to change by $9.3 million based on our previous analysis. This attempt at displaying flows by area of management attention is merely an example of the useful picture funds flows analysis can provide for an overview and understanding of management decisions. It is increasingly considered to be a more convenient way to think about a company's operations than the review of the ac-counting statements in their original form. The particular ap-proach we used here has employed the key elements of both the balance sheet and the operating statements, and has com-bined these into a decisional framework from which to ask and begin to answer significant questions, particularly if the review is made over a series of periods.

For *external presentation*, a more accounting-oriented set of data is usually provided. In line with this custom, Crown Zeller-bach presented its funds flow picture in an arrangement shown in Figure 1–11. This material has been adapted from the 1970 annual report without the footnotes explaining many of the intricacies. A review and comparison between Figures 1–9 and

Figure 1–11

CROWN ZELLERBACH AND SUBSIDIARIES

Statement of Source and Application of Funds
(thousands of dollars)

Source of Funds	Year Ended December 31, 1970	Year Ended December 31, 1969
Net income	$ 41,905	$ 53,963
Expenses which did not require current cash outlay:		
Depreciation, depletion and amortization	51,935	48,377
Net book value of assets sold or abandoned	2,784	4,503
Provision for deferred income taxes ...	3,451	1,200
Internal funds generated	$100,075	$108,043
Increase in long-term debt	125,983	10,000
Investments in affiliated companies ...	885	(2,147)
Proceeds from sale of common stock under option plan	378	3,827
Reduction of long-term receivables ...	–0–	6,000
Miscellaneous—Net	1,292	(2,573)
	$228,613	$123,150
Application of Funds		
Long-term debt paid or currently maturing	$ 79,674	$ 7,322
Additions to properties	68,351	82,739
Dividends declared	35,721	37,210
Preferred stock redemptions	–0–	1,220
Net increase (decrease) in working capital	44,867	(5,341)
	$228,613	$123,150

Source: 1970 annual report. Shown here without accompanying notes to financial statements.

1–11 shows that most elements are reflected in the way we would have predicted from our earlier analysis. Only in a few cases does inside knowledge provide extra touches, such as the information about the proceeds from sale of common stock, or the somewhat lower increase in deferred income taxes which is due to a variety of adjustments made in connection with the abandoned assets.

A few more examples of presentations of funds flows analysis to the financial community are given as Figures 1–12 through 1–16. While details and layout vary, all presentations have in common the highlighting of key elements of importance to the respective business, and they all tend to concentrate on major funds movements, with some attention given to nonfunds elements.

SUMMARY

In this chapter we have laid the foundation for the many techniques to follow in this book. In essence, funds flow analysis is a decisional display of management's disposition of short- and long-term funds available for operations and investment. By tracing through the operations of a simple fictional business, we have shown the funds pattern as the "third dimension" of the reporting of results, and at the same time have gained more insight into the effects of particular management decisions. Applying the techniques to the statements of a major corporation, we recognize that most of the difficulties in this process stem from the need to translate accounting practices represented in the statement back towards a simple "cash transaction" framework, which is based on commonsense reasoning.

The increasing use of funds flow analysis and the requirement for displaying this approach for publicly held companies is an indication of the importance of the technique. The concepts will appear frequently in part or in total in the later chapters of this book.

Figure 1–12

PACIFIC GAS AND ELECTRIC COMPANY
Statement of Source and Application of Funds
for the Years Ended December 31, 1970 and 1969
(thousands of dollars)

Source of Funds	1970	1969
Funds derived from operations:		
Net income	$166,219	$169,749
Nonfund items in net income:		
Depreciation (including charges to other accounts)	129,504	121,780
Gain on bonds purchased for sinking fund	(14,099)	(8,351)
Allowance for funds used during construction	(18,153)	(10,393)
Other—net	(4,879)	(4,550)
Total funds derived from operations	$258,592	$268,235

Figure 1–12   (continued)

	1970	1969
Preferred and common stock sold—net	66,699	–0–
Mortgage bonds sold—net	174,183	159,912
Utility plant sold and salvaged	18,885	15,250
Increase in short-term borrowing	55,350	–0–
Decrease in other working capital items	–0–	30,352
Other changes—net	977	–0–
Total Sources	$574,686	$473,749

Application of Funds

	1970	1969
Capital expenditures	$415,331	$339,990
Allowance for funds used during construction	(18,153)	(10,393)
Funds used for capital expenditures	$397,178	$329,597
Mortgage bonds retired (at cost)	39,390	22,672
Dividends—preferred and common stock	108,204	106,442
Decrease in short-term borrowing	–0–	3,800
Increase in other working capital items	29,914	–0–
Other changes—net	–0–	11,238
Total Applications	$574,686	$473,749

Source: 1970 annual report. Shown here without accompanying notes to financial statements.

Figure 1–13

ATLANTIC RICHFIELD COMPANY

Statement of Source and Application of Funds
(thousands of dollars)

	1970	1969
Source of Funds		
Net income	$205,630	$ 227,174
Add: Depreciation, depletion, etc.	232,640	227,193
Dry hole expenditures charged to income	27,435	38,965
Funds generated from operations	$465,705	$ 493,332
Sale of property, plant, equipment, and investments ...	34,443	416,826
Proceeds from issuance of capital stock,		
including conversion of convertible securities	9,696	245,034
Additional long-term borrowing	400,000	–0–
	$909,844	$ 1,155,192
Application of Funds		
Capital expenditures	$462,944	$ 418,381
Dividends to shareholders	131,306	120,838
Reduction of long-term debt	120,654	386,247
Liquidation of production payments	4,479	24,879
Receivable from sale of assets to BP (note 2)	15,834	286,196
Other (net)	26,926	40,300
	$762,143	$ 1,276,841
Increase (decrease) in working capital	$147,701	$(121,649)

Source: 1970 annual report. Shown here without accompanying notes to financial statements.

Figure 1–14

FORD MOTOR COMPANY AND CONSOLIDATED SUBSIDIARIES
Statement of Source and Application of Funds
(millions of dollars)

	1970	1969
Working capital, January 1	$1,107.7	$1,134.3
Additions to working capital:		
Net income	$ 515.7	$ 546.5
Depreciation	413.6	385.2
Amortization of special tools	409.9	418.5
Proceeds from issuance of long-term debt	228.5	35.7
Increase in other liabilities and reserves	14.8	24.4
Proceeds from issuance of shares of common stock	3.2	2.5
Total additions	$1,585.7	$1,412.8
Dispositions of working capital:		
Cash dividends paid	$ 259.2	$ 260.8
Additions to property, plant and equipment, net of proceeds from disposals	1,037.2	950.0
Increase in equities in net assets of unconsolidated subsidiaries	202.1	107.4
Reductions in principal amount of long-term debt	76.3	72.9
Increase in other investments	18.1	33.6
Class A stock purchased and retired	13.8	12.8
Decrease in minority interests in net assets	3.7	1.9
Total dispositions	$1,610.4	$1,439.4
Decrease in working capital	$ (24.7)	$ (26.6)
Working capital, December 31	$1,083.0	$1,107.7

Source: 1970 annual report. Shown here without accompanying notes to financial statements.

Figure 1–15

JANTZEN INC. AND CONSOLIDATED SUBSIDIARIES
Statement of Consolidated Source and Use of Funds
for the Year Ended August 29, 1970

Source of Funds

Net income	$ 2,002,515
Depreciation and amortization	1,066,677
Decrease in working capital	120,615
Additional long-term debt	267,450
Other	24,994
Total Source of Funds	$ 3,482,251

Use of Funds

Net addition to plant and equipment	$ 1,815,912
Payments on long-term debt	764,002
Cash dividends	902,337
Total Use of Funds	$ 3,482,251

Source: 1970 annual report. Shown here without accompanying notes to financial statements.

Figure 1–16

TRANSAMERICA CORPORATION AND SUBSIDIARIES
Statement of Source and Application of Funds
(thousands of dollars)

	Years Ended December 31	
Source of Funds	1970	1969
Net income before depreciation and amortization ....$ 78,558		$109,823
Increase in liabilities:		
Notes and debentures payable 168,565		61,479
Insurance reserves and claims 35,853		103,045
Accounts payable and other liabilities 10,720		17,690
Decrease (increase) in assets:		
Finance receivables 24,557		24,228
Trade and other accounts receivable 10,412		(26,192)
	$328,665	$290,073
Application of Funds		
Cash dividends ....$ 35,657		$ 31,792
Increase (decrease) in assets:		
Additions to property and equipment 122,775		161,511
Securities, mortgages and loans		
of insurance companies 93,886		54,713
Broadcasting rights and other		
miscellaneous investments 25,876		2,890
Film productions and record inventories 10,838		(52)
Real estate and related enterprises 7,926		(18,180)
Cash 3,424		10,842
Other 20,907		41,202
Decrease in all other liabilities 7,376		5,355
	$328,665	$290,073

Source: 1970 annual report. Shown here without accompanying notes to financial statements.

SELECTED REFERENCES

ANTHONY, ROBERT N. *Management Accounting, Text and Cases,* chap. 12. 4th ed. Homewood, Ill.: Richard D. Irwin, 1970.

HUNT, PEARSON; WILLIAMS, CHARLES M.; and DONALDSON, GORDON. *Basic Business Finance,* part I and chap. 7. 3d ed. Homewood, Ill.: Richard D. Irwin, 1966.

JAEDICKE, ROBERT K., and SPROUSE, ROBERT T. *Accounting Flows: Income, Funds and Cash.* Englewood Cliffs, N.J.: Prentice-Hall, 1965.

MOORE, CARL L., and JAEDICKE, ROBERT K. *Managerial Accounting,* chap. 7. Cincinnati, Ohio: South-Western Publishing Co., 1963.

VANCIL, RICHARD F. (ed.). *Financial Executive's Handbook,* chap. 40. Homewood, Ill.: Dow-Jones-Irwin, 1970.

VAN HORNE, JAMES C. *Financial Management and Policy,* chap. 25. Englewood Cliffs, N.J.: Prentice-Hall, 1968.

WESTON, J. FRED, and BRIGHAM, EUGENE F.   *Managerial Finance,* chaps. 4, 13. 3d ed. New York: Holt, Rinehart & Winston, 1971.

CHAPTER
2
MEASUREMENT OF BUSINESS RESULTS

Up to now the focus of discussion has been on depicting the decision process of resource deployment. This has provided some insights, but has also raised a number of questions which only a more specific analysis could answer. The performance measurement of business results is more complex and difficult, since it must deal with the effectiveness with which capital is employed, the efficiency and profitability of operations, and the value and safety of various claims against the business. The reader will again recognize the pattern of the previous chapter: results should be related to the basic decisions on investment, operations, and financing.

Many techniques of analysis—a large proportion based on a variety of ratios—exist in results measurement. Only the most important can be discussed here. It is particularly important, however, that the person analyzing the business results have clearly in mind which tests he wishes to apply and for what specific reasons. He must define the viewpoints to be taken, the objectives of the analysis, and possible standards of comparison. The temptation arises in financial ratio analysis to "run all the numbers"—yet normally only a selected few relationships will provide clues for judgment. A ratio can relate any

41

magnitude to any other, such as profit to total assets, or current liabilities to current assets. The choices are wide and numerous, as literally hundreds of relationships could be drawn; but the usefulness of any particular one is severely limited. Meaningful ratios serve best to point up changes in direction and patterns of change, which in turn may indicate risks and opportunities for the business under review.

The analyst must realize, moreover, that an appraisal of results deals with past data and conditions, from which it may be difficult to extrapolate future expectations. It is the future that can be affected by decisions—the past is gone and cannot be changed.

No attempt to measure business results can provide absolute answers. Only relative insights can be gained, since business conditions vary so much from company to company and industry to industry. Comparisons and standards have been further weakened by the trend of recent years towards multibusiness companies and conglomerates. Differences exist in location, types of facilities, products and services, accounting policies, capital structures, levels of efficiency, and caliber of management, to name but a few. To develop a rationale for dealing with all of these aspects is far beyond the scope of this book. Nevertheless, they must be kept in mind when dealing with the numerical results on which performance measurement depends.

We shall discuss the key ratios and measures commonly applied in financial analysis for expressing business results and characterize each. The chapter will be developed along the major viewpoints which may govern this analysis, and in the end an attempt at integrating the measures will be made.

IMPORTANCE OF POINT OF VIEW

Many persons and groups normally take an interest in the success or failure of a business operation. The most important are owners (investors), managers, lenders, labor organizations, governmental agencies, and social groups. Depending on their objectives, they will view business results selectively as to financial measures, and beyond this will often include intangible values. Since viewpoints and objectives cannot be separated, we shall deal with major interested parties and those measures most meaningful to them.

Closest to the business from a day-to-day standpoint, but also responsible for long-range plans, is the *management* of the operation—whether it comprises professional managers or owner/managers. The managers are responsible for efficiency, current and long-term profit from operations, and effective deployment of capital and other resources in the process. The *owners* of the business, in contrast, are interested in the current and long-term profitability of their equity investment, expressed in growing earnings and dividends and in the rise of the economic value of their "stake" relative to the risk encountered. At the same time, the providers of "other people's money," *creditors and lenders* of short- and long-term nature, are oriented towards steady interest payments, the ability of the business to repay the principal, and reasonable specific or residual asset values as a margin of protection for risk. In addition, other groups such as the *government, labor,* and other groupings in *society* will have some specific objectives—reliability of tax receipts, ability to pay wages, or financial strength to carry out social and environmental obligations, for instance.

The ensuing analysis of business operations by means of ratios and other measures will be developed along the first three viewpoints, which are not independent of each other but differ only in focus. The reader is encouraged to consider the applicability of the measures to the interests of the other groups mentioned.

MANAGEMENT'S VIEW OF OPERATIONS

As stated before, management has a twofold interest in the analysis of financial statements—efficient and profitable operations, and effective use of capital entrusted to it. The operational analysis is generally based on the operating (income) statements of the company, while the effective use of capital is usually measured from a review of the balance sheet and the income statement combined. For purposes of illustration we shall again use the sample statements of Crown Zellerbach for 1969 and 1970, which are reproduced as Figures 2–1 and 2–2.

Figure 2–1

CROWN ZELLERBACH
Condensed Operating Statements
Years Ending December 31, 1969 and 1970
(millions of dollars)

	1970		1969	
Net sales	$955.3	100.0%	$919.3	100.0%
Cost of goods sold°	788.0	82.5	747.0	81.2
Gross margin	$167.3	17.5%	$172.3	18.8%
Selling and administrative	86.9	9.1	82.4	9.0
Operating profit	$ 80.4	8.4%	$ 89.9	9.8%
Other operating income	2.8	0.3	3.1	0.3
Miscellaneous (net)	0.7	–0–	2.5	0.3
Earnings before interest and taxes	$ 83.9	8.7%	$ 95.5	10.4%
Interest on debt	17.6	1.8	12.9	1.4
Earnings before taxes	$ 66.3	6.9%	$ 82.6	9.0%
Federal and foreign income taxes	24.4	2.5	28.6	3.1
Net income	$ 41.9	4.4%	$ 54.0	5.9%
Net income per share of common stock	$ 1.77		$ 2.29	
Net income	$ 41.9	100.0%	$ 54.0	100.0%
Common dividends	$ 34.9		$ 36.4	
Preferred dividends	0.8		.8	
Total dividends paid	$ 35.7	85.2%	$ 37.2	69.0%
Retained earnings	$ 6.2	14.8%	$ 16.8	31.0%

° Contains depreciation, depletion, and amortization of $51.9 in 1970 and $48.4 in 1969.
Source: Adapted from 1970 annual report.

Operational analysis for a business as a whole is generally performed by means of a "common numbers" or percentage analysis of the income statement. The basis against which the ratios are usually developed is *net sales,* that is, gross sales revenues after any returns or allowances. The use of net sales as the base provides a reasonably comparable standard of measurement, which is particularly useful when tracing results over a series of past periods or making intercompany comparisons.

Figure 2–2

CROWN ZELLERBACH

Condensed Balance Sheets
December 31, 1969 and 1970
(millions of dollars)

Assets	1970	1969
Cash	$ 13.8	$ 23.1
Short-term investments	17.4	3.7
Accounts receivable (net)	116.2	110.9
Inventories	159.3	162.3
Prepaid expenses	15.6	14.5
Total Current Assets	$ 322.3	$ 314.5
Properties: Timberlands,* buildings, machinery, and equipment	$1,109.5	$1,059.0
Less accumulated depreciation	445.0	408.1
Net Properties	$ 664.5	$ 650.9
Investments in affiliated companies	28.0	28.9
Other investments and receivables	6.7	10.3
Deferred charges	9.4	4.4
Total Assets	$1,030.9	$1,009.0
Liabilities		
Accounts payable	$ 82.5	$ 82.6
Dividends payable	7.0	9.3
Notes payable	7.7	37.5
Long-term debt due in one year	5.3	8.0
Accrued U.S. and foreign taxes	8.5	10.7
Total Current Liabilities	$ 111.0	$ 148.1
Long-term debt	266.6	220.2
Deferred income taxes†	67.0	61.9
Reserve for self-insurance‡	4.5	4.7
Minority interests—Canadian subs.	12.1	11.0
Cumulative preferred stock	20.0	20.0
Common stock	116.3	116.2
Other capital	63.5	63.2
Income retained in business	369.9	363.7
Total Liabilities and Net Worth	$1,030.9	$1,009.0

° Shown net of depletion allowance.
† Result of using different depreciation methods for reporting and federal income tax purposes.
‡ So-called surplus reserves are not counted as part of the capitalization or net worth of the company. As a general rule, only surplus items not specifically set aside for a definite purpose are so counted, which includes most "contingency" reserves.
SOURCE: Adapted from 1970 annual report.

We distinguish among the following types of ratios for operational evaluation:

1. Cost of goods sold and gross margin analysis.
2. Profit (net income) analysis.

3. Operating expense analysis.
4. Contribution analysis.

The purpose of deriving these ratios is to judge the relative magnitudes of selected key elements and to determine any trends towards improvement or worsening of performance. In this process we must keep in mind the industry involved and its particular characteristics, as well as the individual trends of the company under analysis. For example, the gross margin percentage of a jewelry store with slow turnover of merchandise and high markups will be much higher (50 percent is not uncommon) than that of a supermarket which depends on low margins and high volume for its success (gross margins of 10 to 15 percent are typical). In fact, the comparison of a particular company's ratios to those of similar companies in its industry *over a period of time* will provide the best clues as to whether the company is improving or worsening its position.

Cost of Goods Sold and Gross Margin Analysis. One of the most common ratios in operational analysis is the determination of the cost of goods sold as a percentage of net sales. This ratio indicates the magnitude of the cost of goods purchased or manufactured in relation to the margin left over for operating expenses and profit. The ratios for analysis appear as follows:

$$\text{Cost of goods sold} = \frac{\text{Cost of goods sold}}{\text{Net sales}} = \frac{\$788}{\$955.3} = 82.49\% \ (1969: 81.26\%)$$

$$\text{Gross margin} = \frac{\text{Net Sales} - \text{cost of goods sold}}{\text{Net sales}} = \frac{\$955.3 - \$788}{\$955.3}$$

$$= 17.51\% \ (1969: 18.74\%)$$

The cost of goods sold of 82.49 percent and the gross margin of 17.51 percent indicate to us the margin of "raw profit." We must keep in mind that gross margin is the result of the relationship of prices, volumes, and costs. A change in gross margin can be a combination of changes in the price of the product and in the level of manufacturing costs, if the product was made by the company. In a trading or service organization, gross margin can be affected by the price of the product or service provided and price levels paid for merchandise or services purchased on the outside. Volume of operations can be significant if, for example, a manufacturing company has a high level of fixed costs (see Chapter 6 for further discussion) or the trading company has less buying power and efficiencies of scale than a large competitor. Complications are found particularly in manufacturing companies, where the nature of the cost accounting system determines the specific costing of products for inventory and for current sale. There can be significant differences between the apparent cost performance of companies using standard full cost systems and those using direct costing, for example, since the level of charges for a period of operations can be affected differently by this choice.

A significant change over an appropriate period of time—in many businesses seasonal fluctuations will be normal—in the cost of goods sold or gross margin would call for further analysis to investigate where the cause of the deviation rests. Thus the ratio is a signal rather than an absolute measure, as we shall find to be true of most of the measures discussed.

Profit Analysis. The relationship of reported net profit (net income) to sales indicates management's ability to operate the business with sufficient success not only to recover from revenues of the period the cost of merchandise or services, the expenses of operating the business (including depreciation), and the cost of borrowed funds, but also to leave a margin of reasonable compensation to the owners for providing their capital at risk. The ratio of net profit to sales essentially expresses the cost/price effectiveness of the operation. As we shall demonstrate later, a more significant ratio is the relationship of total profit to the capital investment employed. The simple calculation for net profit appears as follows:

$$\text{Profit margin} = \frac{\text{Net profit}}{\text{Net sales}} = \frac{\$ \ 41.9}{\$955.3} = 4.39\% \ (1969: 5.87\%)$$

A variation of this calculation is the use of net profit *before* interest and taxes. This figure represents the operating profit before any compensation paid to debt holders and before the tax calculations, which are often partly based on a different set of data. The use of this ratio rests on the assumption that it provides a "purer" view of operating effectiveness:

$$\text{Profit margin} = \frac{\text{Net profit before interest and taxes}}{\text{Net sales}} = \frac{\$\ 83.9}{\$955.3}$$
$$= 8.78\% \ (1969: 10.39\%)$$

Increasingly one encounters the argument, however, that income taxes should be considered as an ongoing expense of being in business. Another modification of the calculation, therefore, is the use of profits after taxes but before interest; again, to recognize operating efficiency, but leaving out the question of compensation to the various holders of capital. The formula appears as follows:

$$\text{Profit margin} = \frac{\text{Net profit after taxes before interest}}{\text{Net sales}}$$
$$= \frac{\$41.9 + \$8.8}{\$955.3} = 5.31\% \ (1969: 6.58\%)$$

In the calculation, for simplicity, we add back the after-tax cost of interest on debt, which is pretax interest times $(1 - \text{tax rate})$, to the after-tax net profit, assuming a 50 percent incremental corporate income tax rate; thus 50 percent of $17.6, or $8.8. (See Chapter 5 for the specific discussion of the cost of debt.)

Expense Analysis.   Various expense categories are commonly related to net sales as a matter of routine. These expense comparisons will include such items as administrative expense, selling and promotion expenses, and many other items typical of particular businesses and their industries.

$$\text{Expense ratio} = \frac{\text{Various expense items}}{\text{Net sales}} = \text{percent}$$

Many trade associations collect such data from their members and publish collections of statistics on expense ratios, as well as on most of the other ratios discussed in this chapter. This is done to provide standards of comparison and the basis for trend analysis to the members of the industry. In order to make the comparisons meaningful, great care is often taken to categorize the businesses by size and other characteristics within the industry, in order to reduce the degree of error introduced by large-scale averaging. A sample of such ratios for the paper industry is shown at the end of the chapter in Figure 2–4.

Contribution Analysis. Mostly for internal management use, but increasingly for broader financial analysis, we find the attempt to relate to net sales the "contribution margin" of product groups or total businesses. This calculation involves a very selective analysis or estimate of the fixed and variable costs and expenses of the business. Directly variable costs alone are subtracted from net sales to show the margin provided by operations towards fixed costs for the period and profits. Significant differences exist between the contribution margins of different industries, due to different capital investment requirements and cost/volume conditions. Even within a company, various lines of products may contribute rather differently to fixed costs and profits. The calculation of contribution margin appears as follows:

$$\text{Contribution to fixed cost and profit} = \frac{\text{Net sales} - \text{direct costs (var. costs)}}{\text{Net sales}}$$

$$= \text{percent}$$

Contribution margins are useful in gauging the risk characteristics of a business, i.e., the degree of leeway management enjoys in pricing and expense control under different economic conditions. Break-even analysis and pricing strategies under different levels of operations are related to the concept, and more will be said on this point in Chapter 6.

Management of Capital. Several ratios are useful in judging the effectiveness of management's employment of capital. These are grouped as various turnover relationships.

The most common of these is the relationship of net sales to gross assets, or net sales to net assets. This ratio provides a clue as to the size of asset commitment required for a given level of sales or, conversely, the sales dollars generated for each dollar of investment. While simple to calculate, the overall asset turnover is a crude measure at best, since the balance sheets of most well-established companies contain a variety of assets recorded at widely different cost levels of past periods. These recorded values often bear little resemblance to current economic values. Nevertheless, the turnover ratio is another of several clues which in combination can point towards favorable or unfavorable performance, especially if over time an improvement or worsening in the situation develops. Here are common ways of calculating turnover ratios:

$$\frac{\text{Net sales}}{\text{Gross assets}} = \frac{\$\ 955.3}{\$1,030.9} = 0.93 \text{ times } (1969: 0.91)$$

or:

$$\frac{\text{Gross assets}}{\text{Net sales}} = \frac{\$1,030.9}{\$\ 955.3} = 1.08 \text{ times } (1969: 1.10)$$

If net assets (total assets less current liabilities, which equals the capitalization of the business) are employed, the calculations appear as follows:

$$\frac{\text{Net sales}}{\text{Net assets}} = \frac{\$955.3}{\$919.9} = 1.04 \text{ times } (1969: 1.07)$$

or:

$$\frac{\text{Net assets}}{\text{Net sales}} = \frac{\$919.9}{\$955.3} = 0.96 \text{ times } (1969: 0.94)$$

The difference between the two sets of calculations is the choice of the asset total—gross assets or net assets. The second concept assumes that current liabilities are available to the business as a matter of course, and therefore the assets employed are effectively reduced through these usually available trade credit relationships. This reasoning is especially important in trading firms, where current trade payables are quite sizable. In our example the results are quite close, indicating that forest products companies require roughly $1 of assets for every $1 of sales—a very capital-intensive industry.

Among the assets of a company, inventories and receivables usually receive special attention. The ratio analysis for these categories attempts to establish the relative effectiveness with which inventories and receivables are managed, and seeks to ascertain whether there are signs of deterioration in value or excessive accumulation in these accounts. The attempt is generally to relate the size of the account to the best indicator of activity, such as sales or cost of sales, assuming that there should be a close relationship.

Inventories cannot be judged precisely, short of an actual count, verification, and value appraisal. Since this is seldom possible, the next best step is to relate the recorded inventory on the balance sheet to either net sales or cost of goods sold, to see if there is a shift in magnitude over a period of time. Normally, one employs average inventory values (the average of beginning and ending inventories); but it is also desirable at times to deal with ending inventories alone, especially in rapidly growing firms where buildup of inventories may have to occur in support of steeply rising sales. While often the relationship of sales and inventories will suffice as a broad measure, it is usually more precise to relate inventories to cost of goods sold, since only then will both items in the comparison be stated at a comparable cost level. The use of net sales introduces a distortion, since the sales include a markup not recorded in the inventories themselves. In a manufacturing company, we must particularly consider the problem of accounting measurements so often found in other tests, since the stated value of inventory in such operations can be seriously affected by the particular accounting system employed.

The method of calculating inventory ratios is as follows:

$$\frac{\text{Average inventory}}{\text{Net sales}} = \frac{\frac{1}{2}(\$159.3 + \$162.3)}{\$955.3} = 16.83\% \ (1969: 16.25\%)$$

or:

$$\frac{\text{Average inventory}}{\text{Cost of goods sold}} = \frac{\$160.8}{\$788} = 20.41\% \ (1969: 19.99\%)$$

More commonly we find this format, which expresses the number of times inventory has turned over during the period:

$$\frac{\text{Net sales}}{\text{Average inventory}} = \frac{\$955.3}{\$160.8} = 5.94 \text{ times} \ (1969: 6.16)$$

or:

$$\frac{\text{Cost of goods sold}}{\text{Average inventory}} = \frac{\$788}{\$160.8} = 4.90 \text{ times} \ (1969: 5)$$

The last two calculations reflect the frequency with which the inventory was recouped during the operating period. Generally speaking, the higher this number, the better, since low inventory levels are often interpreted to mean a low risk of unsalable stock and efficient use of capital. Yet, inventory turnover out of proportion to industry conditions may indicate inventory shortages and poor customer service. The final judgment will depend on the specific conditions.

The analysis of *accounts receivable* again uses the basis of net sales. Here the question is raised whether the amount of accounts receivable outstanding at the end of the period closely represents the amount of credit sales we would expect to remain uncollected, assuming normal credit terms. For example, a business selling at n/30 would normally expect to have the last month's sales outstanding. If 40 or 50 days' sales were represented on the balance sheet, one could expect that some customers had difficulty paying or were abusing their credit privileges, or that some sales were made on extended terms. An *exact* analysis of accounts receivable can only be made through an aging process of the accounts on the books of the company. Aging means classifying individual accounts into brackets such as 10 days, 20 days, 30 days, 40 days, etc. outstanding, and relating these groups to the credit terms applicable in the business. Since this type of analysis requires inside knowledge, financial analysts looking at the business from the outside must be satisfied with the crude or overall approach of expressing accounts receivable in terms of average daily sales. This takes the following form:

$$\frac{\text{Net sales}}{\text{Days in the year}} = \frac{\$955.3}{360} = \$2{,}654/\text{day (millions)}$$

and:

$$\frac{\text{Accounts receivable}}{\text{Sales per day}} = \frac{\$116.2}{\$2{,}654} = 43.8 \text{ days (1969: 43.4)}$$

A complication arises if a company's sales are made to different types of customers under different terms, or if the sales are made partly for cash and partly on account. A separation should be made between cash and credit sales where available. If no detailed information is obtainable on this aspect and on the pattern of terms used, the rough average has to suffice for a broad indication of trends.

A similar process can be applied in judging the company's performance regarding the payment of *accounts payable*. The analysis is made a little more difficult, since accounts payable should be specifically related to the purchases made during the operating period. Normally this information is not readily available except in a trading company, where the amount of purchases can be deduced from an analysis of beginning and ending inventories and the cost of goods sold for the period. In a manufacturing company, purchases of goods and services are buried in the cost of goods sold account for the period, and in the inventories at the end of the operating period. A very crude approximation can be made in such a case, by relating the accounts payable to the average daily use of raw materials, if this expense element is provided. If the analyst can obtain the average daily purchases for the period, he can follow the process we demonstrated for the accounts receivable, that is, calculating the number of days of accounts payable outstanding. This figure can then be related to the normal credit terms under which the company purchases, and serious deviations from that norm can be spotted.

Total assets and *net assets* and the effectiveness of their use by management are analyzed by relating profit defined in a variety of ways to the commitment of assets used to generate them. This is one of the more telling analyses, although the character of recorded values will tend to distort the results.

The easiest form of analysis is the ratio of "return on assets," which relates reported net profit (net income) to the total assets on the balance sheet or to the total long-term capital funds, the capitalization. While it is an indicator of effectiveness, the results can be seriously distorted by changes in the company's capital structure (proportion of debt and equity) and the federal income tax calculations applicable to the period:

$$\frac{\text{Net profits}}{\text{Assets}} = \frac{\$\ 41.9}{\$1,030.9} = 4.06\% \ (1969: 5.35\%\ )$$

or:

$$\frac{\text{Net profit}}{\text{Net assets (capitalization)}} = \frac{\$41.9}{\$1,030.9 - \$111} = 4.55\% \ (1969: 6.27\%\ )$$

As we stated before, net income is the final operating result after deduction of interest and taxes, and is therefore affected by the proportion of debt capital in the operation. By eliminating both interest and taxes from the ratio, we obtain a somewhat more meaningful result, which takes the following form:

$$\frac{\text{Net profit before interest and taxes}}{\text{Assets}} = \frac{\$\ 83.9}{\$1,030.9} = 8.14\% \ (1969: 9.46\%\ )$$

or:

$$\frac{\text{Net profit before interest and taxes}}{\text{Net assets (capitalization)}} = \frac{\$\ 83.9}{\$919.9} = 9.12\% \ (1969: 11.09\%\ )$$

If we accept the argument that income taxes are a normal part of doing business, the result can be modified to the extent that operating income before interest but after taxes is employed. We can use the adjustment shown on page 54 to add back to net profit the after-tax cost of interest or, if there is reason to believe that income taxes shown have been modified for a variety of reasons and are not an expression of normal conditions, we can employ a "normal" income tax rate, to arrive at an income figure for the rate of return calculation. The first of the two methods was employed here:

$$\frac{\text{Net profit after taxes, before interest}}{\text{Assets}} = \frac{\$41.9 + \tfrac{1}{2}(\$17.6)}{\$1,030.9}$$
$$= 4.91\% \ (1969: 5.98\%\ )$$

or:

$$\frac{\text{Net profit after taxes, before interest}}{\text{Net assets (capitalization)}} = \frac{\$\ 50.7}{\$919.9}$$
$$= 5.51\% \ (1969: 7.01\%\ )$$

The various ratios available for judging the business from the point of view of management thus deal with the effectiveness of operations and the effectiveness of the deployment of capital.

All suffer in one form or another from accounting and valuation uncertainties, but together they can provide reasonable clues for further study. We now turn to the viewpoint of the owners, to whom management is responsible, for a further discussion of applicable ratios. We have not mentioned these so far, even though it is quite clear that in the timing, execution, and appraisal of business operations, management must be fully aware of the owners' viewpoint of the business, just as much as the lenders' considerations have to be taken into account.

OWNERS' POINT OF VIEW

The main interest of the owners of an enterprise—the stockholders in the case of a corporation—will be the returns achieved by management effort on their share of the invested funds, and the distribution of earnings belonging to them. While there will be an absolute interest in these results, a large portion of the attention paid to these two elements will be directed to the effect of the results on the value of the ownership investment, particularly in the case of publicly traded shares of stock. The second part of Chapter 5 deals with the key concepts in this area, and we can only briefly touch upon some of these here.

The first and most common ratio used for measuring the return on owners' investment is the relationship of net profit to net worth (equity). In this case we have to make no adjustments, since net profit has been properly reduced by the interest charges, if any, paid to holders of debt funds. Thus net income represents a residual result totally belonging to the equity holders, common and preferred. The calculation appears as follows:

$$\frac{\text{Net profit}}{\text{Net worth (equity)}} = \frac{\$41.9}{\$20 + \$549.7} = 7.35\% \ (1969: 9.58\%)$$

Some questions arise regarding the handling of deferred income taxes, which, as we discussed in Chapter 1, result from the difference between accounting treatment and tax treatment of depreciation. Some analysts argue that deferred income taxes are in effect ownership equity set aside against future higher tax levels, while others argue that they represent a form of debt. Often, deferred income taxes are not included in any of the calculations. Many analysts appear to be leaning toward the recognition of deferred income taxes as part of equity, but the point is still in dispute.

A somewhat more refined version of the return calculation is the analysis of earnings ascribed to the common stockholder, as related to the stated value of the common stockholder's equity. The difference is merely the elimination from earnings of dividends to preferred stockholders and other obligatory payments, such as to minority holders. Also, the preferred equity and any minority elements are removed from the net worth to arrive at common equity. The result of this calculation is shown below:

$$\frac{\text{Net profit to common}}{\text{Common equity}} = \frac{\$41.9 - \$0.8}{\$549.7} = 7.45\% \ (1969: 9.79\%)$$

Again, the question of accuracy of recorded values and earnings calculations arises, and adjustments may be necessary if the analyst is aware of major inconsistencies.

The analysis of earnings from the owners' point of view centers around the *earnings per share* concept in the case of a corporate enterprise. This is simply the relationship of net profit (income) to the number of shares of common stock outstanding. Since in many corporations the number of shares changes during the year, either from issuance of new shares (new issues of stock, stock dividends, options, etc.) or retirements of old shares (treasury stock), it is common practice to use the average number of shares outstanding during the year. Earnings per share is a focal concept to which both management and the investor pay a great deal of attention. It looms large in the valuation of common stock (see Chapter 5) and often is the basis for specific corporate objectives and goals in planning for the future.

$$\text{Earnings per share} = \frac{\text{Net income}}{\text{Average number of shares outstanding}}$$

The calculation of earnings per share is normally unnecessary, since earnings per share are announced freely and frequently by corporations large and small. This is done both on a quarterly and annual basis, and wherever publicly traded shares are involved these are matters of public record.

A great deal of current analysis is directed to analyzing past earnings per share, both on a quarterly and annual basis. Much of the financial reporting of corporations is built around this figure, and projections are made by the financial community. Fluctuations and trends are watched closely as indicators of strength and weakness. Again, great caution is advised in the interpretation, however, to make allowances for unusual elements both in earnings and numbers of shares. In recent years it has become mandatory to calculate earnings per share also on a "converted" basis if a corporation has outstanding a number of convertible securities which may be turned into common stock in the future. In this fashion an attempt is made to call attention to the dilution effect of such issues. Moreover, any significant change in the number of shares outstanding (such as that caused by stock splits, for example) requires adjustments in past data for compatibility.

Cash flow per share is found frequently as an additional piece of information. This ratio, which represents per share net income plus depreciation and depletion, is an attempt to indicate the potential availability of cash for dividend and other disbursement purposes. Since the use of funds is largely at the discretion of management, however, this figure is at best only a crude indication of the ability to pay dividends. A much more revealing analysis is the funds flow format we discussed in the previous chapter.

Dividends per share are generally declared specifically and directly by the board of directors, and no calculations are necessary. A useful measure, however, is the so-called payout ratio, which represents the proportion of earnings paid in the form of cash during any given year. Since dividend policy quite commonly is oriented towards a fairly stable dividend by most boards of directors, the payout ratio of a company may fluctuate widely over the short term (two or three years) as earnings performance changes. In the long run, the payout ratio can often be used as one predictive device to judge the tendency of the directors to reinvest funds vis-à-vis paying out the earnings to the stockholder. There are no absolute standards for this ratio, but the relationship is significant in characterizing the "style" of corporate management. High-growth companies tend to pay out relatively low proportions of earnings, preferring to reinvest funds, while stable or moderate-growth companies tend to pay out larger proportions. Much more background, of course, must be considered in this as in many other questions of ratio analysis, and the reader is directed to the references at the end of the chapter.

Owners will also be interested in the degree to which their dividends are "covered" by earnings and cash flow. Furthermore, they will be interested in the degree to which the proportions in the capital structure of debt, fixed interest cost, and cash repayment requirements will affect management's ability to achieve reasonably stable and growing earnings and dividends commensurate with their expectations. A variety of "coverage" ratios are calculated, but they hardly differ from the ones we shall take up in the discussion of the lenders' point of view.

On balance, the judgment of a company's performance by the owner will be based on the return on his "stake," in terms of growth of the value of his commitment and cash rewards in the form of dividends. All of these are related to earnings power and management policies regarding the use of leverage and dividend policy. More details will be provided on these points in Chapter 6.

LENDERS' VIEW

While the main orientation of management and ownership is towards the business as a going concern, the viewpoint of the lender of necessity has to be split. He has an interest both in funding a successful business operation and a cautious view towards the possibility of default and liquidation. Sharing none of the rewards of success other than the regular interest and principal payments, the lender must carefully assess the risk of recovering his funds. Part of that assessment must be the value of his claims in case of serious difficulty. The general creditor ranks right after federal tax claims and secured creditors (who lend against a specific asset, such as a building or mobile equipment) in the satisfaction of his claims—and cautious practice dictates the existence of a "cushion" against default. Several ratios appeal to this protective motive, while others, particularly coverage of debt service, are directed to an operational view.

Debt Proportions. The most commonly quoted ratio in appraising the debt exposure represented on a balance sheet is the current ratio, which relates current assets to current liabilities in an attempt to show the safety of the claims of the current debt holders:

$$\frac{\text{Current assets}}{\text{Current liabilities}} = \frac{\$322.3}{\$111} = 2.9\text{:}1 \ (1969\text{: } 2.1\text{:}1)$$

Presumably, the larger the ratio, the better the position of the debt holders. From the lender's viewpoint, a higher ratio would certainly appear to protect his claim against drastic losses in value in case of liquidation. In that sense, a large excess of current assets over current liabilities would provide for a cushion should inventories have to be disposed of at a forced sale and should accounts receivable contain sizable credit risks. Seen from another angle, however, an excessively high current ratio would indicate slack management practices, since it might signal excessive inventories for the current requirements and poor credit management in terms of overextended accounts receivable. At the same time, the business might not be making the full use of its current borrowing power.

A very commonly encountered rule of thumb is the belief that a 2:1 current ratio is about right for most businesses, since it would allow a shrinkage of up to 50 percent in value of current assets and still cover current liabilities. The difficulty with this concept is that the current ratio is an essentially static measure which looks upon a business at the brink of liquidation and does not take the point of view of a going concern with which management should be engrossed. An even more stringent test of static nature is the acid test ratio, which employs only a portion of current assets—namely cash, marketable securities, and receivables—which are related to current liabilities as follows:

$$\frac{\text{Cash} + \text{marketable securities} + \text{receivables}}{\text{Current liabilities}} = \frac{\$13.8 + \$17.4 + \$116.2}{\$111}$$
$$= 1.3{:}1 \ (1969{:}\ 0.9{:}1)$$

As this ratio implies, the whole orientation here is to test the collectibility of current liabilities in case of real crisis, assuming that there will be no value remaining in inventories at all. As drastic tests of ability to pay in the face of disaster, these ratios are quite useful. From an operational standpoint, however, it is better to analyze a business operation in terms of expected future operating conditions, of which the proportion of current assets to current liabilities will only be a small part.

A more overall view of measuring the riskiness of a business from the lenders' point of view is given by a variety of ratios dealing with *total debt* or *long-term debt* in relation to various parts of the balance sheet. These ratios again are an attempt to express the risk exposure of a business in relation to the asset values against which all claims, debt or equity, are held. The first and most overall test is that of relating total debt, current and long-term, to total assets, as follows:

$$\frac{\text{Total debt}}{\text{Total assets}} = \frac{\$111 + \$266.6}{\$1,030.9} = 36.6\% \ (1969{:}\ 36.5\%)$$

This test merely indicates the proportion of "other people's money" to the total claims against the assets of the business. It is not necessarily a true test of the ability of the business to cover its debt, since, as we already observed, the values recorded on the balance sheet are not necessarily indicative of economic values.

A more refined version of debt proportion analysis is the relationship of long-term debt to the capitalization of the corporation, the latter again being defined as the total claims against the business, both debt and equity, other than short-term trade and tax obligations. A great deal of emphasis has been placed upon this particular ratio, since many lending agreements in publicly held and private corporations contain covenants regulating maximum debt exposure in these terms.

$$\frac{\text{Long-term debt}}{\text{Capitalization (net assets)}} = \frac{\$266.6}{\$919.9} = 29\% \ (1969: 25.6\%)$$

As we shall see later, however, there is increasing recognition that the most relevant aspect of analyzing debt exposure is not so much the proportion in the capital structure but the ability to *service* the debt.

Another version of this relationship is the ratio of total debt, normally all short and long-term debt, to total net worth (equity). In this ratio, as in some instances before, the question of deferred income taxes is sidestepped by leaving that portion of the capitalization out altogether. The ratio is an attempt to show, in another form, the relative proportions of debt to equity, and again it is used as a measure of debt exposure:

$$\frac{\text{Total debt}}{\text{Net worth (equity)}} = \frac{\$111 + \$266.6}{\$569.7} = 66.3\% \ (1969: 65.4\%)$$

A specific refinement of this formula uses long-term debt *only,* as related to net worth, while a final refinement calls for long-term debt as a proportion of the total capitalization, in which such elements as deferred income taxes and a variety of other claims might or might not be contained:

$$\frac{\text{Long-term debt}}{\text{Net worth (equity)}} = \frac{\$266.6}{\$569.7}$$
$$= 46.8\% \ (1969: 39.1\%)$$

or

$$\frac{\text{Long-term debt}}{\text{Capitalization} - \text{long-term debt}} = \frac{\$266.6}{\$919.9 - \$266.6}$$
$$= 40.8\% \ (1969: 34.4\%)$$

Regardless of the specific choice of the several ratios just discussed, the debt proportion analysis is essentially a *static* analysis which does not take into account the operational dynamics of the business organization. The analysis is derived totally from the balance sheet, which in itself is a static snapshot of the financial condition of a business at any one point in time. Only the relative ease with which the ratios are calculated probably accounts for their popularity. While useful as indicators of trends, when applied over a long period of time, the ratios still do not get at the heart of the analysis of the debt-worthiness of a business, which lies in its ability to repay both principal and interest.

Somewhat more in line with that thinking are the various "coverages" of debt service in contrast to examining debt as a proportion of the funding of the business. One of the very frequently encountered ratios is the relationship of net profit before taxes and interest to the size of the interest payments themselves. This ratio is developed in the hope that the annual operating profit can be considered a basic source of debt service funds, and any significant change in the ratio might signal difficulties. No hard and fast standards are in existence; rather, after an exhaustive analysis of a business's condition, the debt holders might require some covenants concerning the number of times the business is expected to cover its debt service obligations, based on their best judgment.

$$\frac{\text{Net profit before taxes and interest}}{\text{Interest}} = \frac{\$83.9}{\$17.6} = 4.8 \text{ times } (1969: 7.4)$$

A somewhat more refined coverage analysis relates the *cash flow* of the business before taxes and interest to the total of interest and principal repayments, in an attempt to indicate the ability of the business to service its debts. Several problems arise with this particular analysis, since interest payments are tax deductible while principal repayments are not. Care must be taken to develop these figures on a comparable basis.

As indicated before, there is growing interest on the part of the financial community to develop a form of "sensitivity analysis" with which to test the ability of a business to take care of its debt obligations. Lease obligations, which up to the present have not been shown on the balance sheet, are analyzed along with debt service requirements if they are significant and available to the analyst. For this purpose, an analysis is made over an appropriately long period of time to determine the major operational fluctuations which are normal for the type of company and industry. Such a range of past analysis might extend over several years or several seasons, as the case may be, in an attempt to determine characteristic high and low points in earnings and cash flow fluctuations. The analysis of past conditions is then projected into the future, along the lines of our funds flow analysis in Chapter 1 and our earnings projections in Chapter 3, to determine what problems, under presently known conditions, the operation might encounter in servicing its debt. It is possible to chart the pretax operating profit, the after-tax operating profit, and the cash flow likely to be encountered, and to draw high and low limits of these conditions from which to judge the maximum debt exposure which might be appropriate for the company. Debt service in this analysis would be defined as the size of the yearly principal repayments, as well as the after-tax interest cost encountered on the debt outstanding. If a business is subject to sizable fluctuations in after-tax cash flow, lenders may be more reluctant to provide debt which could not be serviced several times over at the low point. In contrast, when dealing with a public utility or a fairly stable corporation, the lenders may be satisfied to have a coverage of only one to one and a half times the debt service at the low point of the cyclical experience.

The type of reasoning described here is very much related to the concept of financial modeling touched upon in Chapters 1 and 3, which is nothing more than a simultaneous expression of the key relationships governing a business operation. With the help of computer models it is possible to make projections of a variety of likely conditions, given knowledge about the interrelationships of key elements in a company's operating and financial performance. When viewed in this light, simple ratio analysis or the insistence upon a minimum standard in one or two key ratios appear somewhat simplistic; since it is to the lenders' advantage, as well as in the management's and owners' interest, to have a business succeed in total, given all of the surrounding conditions. The simulation of a business and the use of the results to make judgments about its total debt-worthiness is therefore much more meaningful and has become increasingly accepted.

RATIOS AS A SYSTEM

In recognition of these complexities, many attempts were made in the past to demonstrate the interrelationship of the various ratios discussed in this chapter. One of the first to recognize and display the system of ratios was the DuPont company, which in its planning activities developed the "DuPont charts." These illustrate the fact that, for example, asset turnover and net profit as a percentage of sales are related, since the elements contained in them lead to net profit on assets. Figure 2–3 shows such a pictorial display, which highlights the interconnections of major ratios. As computerized analysis and models have come into use, these and many other interrelationships are quite easily exploited, allowing management to think of the business as a system rather than as a loose combination of checkpoints.

SUMMARY

In this chapter we have shown that the assessment of business performance is inseparable from the viewpoints of the persons or groups analyzing this performance. We have chosen to talk about only three major viewpoints—management, owners, and lenders—leaving out detailed discussions of other interested groups. The various analyses displayed lead very quickly to the recognition that, in the end, the crucial test is the return on the investment employed in the business and its attendant effect on the value of ownership. All three parties are concerned about the success of the operation, each from its own interest; but it is management's duty to bring about stability, growth, and reliability of earnings performance relative to the investment en-

Figure 2-3

KEY RATIOS AS A SYSTEM

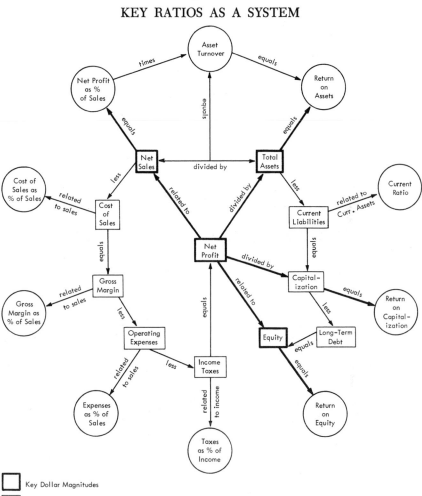

☐ Key Dollar Magnitudes

□ Subsidiary Dollar Magnitudes

◯ Key Ratios

trusted to it. All the ratios are intertwined and are best interpreted when viewing the business as a system of interconnected conditions. To this end, modeling and computerized simulation are increasingly becoming useful, since many ratios are by their nature only fairly static tests which cannot do justice to the dynamics of a business operation. Chapter 6 will provide a fuller treatment of this concept.

Figure 2-4

CROWN ZELLERBACH COMPARED WITH FOUR MAJOR PAPER COMPANIES AND 38 INTEGRATED COMPANIES IN THE PAPER INDUSTRY

Selected Ratios for 1969 and 1970

(dollar figures in millions except per share)

	Crown Zellerbach	International Paper	Mead Paper	St. Regis Paper	Kimberly Clark	38 Integrated* Companies
Net sales						
1969	$ 919	$1,777	$1,032	$ 868	$ 835	—
1970	$ 955	$1,841	$1,038	$ 857	$ 866	—
Total assets						
1969	$1,009	$1,887	$ 811	$ 949	$ 904	—
1970	$1,031	$2,047	$ 862	$ 937	$ 956	—
Net profit						
1969	$ 54.0	$115.6	$ 35.9	$41.2	$49.9	—
1970	$ 41.9	$ 42.9	$ 19.9	$32.0	$38.3	—
Capitalization						
1969	$ 861	$1,563	$ 668	$ 821	$ 778	—
1970	$ 920	$1,682	$ 712	$ 823	$ 825	—
Gross margin						
1969	18.7%	24.9%	17.2%	15.4%	30.1%	20.4%
1970	17.5%	22.7%	14.6%	15.8%	29.0%	18.7%
Net profit to sales						
1969	5.8%	6.5%	3.5%	4.7%	6.0%	5.4%
1970	4.4%	4.5%	1.9%	3.7%	4.4%	4.2%
Net sales to total assets						
1969	.91:1	.94:1	1.27:1	.91:1	.92:1	1.01:1
1970	.93:1	.89:1	1.20:1	.91:1	.91:1	91:1
Ending inventory to sales						
1969	17.6%	14.1%	14.9%	15.5%	16.2%	14.6%
1970	16.6%	15.8%	14.0%	15.0%	18.4%	15.5%

	1	2	3	4	5	6
Days receivables						
1969	43.4	54.5	46.7	46.0	42.3	44.6
1970	43.7	54.6	45.4	45.8	42.8	45.0
Net profit to capitalization (before interest)						
1969	7.0%	8.2%	6.1%	6.1%	7.1%	—
1970	5.5%	3.8%	3.8%	4.9%	5.4%	—
Net profit to common equity						
1969	9.6%	10.3%	7.0%	7.9%	9.0%	9.7%
1970	7.4%	3.8%	4.5%	6.0%	6.7%	7.3%
Current ratio						
1969	2.9:1	1.8:1	2.3:1	2.3:1	2.3:1	2.1:1
1970	2.1:1	2.2:1	2.3:1	2.6:1	2.2:1	2.2:1
Debt as percent of capitalization						
1969	26%	24%	28%	33%	22%	33%**
1970	29%	32%	33%	31%	23%	36%**
Earnings per share						
1969	$2.29	$2.59	$1.72	$2.98	$2.31	—
1970	$1.77	$1.85	$0.70	$2.29	$1.64	—
Year-end price/earnings ratio						
1969	15X	14X	12X	12X	17X	—
1970	17X	19X	23X	16X	19X	—

Source: Annual Reports.
* Adapted from 1970 Capital and Income Survey, American Paper Institute.
** Debt and deferred taxes.

SELECTED REFERENCES

ANTHONY, ROBERT N. *Management Accounting, Text and Cases,* chaps. 10, 11. 4th ed. Homewood, Ill.: Richard D. Irwin, 1970.

COHEN, JEROME B., and ROBBINS, SIDNEY M. *The Financial Manager, Basic Aspects of Financial Administration.* New York: Harper & Row, 1966.

GRAHAM, B.; DODD, D. L.; and COTTLE, S. *Security Analysis,* part II. 4th ed. New York: McGraw-Hill Book Co., 1962.

FOULKE, ROY A. *Practical Financial Statement Analysis.* 6th ed. New York: McGraw-Hill Book Co., 1968.

HAYES, DOUGLAS A. *Investments, Analysis and Management.* 2d ed. New York: Macmillan Co., 1966.

HUNT, PEARSON; WILLIAMS, CHARLES M.; and DONALDSON, GORDON. *Basic Business Finance,* chap. 7. 3d ed. Homewood, Ill.: Richard D. Irwin, 1966.

ROBERT MORRIS ASSOCIATES. *Annual Statement Studies.*

TROY, LEO. *Almanac of Business and Industrial Financial Ratios.* Englewood Cliffs, N.J.: Prentice-Hall, 1971.

VAN HORNE, JAMES C. *Financial Management and Policy,* chap. 24. Englewood Cliffs, N.J.: Prentice-Hall, 1968.

WESTON, J. FRED, and BRIGHAM, EUGENE F. *Managerial Finance,* chap. 4. 3d ed. New York: Holt, Rinehart & Winston, 1971.

CHAPTER
3
PROJECTION OF BUSINESS RESULTS

Our discussion so far has dealt with an appraisal and judgment of the results of *past* business decisions about investments, operations, and financing. This chapter will be the first of three chapters to deal with a *forward* look towards likely future conditions—the projection of operating and financial results and the analysis of various alternative plans under different conditions. The projection of financial results is only part of the business planning process in which management takes account of the economic, competitive, technical, and social environment. During the total planning effort, management sets objectives and goals, with strategies for achieving desired short-run, intermediate, and long-term results. In the specific, narrower analysis of financial projections, the manager or analyst can employ the useful ratios illustrated in Chapter 2 to the extent they apply, in addition to various statistical techniques. Regardless of the techniques employed, however, financial projections are essential to the foundation of the planning structure.

The scope of this book permits a focus only on major specific methodology regarding formats of financial projection, without explicitly taking account of the broader planning framework. Also, discussion of the increasingly popular use of statistical projection techniques through easy access to time-shared computer systems will be left out because of space limitations. Such specialized techniques are adequately covered in the common textbooks on statistics and the specific descriptive materials available with time-sharing services. The reader is also referred to planning literature at the end of Chapter 6 for a broader framework within which to view the process discussed here.

The main techniques for financial projection fall into three categories—operating budgets, financial budgets, and pro forma financial statements. Operating and financial (cash) budgets are projections dealing with key sections and elements of the the business operation, while pro forma financial statements represent a forward look for the business as a whole, in the form of the usual balance sheet and income statements. In all three cases we are talking about an arrangement of basic physical and financial data as the starting point for planning activities. These efforts are not only necessary for the short run, but also become a basis for truly strategic long-range thinking. Each of the three areas will be dealt with specifically in this chapter, and the most important techniques will be highlighted. At the end of the chapter the concept of financial modeling will be related to these techniques, since such models can provide a fully integrated set of concepts for projection.

OPERATING BUDGETS

The most frequently encountered type of projection, and the one with the greatest variability, is the operating budget. As an expression of ongoing operations, the operating budget is linked closely to the organizational structure of the business operation and to its performance measurement. Most managements will attempt to structure the total company into manageable parts, for each of which a manager or executive is held responsible. This separation may take the form of a functional organization—i.e., one person is responsible for sales, another for production, a third for purchasing resources, etc. In other cases, the organization may be composed of a series of smaller "profit centers," each of which is expected to provide a profit contribution to the corporation.

While there are countless variations of organizational structure and performance evaluation, the principles are quite simple. Projection of operating results must take a form which expresses the scope of the business unit involved. It must be related to the elements under the control of the responsible manager, and should be the basis on which the manager's performance is measured. These criteria quite obviously require that operating budgets be carefully structured to fit the particular unit's conditions and the management style of the company as a whole. This means that there will be a great deal of difference in the approaches taken by various companies, even within the same industry, and differences will have to be recognized also within a given company. A growing body of literature on the concept of responsibility accounting has taken recognition of these aspects.

For purposes of illustration within the scope of our discussion, let us take two simple examples of the process: (1) the sales manager of all product groups of XYZ Corporation is asked to establish a quarterly sales budget for the year 1972, which is to show his contribution to corporate profits; and (2) the manager of a factory of XYZ Corporation is to prepare his operating budget for the third quarter of 1972, which is to show the output expected and the total costs incurred in the process.

Our sales manager first must project the level of unit sales he expects in the territories served, by major product line. He most likely will build this up from his and his people's judgments about the expected demand from his major current and potential customers, based on the strategies he and his competitors are likely to follow. Next, he has to estimate the price levels under which he will have to operate. This will commonly be a function of industry pricing practices, the strategic balance, and to some extent the cost performance of his company's manufacturing operations. Furthermore, he must estimate the cost of the products transferred internally or purchased from the outside. In addition, he must project the manpower requirements for his sales activities, the travel and entertainment expenses, and other direct sales support costs. Another element will be delivery expense to the customer, if borne by the company. Finally, estimates of sales support costs provided by the company, general marketing and advertising expense, and the share of corporate overhead ascribed to his operations will normally be projected.

In all of these estimating efforts, our manager can make use of past relationships and selected ratios, tempered by his best judgment of changes in future conditions. The operating budget for his organization may take shape as shown in Figure 3–1. In this sample, both basic data and dollar elements have been set out by four quarters and for the total year 1972. There is nothing unique about the format selected here, since many arrangements of the information are possible. Generally, a company will have prescribed formats which its managers have to follow, both to maintain a certain amount of uniformity and to ease the accounting problem of consolidation. From a financial projection standpoint, the sales and contribution data shown in the example are pieces of raw material which go into making up the total operating plan of the company.

Another example of an operating budget is the factory budget shown in Figure 3–2. This time, the data are displayed in a monthly format highlighting three months of the year and a quarterly total. Again, the format selection must suit the particular preferences of the organization. In this case we have chosen to show, in the arrangement of the data and headings, the fact that certain items of cost are under the control of the local manager. Other costs will be transferred in from corporate headquarters and are thus only to a very limited extent under his control. This type of structuring becomes useful if the operating plan as displayed is to serve as a control device on which to measure the performance of the unit during the projected time period.

In both the sales and the manufacturing operating budgets, it is possible to include additional columns in which to record

Figure 3–1

XYZ CORPORATION

Sample Quarterly Sales Budget
Year Ended December 31, 1972

Basic Data:	Quarter				Total
	First	*Second*	*Third*	*Fourth*	*Total*
Unit sales (number of units):					
Product A	2,700	2,900	3,000	2,800	11,400
Product B	8,000	8,500	10,000	8,000	34,500
Product C	17,500	18,500	21,000	16,000	73,000
Price level (per unit):					
Product A	$145	$145	$150	$150	....
Product B	$ 92	$ 92	$ 95	$ 95	....
Product C	$ 74	$ 74	$ 74	$ 74	....
Number of salesmen	25	25	25	26	....
Operating Budget (in thousands):					
Sales revenue	$2,423	$2,572	$2,954	$2,364	$10,313
Less: Returns, allowances	25	26	28	24	103
Net sales	$2,398	$2,546	$2,926	$2,340	$10,210
Cost of goods sold	1,916	2,051	2,322	1,868	8,159
Margin before delivery	$ 482	$ 495	$ 604	$ 472	$ 2,053
Delivery expense	56	60	68	54	238
Gross margin	$ 426	$ 435	$ 536	$ 418	$ 1,815
Selling expense (controllable):					
Salesmen's compensation	$ 94	$ 94	$ 94	$ 98	$ 380
Travel and entertainment	32	32	32	33	129
Sales support costs	23	23	26	24	96
Total selling expense	$ 149	$ 149	$ 152	$ 155	$ 605
Gross contribution	$ 277	$ 286	$ 384	$ 263	$ 1,210
Departmental period costs	18	18	18	18	72
Net contribution	$ 259	$ 268	$ 366	$ 245	$ 1,138
Corporate support (transferred):					
Staff support	$ 23	$ 25	$ 25	$ 27	$ 100
Advertising	50	50	75	50	225
General overhead	63	63	63	63	252
Total corporate support	$ 136	$ 138	$ 163	$ 140	$ 577
Profit contribution (before taxes)	$ 123	$ 130	$ 203	$ 105	$ 561

the actual experience. Also, variance columns can be provided to measure deviations from the plan. We shall not go into such refinements, since the purpose of showing the examples was to highlight the type of analysis and projection that takes place, formally or informally, in parts of an organization, preparatory to developing a financial plan.

Figure 3–2

XYZ CORPORATION
Sample Factory Budget
For the Quarter Ended June 30, 1972

Basic data:	April	May	June	Total
Number of shifts (5-day week) ...	3	3	3	3
Days worked	20	21	22	63
Hourly employees per shift	33	33	33	33
Number of machines	35	35	34	....
Unit production:				
Product A	1,000	1,050	1,100	3,150
Product B	2,400	2,510	2,640	7,550
Capacity utilization	94%	94%	96%	95%
Down time for repairs (hours) ...	–0–	36	–0–	36
Operating budget:				
Direct costs (controllable):*				
Manufacturing labor ....$ 57,600		$ 60,500	$ 63,400	$181,500
Raw materials	53,800	56,400	59,200	169,400
Operating supplies	6,500	6,900	7,300	20,700
Repair labor and parts	7,300	12,400	6,500	26,200
Power, heat, light	4,200	4,500	4,800	13,500
Total direct costs $129,400		$140,700	$141,200	$411,300
Period costs (controllable):				
Supervision ....$ 5,500		$ 5,500	$ 5,500	$ 16,500
Support labor	28,500	28,500	28,500	85,500
Insurance, taxes	8,700	8,700	8,700	26,100
Depreciation	20,500	20,500	20,500	61,500
Total period costs ....$ 63,200		$ 63,200	$ 63,200	$189,600
Total controllable costs $192,600		$203,900	$204,400	$600,900
General overhead (allocated)	72,000	72,000	72,000	216,000
Total cost $264,600		$275,900	$276,400	$816,900

* Where appropriate, unit costs can be shown.

CASH BUDGETS

Of more specific interest to the financial analyst and the financial manager within a company will be the detailed projection of cash requirements, which normally takes the form of a cash budget. In contrast to the activity plans highlighted in the earlier section, which are a reflection of selling or manufacturing operations as they will be recorded through the accounting system, the cash budget is an attempt to focus very specifically on the incidence of cash receipts and payments. Our sales manager or factory manager was not overly concerned as to when the actual payment for the expenses incurred by him would be made, or when collection for sales on credit would take place. The accounting system under which he is measured concentrates on recording the transactions for revenues and expenses as they are committed, with the accrual method ascribing to each time period the appropriate amounts, irrespective of cash movement.

In contrast, our financial manager is very much concerned with observing the activity in the cash account, which he must maintain at a level high enough to allow payment of amounts due. As a consequence, he must develop a cash activity plan which reflects the very specific timing of the inflows and outflows of cash in response to the operational activities planned.

The process of cash budgeting is quite simple when one remembers the need to estimate cash incidence. The approach is similar to personal budgeting, where bills due are matched with receipts from paychecks, dividend checks, bank interest payments, etc. The purpose of the effort is, of course, an analysis of funds requirements as reflected by changes in the cash balance available for payment. This balance may fluctuate from day to day, week to week, or month to month. If a company's collections from credit sales tend to lag for weeks while wages and purchases must be paid for currently, serious cash shortages can occur. Similarly, cash payments for nonperiodic elements, such as capital equipment, can cause temporary problems which must be met by a cash provision. It is necessary, therefore, to lay out a *time schedule* of the estimated receipts and payments of cash, and to observe the net effect of projected activity. The selection of the time period depends on the nature of the business and the trade terms under which it operates. If daily fluctuations are likely to be large, as in some parts of the banking business, daily projections will be helpful; in other cases, monthly or even quarterly projections will suffice.

In the example used for illustration, Figure 3–3, we have chosen to show a monthly cash budget for XYZ Corporation which covers the quarter ended December 31, 1972. The process begins with a presentation of the basic data of the company's operations regarding sales, production, and purchases. Two

Figure 3–3

XYZ CORPORATION

Sample Cash Budget for the Quarter Ended December 31, 1972

(thousands of dollars)

	August	September	October	November	December	Total
Basic data:						
Unit sales	48,000	46,000	42,000	36,000	33,000	111,000
Unit production	50,000	50,000	35,000	34,000	31,000	100,000
Change in inventory	+2,000	+4,000	−7,000	−2,000	−2,000	−11,000
Sales volume (on credit)	$4,450	$4,250	$3,850	$3,350	$3,050	$10,250
Purchases (on credit)	$ 760	$ 740	$ 520	$ 500	$ 460	$ 1,480
Cash receipts:						
Collection of receivables—prior months' sales; normal terms of 30 days assumed			$4,250	$ 3,850	$ 3,350	$11,450
Proceeds from sale of stock options			–0–	250	–0–	250
Proceeds from sale of used machines at book value			–0–	–0–	550	550
Total cash receipts			$4,250	$ 4,100	$ 3,900	$12,250
Cash disbursements:						
Payment for purchases*			$ 750	$ 630	$ 510	$ 1,890
Production payroll (from operating budget)			560	545	490	1,595
Manufacturing expenses (from operating budget)			1,265	1,260	1,235	3,760
Selling and delivery (from sales budget)			350	345	335	1,030
General overhead (from administrative budget)			200	200	200	600
Interest payment on debt			–0–	–0–	175	175
Principal payment on note payable			1,500	–0–	–0–	1,500
Federal tax payment			400	–0–	–0–	400
Payments on contruction of new plant			–0–	2,000	900	2,900
Total cash disbursements			$5,025	$ 4,980	$ 3,845	$13,850
Net cash receipts (disbursements)			$ (775)	$ (880)	$ 55	$ (1,600)
Cumulative net cash flow			$ (775)	$(1,655)	$(1,600)	$ (1,600)
Analysis of cash requirements:						
Beginning cash balance			$1,450	$ 675	$ (205)	$ 1,450
Net cash receipts (disbursements)			(775)	(880)	55	(1,600)
Ending cash balance			$ 675	$ (205)	$ (150)	$ (150)
Minimum cash balance			1,250	1,250	1,250	1,250
Cash requirements			$ 575	$ 1,455	$ 1,400	$ 1,400

* One month's purchases prior to past 1.5 months; normal terms of 45 days assumed (e.g., half of August and half of September paid during October).

months' activities prior to the quarter analyzed are shown, since under the sales and purchase terms assumed here the cash effect from these months will lag into this period. This condition is clearly reflected in the first item of cash receipts, the collection of receivables. If we can assume that the company's customers will continue to pay within the 30-day terms, then the cash receipts of any one month should be the sales of the previous month. Any change in expected customer behavior, or in the credit terms themselves, would have to be reflected in a different receipts pattern. Other cash receipts are shown according to the best estimate of incidence.

Another lag is reflected in the payment for purchases, on the assumption that normal payment terms of 45 days will be observed by XYZ Corporation. Part of August and September purchases will, therefore, be paid for in October, with a similar lag observed for November and December. Since the last quarter is projected as a seasonal low in sales and manufacturing activities, the effect of the timing pattern is to shift somewhat higher cash receipts and payments into a period of low activity. In contrast, a rising volume of operations would have resulted in lower cash incidence, as the current budget would partly reflect earlier low-level conditions. This observation supports the critical need for cash budgeting in a business where operating levels and payment conditions may vary widely from period to period.

Other cash disbursements are listed on the assumption that payments for the expenses and obligations are made within the time period indicated. This could be slightly incorrect in the case of payroll and certain manufacturing expenses. Such items could lag by one or two weeks. The degree of precision required will have to be judged by the seriousness of any indicated cash problems. Note also that production-related payments are based on the operating plan, which calls for an inventory reduction (see "Basic Data"). This is a major difference from the income statement for the period, where cost of goods sold will be based on selling activities.

The result of the cash budget is a picture of the cash effect of the various operating plans on which the budget is based. In this case, the first two months of the quarter show sizable net cash disbursements, while the third month provides a slight cash surplus. Overall, a net cash outflow of $1.6 million is indicated. A further analysis of the effect on the corporate cash balance shows a funds requirement building up from over $0.6 million to $1.4 million, with a slightly larger requirement in November. It is possible to show the total corporate borrowing requirement by adding any outstanding loans to the funds requirements of each period.

It is important to remember that the monthly picture shown here could indeed hide some more serious cash shortages during certain days or weeks of the quarter. Only a more detailed analysis would reveal these. Also, any change in the assumptions about receipts and collections could seriously affect the picture. The advantage of such a format, on the other hand, is that one can test the likely effect of significant changes by working through the figures under different assumptions. The cash budget thus becomes a financial planning tool on the basis of which arrangements can be made for future cash needs.

PRO FORMA STATEMENTS

So far we have dealt with segments of projection needs for XYZ Corporation. The most comprehensive look at likely future conditions for a company can be taken by developing a set of pro forma statements. These statements are but an income statement and balance sheet extended into the future, and in that sense present an "operating plan" of the company as a whole. They are prepared by taking the most readily available estimates of activity and projecting, account by account, the expected results and conditions. This is one of the most widely used quick ways of estimating future profitability and financial condition, and is particularly in favor with bank loan officers, who must assess the credit of the company from the total financial picture.

It is not really necessary to have all the detailed plan segments (sales budgets, manufacturing and service plans, etc.) available from which to build up the pro forma statement— although the degree of precision will be better—since a heavy use of ratios can produce entirely satisfactory statements for a first look. As will be shown later, pro forma balance sheets can also be used to find funds requirements necessary to support operations as of the projected balance sheet date.

Having worked with key planning segments of XYZ Corporation earlier in this chapter, let us now develop a set of pro forma statements for the last quarter of 1972. We start with the income statement, Figure 3–4, since the profit (retained earnings) will have to be reflected in the pro forma balance sheet. We begin with a unit and dollar projection of sales, and we already know from the sales plan that the last part of 1972 is a seasonal low. Price and product mix are assumed unchanged for this purpose, although more specific analyses could take place. Cost of goods sold is projected by using a modified ratio approach, which assumes that lower volume production will result in inefficiencies and will cause a one percentage point rise in cost. The breakdown into cost elements is based on ratios experienced in the past. If no details had been available, the projection might be made on broad cost-to-sales assumptions.

Selling and general and administrative expenses in XYZ Corporation are assumed to be essentially fixed. The projection therefore shows a higher percentage of costs relative to sales than in the previous quarter. If detailed knowledge about such elements were not available, a more arbitrary judgment might have to suffice. An unchanged ratio of selling expenses to sales might be used, for example. The analyst must use his best judgment in any case. Interest expense is based on outstanding obligations, while taxes are projected at 48 percent. Often a tax rate of 50 percent is assumed for ease of calculation.

The results of the projections provide net income for the period, which is only one third of that of the previous quarter. This is largely a reflection of the lower operating rate. Also shown, for interest, is the so-called cash flow, which is a quick estimate of cash provided by operations, but which has to be

Figure 3-4

XYZ CORPORATION

Pro Forma Income Statement for the Quarter Ended December 31, 1972
(thousands of dollars)

	Actual Quarter Ended 9-30-72		Pro Forma* Quarter Ended 12-31-72		Remarks
Units sold	137,000		111,000		Last quarter is seasonal low (see sample sales budget).
Net sales	$12,650	100.0%	$10,250	100.0%	Projected from sales plan.
Cost of goods sold:					Expected to reflect low volume inefficiencies— rise of 1%.
Labor	$ 2,210		$ 1,810		21.5% of cost of goods.
Materials	2,045		1,680		20.0% of cost of goods.
Overhead	5,685		4,660		55.5% of cost of goods.
Delivery	305		250		3.0% of cost of goods.
Total	$10,245	81.0%	$ 8,400	82.0%	
Gross margin	$ 2,405	19.0%	$ 1,850	18.0%	
Selling expense	875	6.9%	825	8.1%	From sales plan, essentially fixed.
General and administrative	585	4.6	600	5.9	From administrative budget.
Total	$ 1,460	11.5%	$ 1,425	14.0%	
Operating profit	$ 945	7.5%	$ 425	4.0%	Shows effect of fixed costs.
Interest	190	1.5	175	1.7	Based on outstanding debt.
Profit before taxes	$ 755	6.0%	$ 250	2.3%	
Income taxes	365	2.9	120	1.1	Projected at 48%.
Net income	$ 390	3.1%	$ 130	1.2%	
Dividends	100	0.8	-0-	-0-	
Retained earnings	$ 290	2.3%	$ 130	1.2%	Carried to balance sheet.
Depreciation	575		600		From overhead plans.
Cash flow	$ 865		$ 730		Rough measure of cash from operations.

* All projections are rounded off.

viewed in connection with other cash movements to be truly meaningful. It is obvious that a cash budget, if available, would be much more precise for judging the cash flow pattern for the period.

We can now turn to the pro forma balance sheet which has been constructed in Figure 3–5. We note that each account has been changed in anticipation of known or expected conditions. The analyst has relative freedom to assume various conditions, since the desired result of the analysis is not to have a completely balanced statement in the accounting sense, but rather to gauge the approximate funds need and the overall financial condition. Consequently, the projection process can be built on a variety of assumptions about key items, such as accounts receivable, inventory levels, payable periods, etc., as long as consistency is observed between the assumptions about the operating statement and the balance sheet.

For example, the assumptions about accounts receivable outstanding at the end of the period should tie to the pro forma operating statement, since the normal process will be to consider outstanding an appropriate number of days' sales of recent months. If there is a significant rise or fall in sales during the period projected, care must be taken to reflect a realistic accounts receivable balance in correspondence with this sales pattern.

In a similar fashion, the assumptions about inventories should represent the projected operating pattern of the business. In a trading company, the projection of inventories is relatively simple, since the two main elements to be watched are purchases and sales, with ending inventories a net result. In a manufacturing company, however, we must think through the effect of the level of production as well as the pattern of sales and materials purchases. For high precision, it will be necessary to develop the projected operating plan typified in the factory budget in Figure 3–2, except that the analysis must cover the business as a whole. The type of cost accounting used will have a major impact here, and a reasonable attempt should be made to simulate the pattern expected. Nevertheless, if only quick and overall

Figure 3-5

XYZ CORPORATION
Pro Forma Balance Sheet as of December 31, 1972
(thousands of dollars)

Assets	Actual 9–30–72	Change	Pro Forma 12–31–72	Remarks
Current assets:				
Cash	$ 1,450	–$ 200	$ 1,250	Cash brought to minimum balance.
Accounts receivable	4,250	– 1,200	3,050	Represents 30 days' sales.
Raw materials	1,500	–0–	1,500	Safety level; purchase requirements as needed.
Finished goods	4,050	– 760	3,290	Reduced production, per plan.
Total current assets	$11,250	–$2,160	$ 9,090	Reflects seasonal pattern.
Fixed assets:				
Land	2,500	–0–	2,500	No change assumed.
Plant and equipment	20,800	–0–	19,300	Sale of machines; original cost $1,500, acc. dep.
Less: Accum. depreciation	8,350	–0–	8,000	$950, per cash budget; depreciation for pe-
Net plant and equipment	$12,450	–$1,150	$11,300	riod $600; net, –$1,150.
Total fixed assets	$14,950	–$1,150	$13,800	
Other assets	1,250	–0–	1,250	No change assumed.
Total assets	$27,450	–$3,310	$24,140	
Liabilities and Net Worth				
Current liabilities:				
Accounts payable	$ 1,120	–$ 410	$ 710	45 days' purchases, per plan.
Notes payable	3,000	– 1,500	1,500	Repayment as required.
Due contractor	3,400	– 2,900	500	From payment schedule.
Accruals	1,250	– 280	970	Tax payments (–$400) and accrual (+$120).
Total current liabilities	$ 8,770	–$5,090	$ 3,680	Reflects heavy current repayments.
Long-term liabilities	$ 8,500	–0–	$ 8,500	No change.
Common stock	4,250	+ 250	4,500	Sale of stock under option.
Retained earnings	5,930	+ 130	6,060	Retained earnings per income statement.
Total liabilities and net worth	$27,450	–$4,710	$22,740	
Funds required		+ 1,400	1,400	"Plug" figure representing financing need as of
		–$3,310	$24,140	12–31–72, the same as in Figure 3–3.

results are desired, a rough assumption about the inventory balance will suffice.

Similar thought must be given to accounts payable, which result from purchase activities, and to wages and taxes payable, etc. Quite clearly, items like depreciation and net profit on the income statement should be tied to the respective changes in the balance sheet. There is, however, a degree of freedom of choice in pro forma statements which makes them clear and quick media for simulating future conditions.

Assumptions chosen will reflect themselves on the balance sheet in the resulting funds need or surplus—the "plug" figure which is the difference between the projected asset and liability accounts. This last item on the pro forma balance sheet will show the funds condition on the specific date of the balance sheet. Any intervening peaks and valleys of cash requirements would have to be found by intermediate balance sheets or by developing cash budgets as shown in the previous section of this chapter.

In the case of XYZ Corporation, we have shown a set of assumptions which matches those underlying the earlier analyses. Therefore, the plug figure of $1.4 million is exactly that shown in the detailed cash budget. One of the keys in this example is the recognition that lower production plans will result in a reduction in finished goods inventory of three-quarter million dollars. This drop was reflected both in the cash projections and the balance sheet. If a more cursory approach to pro forma analysis had ignored this fact, the funds need (plug figure) would have risen to over two million dollars. The assumption would have simply been that production levels would match sales levels, and the inventory would not have been reduced. Similarly, different projections could be made for other accounts, with resultant effects on the funds requirements. The main caution is to observe reasonable consistency between the pro forma income statement and the balance sheet—otherwise, too much deviation might occur. Together, the set of pro forma statements summarizes in a convenient form the effect of planning assumptions, and provides a basis for judging the viability of the projected operations, trends in key ratios, the financial requirements on specific dates, and the effect of alternative plans.

INTERRELATIONSHIP OF FINANCIAL PROJECTIONS

It should be obvious by now that the various analyses presented in this chapter are closely related. If all three types of analyses—operating budgets, cash budgets, and pro forma statements—are based on the *same* set of assumptions about operating rates, receipts and collections, payment rates, inventory levels, and so on, they all fit precisely together in the fashion illustrated in Figure 3–6. Differences in the plans arise only if

Figure 3–6

INTERRELATIONSHIP OF FINANCIAL PROJECTIONS

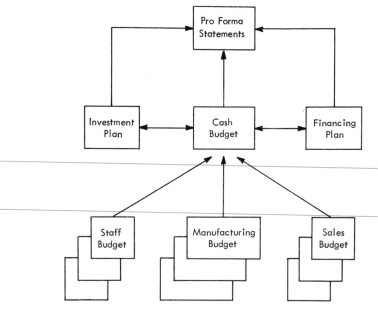

such assumptions are allowed to differ between the analyses, particularly between the cash budget and the pro forma statements. It is quite easy to reconcile cash budgets and pro forma statements, however, by carefully thinking through the operational assumptions, one by one, and by laying out formats with sufficient detail on background conditions.

The diagram in Figure 3–6 shows how the various operational budgets flow into a combined cash budget, which is reinforced by information from the investment and financing plans. The combination of this information goes into making up the pro forma statements. The picture also shows that pro forma statements, at the top of the figure, are the all-encompassing expression of the conditions of the period ahead. If pro forma statements alone are developed, they in effect imply assumptions about all the other elements in the diagram.

We have not yet specifically mentioned *staff budgets*, which are spending plans based on operating various service functions. These budgets find their way into the total financial picture in the same way as other expense budgets. *Investment plans* are the projection of spending on new land, plant, equipment, and related working capital, or reduction in any of these. In the case of XYZ Corporation, we had assumed a minor reduction in investment through the sale of used machines (see cash budget). The obligation for the building of a new plant had already been reflected on the actual balance sheet as of September 30, 1972, and only the payment due the contractor was properly included in the cash disbursements. The *financing plan* is an expression of the proposed future additions or reductions in obligations and equity funds contemplated by a company. In the case of XYZ Corporation, we left the specific nature of future financing open and only developed the cash requirements as shown in the cash budget and the pro forma balance sheet.

FINANCIAL MODELING

The capabilities of the computer and the increasing application of its computational speed to financial analysis has, in recent years, lead to the concept of financial modeling. In principle, this is no more than a mathematical representation of the key operational and financial relationships peculiar to a company. A financial model will include such items as key accounting procedures, tax calculations, depreciation schedules, debt service and repayments, financial restrictions and covenants, inventory policies, etc. The computer will calculate from these relationships the projected results of the conditions to be encountered by the company, given the assumptions made by management.

The major difference between the projection techniques discussed in this chapter and financial modeling is only the degree of automation of the process. A cash budget, done by hand, is essentially a model of the cash flow pattern of the company wherein the analyst must refer to corporate accounting, tax, and other procedures and policies. By incorporating into computer programs the concepts and logic applied in developing such a cash budget, for example, it is possible to run many different financial plans with ease and speed. Moreover, the computer is capable of simultaneously tracking all interrelationships considered to be of importance.

The nature of financial models ranges all the way from a simple calculation of condensed pro forma statements to a highly sophisticated full representation of a company's accounting system, to which are often added projectional capabilities. In such cases, the model will contain routines which use various statistical methods for projecting past trends in key accounts, while observing interrelationships. The use of this kind of model enables the management of a firm to calculate, on paper, a variety of operating conditions and financing options and to gauge the impact of different alternatives before making a real commitment. Some companies have proceeded to develop models which not only, in a deterministic sense, will calculate the results of specified assumptions, but also include "optimizing routines" which will indicate the most desirable alternative investment patterns, as well as financing arrangements based on criteria submitted to the model.

It is clearly beyond the scope of this book to treat in detail the vast number of concepts and specialized techniques involved in computerized models. Figure 3–7 depicts the nature of the relationships of a full computer model, whose central element consists of the various computer programs in the center of the diagram. The reader should keep in mind, however, that financial projection at almost any level is a "modeling" effort. The main advantage of sophisticated financial models is that they are able to analyze and relate simultaneously a great number of variables affecting a business operation, and to indicate the results of different possible actions with high speed and accuracy of calculation.

Figure 3–7

FINANCIAL MODELING
An Overview of Relationships

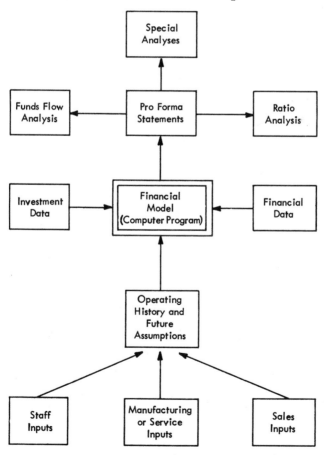

SUMMARY

The principles of financial projection discussed in this chapter revolve around the use of budgets and pro forma statements. We have observed that financial projection is a part of business planning which is expressed in the familiar form of financial statements and specifically tailored budget formats. The process is simple in that an orderly way of sorting out the financial impact of operational, investment, and financing decisions is observed. The process is difficult in that the nature of the judgments about *future* conditions is fraught with uncertainty—as any planning must be. It is here that the calculation of alternative assumptions can narrow the range of uncertainty, and computerized financial models can be of material assistance.

SELECTED REFERENCES

ANTHONY, ROBERT N.   *Management Accounting, Text and Cases,* chap. 16. 4th ed. Homewood, Ill.: Richard D. Irwin, 1970.

GUTHMANN, H. G., and DOUGALL, H. E.   *Corporate Financial Policy,* chaps. 5, 6. 4th ed. Englewood Cliffs, N.J.: Prentice-Hall, 1962.

GERSHEFSKI, GEORGE W.   *The Development and Application of a Corporate Financial Model.* Sun Oil Co. Oxford, Ohio: Planning Executives Institute, 1968.

HORNGREN, CHARLES T.   *Cost Accounting, A Managerial Emphasis,* chap. 6. Englewood Cliffs, N.J.: Prentice-Hall, 1962.

HUNT, PEARSON; WILLIAMS, CHARLES M.; and DONALDSON, GORDON.   *Basic Business Finance,* chap. 8. 3d ed. Homewood, Ill.: Richard D. Irwin, 1966.

JOHNSON, ROBERT W.   *Financial Management,* chaps. 4, 5. 2d ed. Boston: Allyn & Bacon, 1962.

KENT, RAYMOND P.   *Corporate Financial Management,* chaps. 11, 12. 3d ed. Homewood, Ill.: Richard D. Irwin, 1969.

VANCIL, RICHARD F. (ed.).   *Financial Executive's Handbook,* part VI. Homewood, Ill.: Dow-Jones-Irwin, 1970.

VAN HORNE, JAMES C.   *Financial Management and Policy,* chap. 8. Englewood Cliffs, N.J.: Prentice-Hall, 1968.

CHAPTER

4

ANALYSIS OF CAPITAL
INVESTMENT DECISIONS

In the previous chapters we have dealt with the operational aspects of a business—the analysis of results and the projection of operating conditions. In both cases we had to assume that the decisions to invest and to finance these operations had been made in an appropriate fashion to permit profitable operation to take place. In this chapter, we shall concentrate on the analytical techniques which are used to support business investment decisions. We shall assume that there exists in a company the capability to operate new facilities and other investments, and that the necessary capital can be provided to finance the investments under review.

The process of investment in land, productive equipment, buildings, working capital, raw material deposits, and other assets for future economic gain is particularly difficult and a cause for careful analysis. Decisions in this area usually commit a business enterprise for a considerable time period to an activity, line of business, or geographic region. As one of the three basic areas of decision making—investment, operations and financing—the investment process has the longest time horizon and rests most heavily on careful forecasts and detailed assumptions about the likely future conditions which will provide the economic gain to justify the contemplated outlay of funds.

Before we turn to specific concepts and the framework for analysis, it should be emphasized that in this book we are viewing the capital investment problem (a part of capital budgeting) in a narrow sense. The critical task of management is to establish the general objectives and specific goals of the enterprise. On the basis of these and the known strengths and limitations in administrative talent, manpower, technical know-how, market standing, financing possibilities, and so on, management must formulate appropriate strategies. Many objectives will call for the commitment of long-term capital investments—and at times also for the opposite, capital disinvestment. Thus every time one considers a capital outlay, it should take place in the framework suggested in Figure 4–1.

Figure 4–1

INVESTMENT ANALYSIS IN PERSPECTIVE

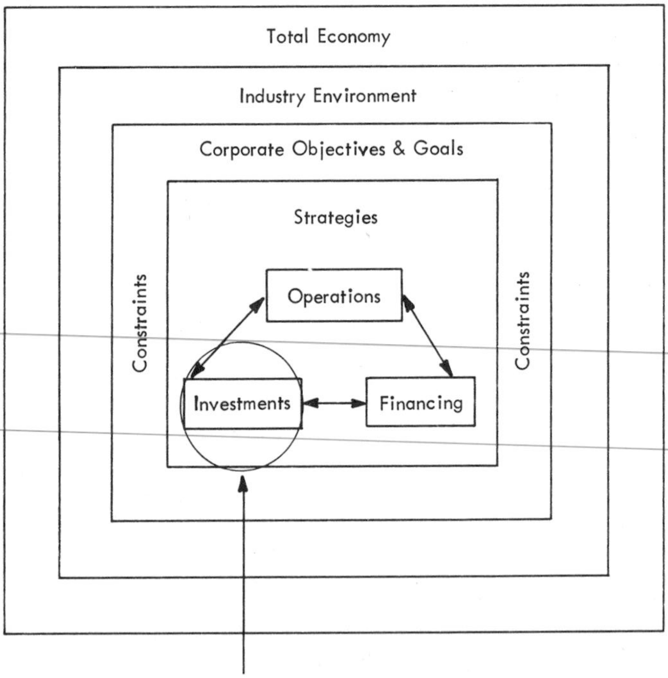

Capital budgeting has been the subject of learned dispute for many years. Ideally, it would be a simple process of listing all investment opportunities against all sources of financing. The theoretical economist's argument is to accept all investments up to the point at which incremental benefits equal incremental cost. In reality, it is not possible to see ahead to all investment opportunities, since management is faced with a revolving planning horizon over which opportunities keep appearing. Even if it were possible to view all investments, it would be difficult to be certain of the right decisions at any one time. There are restrictions on a company's ability to take care of the investment opportunities. Management must, therefore, concentrate on enhancing the idea flow throughout the organization and hope that in the long run the results from accepting and rejecting investment opportunities will come out ahead of competition.

The capital budgeting process also distinguishes among types of investment opportunities. There are such obvious needs as replacing a washed-out railroad bridge, where any detailed economic analysis would be waste motion. The decision would be so obvious that it would be folly to run an analysis. At the other extreme, there are many investment projects which have implications far beyond the detailed and rational economics that can be expressed in numbers. Management's obligation is to steer a course which provides sufficient economic investment opportunities to carry the load of those investments which may be necessary for a variety of reasons other than pure profit.

In this book we are dealing with a partial approach to investment analysis, namely, the specific tools which determine the relative attractiveness of projects. We must stress that the calculation and methodology are only the underpinning for the broader questions involved.

THE FRAMEWORK FOR DECISION

Our specific focus on analytical techniques still requires the careful definition and observation of a series of ground rules to ensure consistent and meaningful results. These ground rules have to do with the futurity of the data and estimates employed, careful definition of the problem to be solved and alternative actions available, and economic reasoning based on incremental conditions. Also, there is the need to define truly relevant costs and revenues, and the distinction between accounting data and cash flows. Each of these will now be discussed briefly.

It is critical to recognize that the economic calculations to justify, say, a new machine, the replacement of an outmoded factory, or the acquisition of a plot of land for development must rest on projections and forecasts of *future* revenues and costs. It will not do to assume that the past operating cost of a machine will go on unchanged, or that past experience with land development will be applicable to a new venture. While this may seem obvious, the temptation exists in practice to extrapolate past conditions instead of carefully forecasting likely developments. The past is at best a rough guide to future events, and at worst irrelevant. Investment analysis, with time horizons of 5, 10, or even 25 years, deals entirely with future conditions and the uncertainty surrounding them. It will therefore behoove the analyst of a proposal to gauge as best he can the relative uncertainty surrounding the estimates, and perhaps to run the analysis under different assumed conditions if the uncertainty is too great. Such an approach can be used to test the sensitivity of the result to changes in particular variables such as product prices, raw material costs, etc. This will be taken up in the last part of the chapter. The uncertainty of future conditions thus causes management to be aware of the risk of investments in capital assets—the risk being a function of the relative uncertainty of the key variables of the project. Careful estimates and research are often warranted to narrow the margin of error in the predicted conditions put into the analytical framework.

Careful *definition of the problem* and the alternatives under analysis is equally important to ensure appropriate results of the calculation. While again apparently obvious, the stress on proper problem definition cannot be overdone. For example, the replacement of a machine nearing the end of its useful life is not a simple problem. As a general rule, there are several alternatives, and the specific circumstances can mean an even greater number. The most obvious alternative is to do nothing and to continue to patch up the machine until it falls apart. The ongoing cost pattern becomes the basis for comparison with a replacement; yet, it may be useful to ask the not-so-obvious question of whether the company should stop making the product altogether. "Go out of business" is an alternative which, though often painful, should at least be considered before new resources are committed. The improved efficiency of a new machine or plant may raise the product's profit performance from poor to average; yet, there may be other alternatives to put the funds to use at greater profit. Even if the decision to replace has been made, there exist still other alternatives. Replacement with the same machine, or with a larger, more automatic model, or with one employing a different manufacturing process are some of these choices.

The picture of these alternatives can be represented in the simple decision tree shown in Figure 4–2.

Figure 4–2
OPTIONS FOR REPLACEMENT DECISION

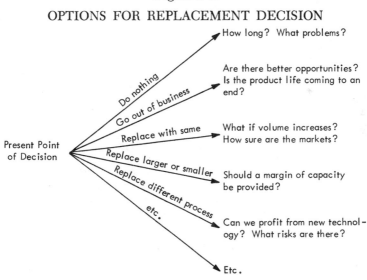

This simple illustration of one type of investment should demonstrate the need to think through the many alternatives usually present with any major or even minor capital outlay. It is crucial to select the appropriate alternatives for analysis and to structure the problem in such a way that the power of the analytical tools is brought to bear on the real decisional issue.

The *economic reasoning* with any capital outlay is based on the conditions which will change because of the action taken. Thus the questions to be dealt with are as follows: What additional funds will be required to carry out the alternative chosen? If the investment proposal results in the sale or other disposition of assets, as well as the addition of new ones, it is the net outlay that counts. What additional revenues will be created over and above any existing ones? If new revenues are brought about but some existing ones are lost, it is the net impact of the action which is relevant for economic analysis. What costs will be added or removed from the business operation? The relevant elements of cost will be those which go up or down because of the decision—anything that remains the same before and after the investment decision is not relevant for the purpose. Thus the economic reasoning is based on incremental changes—a relative rather than absolute approach, which is tied closely to carefully defined alternatives. The specific data developed are therefore differential funds commitments, revenues, and costs caused by the decision.

Finally, a distinction must be drawn between accounting data and relevant revenues and costs. While our analysis will often be based on data taken from the accounting system, particularly in the case of cost elements affected by the investment decision, a clear distinction must be made between those items which vary with the change brought about by the investment and those which only appear to do so. The latter is a reference to accounting allocations which may change in size but do not necessarily represent a true change in costs incurred. For example, a new machine with greater output than the old may be ascribed a larger proportion of general overhead (plant manager's salary, administrative costs, insurance, etc.) if the allocation is based on operating volume. While the overhead costs have thus risen for the specific operation, there has likely been no change in general overhead in total, since we have only substituted one machine for another. The analysis thus comes down to a judgment whether in the overall divisional or corporate picture there has been a change in true outlays and revenues, not whether the accounting system is redistributing the existing costs differently. The emphasis is, therefore, on cash in and cash out, as affected by the decision: an economic cash flow framework. Since federal and state income taxes are a common "expense" of doing business, we are talking about the after-tax cash effect of a decision on the business, and all analytical effort should point in this direction.

METHOD OF ANALYSIS: BASIC CONCEPTS

The investment of capital is, in its simplest form, made for one basic reason: to obtain sufficient economic returns over a future period to justify the original outlay, i.e., enough cash receipts to justify the cash spent. The method of analysis should take into account in one way or another this trade-off of current cash outflow versus future cash inflow. This section of the chapter will deal with an often used simple framework for analysis and its advantages and shortcomings, while also spelling out the key elements of analysis. The next section will deal with more advanced and increasingly common methods, which employ present value concepts—the adjustment for the timing of cash flows and the recognition of economic opportunity costs.

Let us now demonstrate the components of investment analysis on the basis of a simplified example. An investment of $100,000 in facilities for a new product is expected to provide after-tax cash flow benefits of $25,000 over a period of six years, without significant annual fluctuations. Although the equipment will not be fully worn out after six years, it is unlikely that more than scrap value will be obtained due to technical obsolescence. The cost of removal is expected to offset this scrap value. Depreciation over the six years has been appropriately considered in the $25,000 figure, a subject to be taken up later on.

To judge the attractiveness of this investment we thus have three elements: the investment, the operating benefits, and the time period over which these benefits are expected to prevail. Our analysis must relate these three elements to provide a clue whether the investment is worthy of consideration or not. These basic conditions are true of all investment proposals. For the remainder of the chapter, we shall therefore use the following economic terminology.

Net investment refers to the net outlay: gross capital requirements less any capital recovered from trade or sale of existing assets, after adjustment for applicable taxes. If there are any substantial recoveries of capital at the end of the analysis period, some allowance will have to be made for this. Similarly, if additional capital outlays during the period are necessary for the project, this will have to be considered in the net investment figure, as will be seen later on. In our example, the net investment is $100,000.

Operating cash flows are the net economic benefits, period for period, which are caused by an investment. They are such after-tax elements as operating savings caused by a machine replacement, the additional profits earned by a new product line, the profit increase from plant expansion, or the profits created by developing a natural resource. These economic benefits are normally transformed into an after-tax cash flow. In our example, the annual operating cash flow after taxes is $25,000 from new product profits.

The *economic life* of a project is the time period over which one can expect to obtain the benefits of the investment proposition. This is the third element of the investment process. It is very important to distinguish this relevant time period from the *physical* life of any equipment involved or the *technological* life of a particular process. Even though physically a building or piece of equipment may be perfectly usable, the economic life has ceased if the market for the product or service has expired. Technology likewise must be related to economic use— the best process is useless if the product can no longer be sold. The *depreciation life* for accounting or tax purposes is similarly suspect as a clue to the project's true life span, since such write-offs are normally based on standard guidelines, not the particular economic circumstances. In our example, the economic life is six years, the period over which the product is expected to be sold.

How do we relate these basic elements, investments, operating cash flow, and life to find the project's attractiveness? Three simple methods are often employed for this purpose: the payback or payout, the return on investment, and the average return. All of these measures are in essence rules of thumb, which under most conditions provide only an approximation of the economic desirability of a project, and at times can be misleading. Nevertheless, their use is so widespread that they should be discussed here.

Payback

The payback measure is a simple relationship of the annual benefit of a project to the investment required.

$$\text{Payback} = \frac{\text{Net investment}}{\text{Average annual operating cash flow}} = \frac{\$100,000}{\$\ 25,000} = 4 \text{ years}$$

The result of the calculation is the number of years required to achieve repayment of the original outlay. When related to the economic life, the payback figure is used as an indication of whether the investment will be repaid within the economic life span. This is true in our simple example, where payback is achieved in four years versus an estimated life of six years.

While the payback period is easy to calculate—which probably accounts for its popularity—some difficult questions arise in its use. First of all, the concept measures the return of the original investment on, so to speak, the installment basis. "How long will it be until I get my money back?" is the implied query. From an economic viewpoint this is not enough, of course, since one would hope to earn a profit on the funds invested. An analogy can be drawn to a savings account in which $100 is invested and from which $25 is withdrawn at the end of each year. After four years the principal would have been repaid. The saver would be very upset if the bank told him that his account was now depleted. He expected to earn 4 or 5 percent per year on the balance remaining in his account.

In the case of our investment example, the payback period

is insufficient to allow for any economic return on the amount of the investment. We must look to the years beyond the payback to provide some profit. In fact, if economic life and payback were to coincide precisely, an *opportunity loss* would have been suffered, since the same funds invested elsewhere would presumably have earned some return. Table 4–1 illus-

Table 4–1

AMORTIZATION OF $100,000 INVESTMENT AT 10 PERCENT

Year	Beginning Balance	Normal Earnings, 10 Percent	Operating Cash Flow	Ending Balance to Be Recovered
1........	$100,000	$10,000	$(25,000)	$85,000
2........	85,000	8,500	(25,000)	68,500
3........	68,500	6,850	(25,000)	50,350
4........	50,350	5,035	(25,000)	30,385 (payback)
5........	30,385	3,039	(25,000)	8,424
6........	8,424	842	(25,000)	(15,734)

trates these points. If we assume that a normal return earned in our hypothetical company was 10 percent after taxes, our simple example could be represented in the amortization schedule shown in Table 4–1, which takes into account the opportunity of earning a normal 10 percent.

For simplicity, we have assumed that earnings are calculated on the beginning balance and operating cash flows are received at the end of the period. Under these conditions it is quite obvious that a payback of four years could mean an opportunity loss of about $30,400, if the project ended at this point. If the economic life were five years, the opportunity loss vis-à-vis other earnings possibilities at 10 percent would be reduced to about $8,400, while at six years the gain vis-à-vis other earnings possibilities would be a quite favorable $15,700.

This brief illustration points up one of the major drawbacks of the payback calculation; namely, that it is relatively insensitive to the economic life span and does not provide a truly meaningful and comparable criterion of earnings power. The speed with which money is repaid is not a convenient way to think about profitability, because without further calculations all we can say about our example is that the project pays out in four years, with two "extra" years for profit. Moreover, on two similar projects with a five-year and a ten-year life the payback measure would show the same results, namely, four years plus something extra.

Another drawback of the payback measure is its inability to handle projects with varying cash flow patterns. Since an average annual operating cash flow is assumed, a project with rising or declining cash flow patterns will not be reflected properly. A new product, for example, may show slowly rising cash inflows over time, leveling out and sharply declining in the late stages of its economic life. A machine replacement will normally show rising savings as the existing machine deteriorates. Moreover, any additional investment during the period or recoveries at the end will cause distortions. Table 4–2 illustrates the insensitivity of the payout concept to variations in cash flow.

Table 4–2

PAYBACK UNDER VARYING CONDITIONS

	Project 1	Project 2	Project 3
Net investment	$100,000	$100,000	$100,000
Average annual operating cash flow ...	$ 25,000	$ 25,000	$ 33,333
Economic life	6 years	8 years	3 years
Payback	4 years	4 years	3 years
Cash flow pattern:			
Year 1	$ 25,000	$ 20,000	$ 16,667
2	25,000	30,000	33,333
3	25,000	50,000	50,000
4	25,000	40,000	–0–
5	25,000	30,000	–0–
6	25,000	15,000	–0–
7	–0–	10,000	–0–
8	–0–	5,000	–0–
Total	$150,000	$200,000	$100,000
Cumulative first four years	$100,000	$140,000	n.a.
Average first four years	$ 25,000	$ 35,000	n.a.

If we assume similar risks in each project shown in Table 4–2, we would choose Project 2 over Project 1 since over its life it will return $50,000 more than Project 1. Project 3, on the other hand, appears to be most favorable if judged only on the payout criterion of three years. Yet it is obvious that the project involves an opportunity loss, as discussed earlier—it merely repays the original capital without any return. The difference in cash flow pattern of Projects 1 and 2 is also masked by the payout criterion. If we cumulate the first four years of operation we find that Project 2 is far superior to Project 1, since the average cash flow is $35,000 versus $25,000—inasmuch as Project 2 provides heavy operating cash flows in the early years.

From the discussion up to this point it is clear that the payback device must be used with considerable caution. Only if the cash flow patterns of alternative projects are similar and if their economic lives are equal or close will the measure provide a proper ranking. If these conditions do not hold, the measure must be supported by further analysis of the kind just shown, and even then the answers are blurred. Average annual cash flows and extra years of life are concepts which are simply too crude except under very limited circumstances.

A modification of payback involves the use of average accounting profit after taxes in the denominator of the formula. The rationale is that accounting profit, which is net of a depreciation allowance (see Chapter 1), is a better measure, since it implicitly provides for a return of principal and a profit to boot. In our simple example we have employed after-tax cash flows of $25,000, which are represented by an accounting profit of $8,333 plus depreciation of $16,667 ($100,000 over six years). The modified payback would then appear as follows:

$$\frac{\text{Net investment}}{\text{Average annual after-tax profit}} = \frac{\$100,000}{\$\ \ 8,333} = 12 \text{ years}$$

This answer is a distortion of the economic picture, since it in no way represents the cash-in, cash-out reasoning underlying investment analysis. One should be careful not to let accounting profits and write-off rules take the place of economic trade-offs, since each is designed for a valid but different purpose. In Table 4–1 we saw that the project was desirable if its economic life was five years or better. A 12-year payout simply does not ap-

pear valid. Depending on the circumstances, particularly variations in the length of economic life, the distortion introduced
by the use of accounting profits will vary in seriousness—and
one cannot hope for any consistency in this measure. The reader
is invited to test for himself the effect of varying the key elements in our simple example.

Return on Investment (Simple)

This measure is an outgrowth of the payback reasoning, and
it represents the inverse of the payback formula. It is an attempt
to express the economic desirability of an investment project
in terms of a percentage return on the original outlay. The
method shares all of the shortcomings of the payback criterion,
however, since it again relates only two of the three aspects of
a project, net investment and operating cash flows, and leaves
out the life span:

$$\text{Return on investment} = \frac{\text{Average annual operating cash flow}}{\text{Net investment}}$$

$$= \frac{\$\ 25,000}{\$100,000} = 25\%$$

With no reference to economic life and with no recognition
of the fact that, just as in a savings account, regular cash with-
drawals will reduce the principal balance, all the measure indicates is that $25,000 is 25 percent of $100,000. Note that the
same answer would be obtained if the economic life were 1
year, 10 years, or 100 years. In fact, the reading would be true in
an economic sense only if the investment provided $25,000 per
year in perpetuity; only then could we speak of a true return
of 25 percent. The conceptually superior devices of the next
section will provide better economic answers. As in the case of
the payback device, meaningful comparisons can be made only
of alternatives quite similar in life and cash flows.

A modification of the return on investment is the use of
accounting profit as the numerator. Apart from economic criteria, it is an attempt to simulate the effect the project would

have on corporate financial statements. As a very crude approximation it will give such a reading, at least for the early part of the project's life. The measure is still subject, however, to most of the shortcomings discussed earlier.

Average Return

For completeness, it will be necessary to mention the third common measure, which employs the average net investment related to average operating cash flows or accounting profit.

$$\text{Average return} = \frac{\text{Average operating cash flow}}{\text{Average net investment}} = \frac{\$25,000}{\$50,000} = 50\%$$

or:

$$= \frac{\text{Average accounting profit after taxes}}{\text{Average net investment}} = \frac{\$\ 8,333}{\$50,000}$$

$$= 16.7\%$$

The latter figure is, under some conditions (simple projects of medium life), a fair approximation of the economic return. It is still subject to serious distortion when complexities are present in a project, and must therefore be used with extreme caution.

SOME COMPLICATIONS

So far we have used a very simple example to illustrate both the rule-of-thumb measures and the key definitions. Before we go on to the more sophisticated measures of the next section, it will be useful to refine our concepts of economic analysis somewhat. One cannot overstress the need to understand fully the reasoning behind net investment and operating cash flows. The application of the appropriate techniques of measurement then becomes almost automatic.

For purposes of illustration we shall use a more complex investment problem, which involves the replacement of an existing machine tool with a more automatic and faster model. Let us assume that this is the only alternative feasible under the

circumstances. We further assume that five years remain before
the old machine becomes unusable, and that the new machine
will be serviceable for ten years before it must be scrapped.
The old machine cost $25,000 five years ago and has a current
book value of $12,500 (depreciated straight-line at $2,500 per
year). It can be sold for $15,000 cash. The new machine will
cost $40,000, will be depreciated over ten years, and will likely
be worth at least its book value if it should be sold before the
end of its physical life. The product made on the machine is
expected to continue in the market for at least ten years without
any serious threat to its existence. The company can even expect
to sell at least 25 percent more than its current volume, using
additional selling and promotional effort.

The new machine will turn out 125,000 units per year as
compared to 100,000 units on the old equipment, and it will
do so at lower unit costs for both labor and materials. In fact,
the machine will use slightly less labor in total than the old
machine, due to fewer setups, and also will use material more
efficiently. The extra 25,000 units turned out by the new machine
are expected to be sold with some incremental selling and promotional expenses, and therefore will provide an additional contribution before taxes of $5,000.

Conditions as described here are quite common in practice.
We shall discuss the economic analysis of these complications in
detail.

Net Investment

We are looking for the net change in funds committed to the
project, as stated in our earlier definition. Two events are to be
considered. First, there is the outlay of $40,000 for the new ma-
chine (no investment tax credit assumed), which is a straightforward cash commitment. Second, there is a recovery of cash
from the sale of the old machine, which is attributable to our
decision to replace and therefore is relevant. The amount of
cash received is somewhat less than the $15,000 cash value of
the machine, however, since for tax purposes a gain on the sale

must be recognized. We recall that the book value was $12,500, and the company will be taxed on the difference of $2,500, which for simplicity we assume to be at the normal corporate tax rate of 48 percent. The tax due on the transaction thus is $1,200.

We now have all the components of the initial net investment figure relevant in this example:

Cost of new machine $40,000
Price received on sale of old .... (15,000)
Tax due on capital gain 1,200
Net investment $26,200

We must observe that the economic analysis does not recognize for other than tax purposes the fact that a book value remained on the old machine. What was spent in the past is irrelevant and represents a *sunk cost*. We are interested only in the changes that take place now; and the tax due on the transaction is a current item caused by the decision. Had the old machine been unsalable in spite of its book value of $12,500, the only relevant element would have been the tax savings from the capital loss incurred under those conditions, and not the past investment represented by the book value—although the latter is often mistakenly considered.

The net investment thus represents a balance of cash movements, in and out, caused by the investment decision. Additional investments or capital recoveries in later periods are relevant also, but we so far have not described the techniques of handling these. This will be done in the next section.

Operating Cash Flows

As discussed before, the operating cash flows are the after-tax cash changes brought about by an investment proposal. In the present case, we must carefully sort out the comparable conditions to develop *differential* revenues and costs. We must distinguish between the operating savings achieved through greater efficiency for the current volume of operations and the contribution provided through profitable sale of the additional output. The analysis will appear as shown in Table 4–3.

Table 4–3

DIFFERENTIAL COST AND REVENUE ANALYSIS

	Current Volume of 100,000 units		
	Old Machine	New Machine	Annual Difference
Operating savings:			
Labor	$21,000	$20,000	$1,000
Material	38,000	36,000	2,000
Overhead (120 percent of direct labor) ...	25,200	24,000	....*
	$84,200	$80,000	$3,000
Contribution from additional volume:			
25,000 units sold at $1.20 per unit		$30,000	
Less: Material cost at 36¢/unit		(9,000)	
Additional selling expense		(5,500)	
Additional promotional expense		(10,500)	5,000
Total savings and additional contribution			$8,000
Depreciation (additional expense;			
for tax purposes only)	$ 2,500	$ 4,000	(1,500)
Taxable operating improvements			$6,500
Tax at 48 percent			3,120
After-tax profit improvement			$3,380
Add back depreciation			1,500
After-tax operating cash flow			$4,880

* Not relevant.

The calculations in Table 4–3 are carried out in three stages. First, the *operating savings* for the current volume of output (100,000 units) are determined by comparing the annual costs of operating the old machine and the new machine. Labor and materials provide some savings each, while overhead, though different, is not relevant from an economic standpoint. The fact that the cost accounting system, for valid reasons, allocates overhead at 120 percent of direct labor does not alter the reality that our decision has not introduced any change in spending for overhead. What has changed is the basis of allocation, which in this case happens to be direct labor, but not the total amount of overhead. The plant manager and his office staff still receive the same salaries, and other overhead costs are unchanged. Only if the replacement decision had in fact brought a change in spending, such as higher property taxes and insurance fees or additional maintenance or technical support, would such a change have to be recognized in the calculation. We would then estimate the annual amount of expenditure and develop the differential cost. As a general rule it should be observed that it is better to deal with annual totals of cost and revenue elements than with unit cost values, since the latter increase the risk of being trapped into the use of accounting allocations, which are appropriate for costing purposes (cost of goods sold, inventory values, etc.) but generally irrelevant for economic analysis.

Second, we make the calculation of the *additional contribution* from the higher volume of the new machine. This calculation represents incremental profit, since the output increase was not possible to achieve with the old equipment. The relevant elements involved are the sales revenue ($30,000) less those costs which are affected by the additional output. Since no additional operators are required to operate the machine at its top speed, no additional labor cost is charged. Additional materials, however, are used up and these are charged at the usage rate of the new machine (36¢ per unit). Selling and promotional expenses required to move the additional volume are estimated at $5,500 and $10,500 per year.

Third, the *differential depreciation* is calculated. As we discussed in detail in Chapter 1, depreciation has no relevance as an economic funds flow, and in our analysis it has merit only as a tax-deductible expense. The ability to charge depreciation against federal income taxes normally reduces the tax payment of the business, and in that sense the depreciation write-off serves as a "tax shield." If an investment alternative results in higher or lower depreciation charges, the change must be analyzed with regard to the impact on federal income tax. This was done in the present case, where the differential depreciation for the next five years of operations will be $1,500, an increase in write-off due to the higher cost of the new machine. After the tax calculation, the depreciation amount is added back to the after-tax profit improvement of $3,380 to arrive at the operating cash flow of $4,880. In this way the depreciation charge correctly caused a tax reduction, but was not left in the final result to distort the economic change. The same result can, of course, be obtained by doing the analysis in two stages: (*a*) determine the tax on the operating improvement before depreciation and (*b*) determine the tax shield effect of the differential depreciation. In our example, the picture would be as follows, with the exact same result:

Taxable operating improvement $8,000
Tax at 48 percent 3,840
After-tax operating improvement $4,160
Tax shield at 48 percent* of depreciation of $1,500 720
After-tax operating cash flow $4,880

* Note that each dollar of depreciation provides a tax shield of $1 times the tax rate applicable.

Economic Life

A complication has been introduced due to the assumed difference in lives between the old and the new machines. Since the old machine is expected to expire in five years while the new one will last for ten, the period of comparability is only the next five years. After that period, the original alternative no longer exists, and something has to be done at any rate. We can picture the situation as shown in Figure 4–3.

Figure 4–3

OVERLAPPING ECONOMIC LIFE SPANS

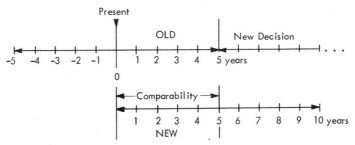

Differential revenues and costs exist only as long as both alternatives exist together, and after five years the old machine is gone. Consequently, we cannot analyze the situation beyond five years without making some assumptions about the life remaining in the new machine. While the economic life of the new machine is likely to be ten years, since we have no doubts about selling the output for that length of time, the economic comparison can be made only over five years. There are two ways of handling this problem. First, we can cut off the analysis at year five, by determining the economic value of the new machine at this point and counting this "capital recovery" as a benefit. This is done quite commonly in practice, but it calls for present value techniques, which will be taken up shortly. Second, we can alternatively assume that a new machine would take the place of the old one at year five, with a life of ten years, and a similar replacement would be made at year ten when our current new machine expires. This approach involves a great deal of guessing about replacement conditions five and ten years hence, and it will be difficult under any circumstances to arrive at a fully comparable life span. Both approaches require the more flexible present value techniques of the next section.

From the preceding discussion it has become clear that rules of thumb and rough analysis can serve only limited purposes, especially if the additional considerations are complex and the timing of cash inflows and outflows varies significantly. For this purpose we now turn to the next section of this chapter, which demonstrates the use of time-adjusted techniques which are generally able to provide us with reasonable economic answers to our investment problems.

METHODS OF ANALYSIS: ADVANCED CONCEPTS

The Time Value of Money

We have described investment analysis as involving a tradeoff between current dollar outlays and future benefits over a period of time. Common sense tells us that the investor cannot be indifferent between otherwise exactly comparable propositions in which the timing of benefits varies widely. More immediate benefits will be preferable to benefits to be obtained further out in time, even if risk and uncertainty are comparable. The reason for this, of course, is the opportunity for an individual or a corporation to invest funds at profit—in a savings account, a government bond, or any of a great variety of other economic propositions. If one has to wait for a period of time to obtain a sum of money instead of having the same sum of money presently, the obvious choice will be to take the immediately available funds and to invest them at a profit commensurate with the risk preferences of the investor. To wait would mean an *opportunity cost* in terms of lost earnings. Conversely, common sense dictates that the choice between an expenditure now versus the same expenditure some time hence will be to defer the outlay, since normally the opportunity exists to earn a profit on the funds in the meantime. Stated another way, money has a value distinctly related to the timing of its receipt or disbursement, and this value is determined by the opportunity to earn from a normal investment.

A simple example can illustrate the point. If an investor normally uses a savings account which provides him with 5 percent per year, $1,000 given to him and invested today will grow to $1,050 one year hence (we ignore daily or monthly compounding, as is practiced by many banks). If our investor were forced to wait one year before receiving his $1,000, he would have lost the opportunity to earn $50. Without question, a sum of $1,000 offered to him one year hence will be worth less to him than the same amount offered him today. Specifically, the value of the delayed $1,000 will be related to his earnings power of 5 percent, and we can calculate the present value of the $1,000 as follows:

$$\text{Present value} = \frac{\$1,000}{1.05} = \$952.38$$

Quite obviously, the $952.38 must be the amount which, invested at 5 percent per year today, will be worth $1,000 at the end of one year from now. The trade-off is thus determined by the length of time and the earnings power available. Ignoring risk for the moment, our investor should be willing to pay $952.38 for a contract for $1,000 to be delivered in one year if he normally earns 5 percent on his money.

Similarly, a lengthening in the time period to receipt or disbursement will reduce the present value of a sum of money. A sum of $1,000 received five years hence will be worth only $783.50 today, since that amount invested today at 5 percent would grow to $1,000 five years hence. The figure was derived from the following calculation:

$$\frac{\$1,000}{1.27628} = \$783.50$$

which relates $1,000 to its compounded value at 5 percent five years hence. We refer to the calculation of present value as discounting, which is nothing more than the reverse of the familiar compound interest process applied to an investment's growth in value due to periodic interest receipts which are reinvested. Through this reasoning process, we are able to fix at any point in time the value of a receipt or disbursement, once the opportunity rate of earnings has been stipulated.

The process of compounding and discounting is as old as moneylending and has been in use in financial institutions since time immemorial, although the application of the process to business investment analysis is of more recent interest. The transformation of cash flows into present values is eased considerably through the use of present value tables, a set of which is provided at the end of the chapter. The tables are based on the concepts discussed earlier. There are four tables, the first of which (Table 4–10) displays the results of discounting a sum of money received or disbursed at year-end, using an annual interest period. The general formula is:

$$\text{Present value} = \frac{1}{(1 + i)^n}$$

where i is the applicable interest (discount) rate and n the number of discount periods. For any number of periods up to 50 years and discount rates from 1 to 50 percent, we can find the present value of a sum of money by simply multiplying the amount involved by the appropriate factor in the table:

$$\text{Present value} = \text{Factor} \times \text{sum}$$

Tables 4–11, 4–12, and 4–13 are variations of Table 4–10 and are helpful for calculating more complex patterns. For example, we may be faced with analyzing the present value of a series of equal receipts or payments over a number of years. While it would be possible to make the calculation by using Table 4–10, repetitively multiplying the annual amounts with the appropriate sequence of factors and adding the results, Table 4–11 eases the task by providing a set of additive factors derived from those of Table 4–10. Thus a single multiplication of the annual amount (annuity) with the appropriate factor will yield the present value of the whole series of equal receipts or disbursements:

$$\text{Present value} = \text{Factor} \times \text{annuity}$$

Tables 4–12 and 4–13 are refinements of Tables 4–10 and 4–11, in that the assumption is made that the amounts received or disbursed will occur in monthly increments rather than in year-end incidence. The forward shift in time provides slightly higher present values, both for single sums and annuities. This pattern represents a closer approximation of operating changes such as labor reductions, material savings, and other weekly and monthly disbursements and receipts.

We are now equipped with the basic tools to deal with time adjustment of money and we shall turn our attention to the concepts of investment evaluation employing these techniques.

Net Present Value

The basic idea of net present value is simply to find the balance of the trade-off between investment outlays and future benefits, in terms of time-adjusted present value dollars. The analysis rests on the assumption that a company's management has determined a normal opportunity rate or standard at which funds can and should be employed in the business. This rate is often referred to as the "cost of capital," that is, the weighted average of the compensation for all long-term funds provided to the company (see Chapter 5). Others prefer to use an estimate of future rates of return at which funds can likely be invested in the company, an "opportunity rate" approach.

Given such a standard, it is possible to determine the present value of all outlays and the present value of all inflows over the economic life of the project, and to net these against each other. The result is a positive or negative (net inflow or net outflow) figure which indicates whether the project, over its life, is meeting or falling short of the earnings standard built into the calculation. Since present value dollars are dependent on timing and earnings opportunity, a positive net present value indicates that over the economic life the project will return the original capital outlay (as well as any future ones), earn the standard return on the outstanding balance, and provide a "cushion" of excess value. Conversely, a negative figure indicates that the project is not achieving the built-in earnings standard and will cause an opportunity loss.

Our simple project on page 113 can serve as an illustration here. It is best to present the information in a time scale format, which permits easy calculation and serves to visualize the problem in a time perspective. This format is shown in Table 4–4.

The result of the calculation is a net present value of almost $20,000, if the company considers 8 percent a normal earnings standard. All of the investment will have been recovered over the six-year period, and 8 percent after taxes will have been earned on the declining outstanding balance during the project life. Moreover, a cushion of $19,750 of extra dollars in present value equivalents can be counted on *if* the project lives out its economic life and the cash flow estimates are correct. We note a similarity to the payback concept discussed earlier, which also referred to a recovery of the investment and something extra. The critical difference, however, is that the net present value concept has a built-in economic earnings requirement beyond

Table 4–4

PRESENT VALUE ANALYSIS BY PERIOD

Time Period	Investment (Outlays)	Benefits (Inflows)	P.V. Factors at 8 Percent*	Present Values	Cumulative P.V.
0	$100,000	....	1.000	−$100,000	−$100,000
1		$ 25,000	.959	+ 23,975	− 76,025
2		25,000	.888	+ 22,200	− 53,825
3		25,000	.823	+ 20,575	− 33,250
4		25,000	.762	+ 19,050	− 14,200
5		25,000	.705	+ 17,625	+ 3,425
6		25,000	.653	+ 16,325	+ 19,750
	$100,000	$150,000		+$ 19,750	

* From Table 4–12, assuming that benefits will come about continuously rather than at year-end. We could instead use, from Table 4–13, 4.790 times $25,000, since the annual cash inflows are equal. The result for the total present value of the inflows is identical.

the recovery of the principal, and thus the cushion of a positive net present value is truly an economic gain beyond satisfying a normal earnings standard.

If a higher earnings standard had been required, say 12 percent, the result would appear as shown in Table 4–5. The net present value remains positive, but the size of the cushion has decreased to $8,325, which we would expect, since we raised the required earnings hurdle. At a 15 percent discount rate, the net present value shrinks to almost nothing ($25,000 × 4.038 − $100,000 = +$950), while at 16 percent the result is slightly

Table 4–5

PRESENT VALUE ANALYSIS AT 12 PERCENT

Time Period	Cash Flows	P.V. Factors at 12 Percent*	Present Values	Cumulative P.V.
0	−$100,000	1.000	−$100,000	−$100,000
1	+ 25,000	.941	+ 23,525	− 76,475
2	+ 25,000	.840	+ 21,000	− 55,475
3	+ 25,000	.750	+ 18,750	− 36,725
4	+ 25,000	.670	+ 16,750	− 19,975
5	+ 25,000	.598	+ 14,950	− 5,025
6	+ 25,000	.534	+ 13,350	+ 8,325
	+$ 50,000		+$ 8,325	

* As in Table 4–4, we could instead use 4.333 times $25,000 from Table 4–13.

negative ($25,000 $\times$ 3.948 $-$ $100,000 = $-$$1,300). We ob-
serve the sensitivity of the net present value measurement to
changes in required earnings, and from the last columns in Tables 4–4 and 4–5 we also note the importance of economic life.
As the earnings standard increases, the time required for the net
present value to turn positive is lengthened. At 8 percent it took
a life of almost five years to do so, while at 12 percent most of
the sixth year of life was necessary. The net present value measure thus appears to reflect properly the trade-off of cash outlays
and cash inflows over time, and it also recognizes both principal
and earnings recovery.

The best use of net present value is as a screening device with
which to ascertain whether, during the economic life, a minimum earnings standard can be obtained. If net present value is
positive, there is earnings potential in excess of the standard; if
net present value is close to or exactly zero, the earnings requirement has just been met, given that the earnings estimate and
length of life are quite certain. If the net present value is negative, the minimum earnings standard and capital recovery cannot be achieved with the cash inflows estimated during the economic life.

The concept of net present value by itself, however, does not
answer all our questions, many of which have been implied in
the discussion just concluded. Given a corporate return standard, the evaluation of the size of the cushion is a little difficult
when comparing projects, particularly if the investments are of
significantly different magnitude. Moreover, the degree to which
one must rely on the project living out its estimated economic
life is often a significant problem. Further, we are interested in
quantifying the amount of error we can afford in our estimates
of cash inflows. Finally, a valid question often asked is: What
level of "true" return will the project provide, if all estimates can
be expected to materialize? Net present value must be fortified
with several other measures for us to be able to make these judgments. The most common measures of this nature are the present value index, the present value payback, the annualized net
present value, and the yield. They will be taken up in this order.

Present Value Index

If the analyst, after calculating net present values, is faced with a choice among several alternative investments of different size, he cannot be indifferent to the fact that even though their net present values may be equal or close, the amount of investment required by the various projects varies widely. In other words, it makes quite a difference if an investment proposal promises a net present value of $1,000 for an outlay of $10,000, and if another investment requires $25,000 for the same net present value, even if we assume equivalent lives and equivalent risk. In the first case, the cushion is a much larger fraction of the commitment than in the second.

A formal way of expressing this relationship is the following ratio:

$$\text{Present value index} = \frac{\text{Present value of operating inflows}}{\text{Present value of net investment}}$$

The present values in this formula are the same amounts we used earlier to derive the net present value, by subtracting one from the other. In this case the question is simply: How much in present value benefits is created per dollar of net investment? The two cases just cited would appear as follows:

$$1. \text{ Present value index} = \frac{\$11,000}{\$10,000} = 1.10$$

$$2. \text{ Present value index} = \frac{\$26,000}{\$25,000} = 1.04$$

As expected, the first project is much more favorable if we assume all other aspects to be reasonably comparable. The higher the index, the better the project. If the index is one or less, the project is just meeting or missing the minimum standard built into the derivation of the present values. The example in Table 4–4 has an index of $119,750 ÷ 100,000 = 1.20$ at 8 percent, and 1.08 at 12 percent. While the measure provides further insight, it still leaves several points unanswered.

Present Value Payback (Minimum Life)

In Table 4–4, we provided a column for cumulative present value. This column was useful for deriving the time required until the net present value turned positive—i.e., until the project became attractive. This test is nothing more than an answer to finding the minimum economic life required for the project to meet the return standard, given the level of cash inflows projected. At the point in time where the trade-off of cash outflows and inflows is even in present value terms, the project will achieve a payback or payout of the investment *plus* an economic return on the outstanding balance at the return standard (opportunity rate) used for the present value analysis.

If a project has uneven and complicated cash flows, as we shall demonstrate shortly, the analysis to find the minimum life requires a year-by-year accumulation of the present values, positive and negative, as was done in Table 4–4. If a project is straightforward in the simple terms used for many of our examples—i.e., a single net investment at point zero and level annual operating cash inflows—use can be made of the annuity factors of Tables 4–11 or 4–13 to find a quick answer. For this purpose, the relationship:

$$\text{Present value} = \text{Factor} \times \text{annuity}$$

can be exploited, as we are looking for the condition at which the present value of the outflows is exactly equal to the present value of the inflows. Since the net investment (outflow) is one of these equal amounts (it has to be recovered by the inflows), we can change the formula to:

$$\text{Net investment} = \text{Factor} \times \text{annuity}$$

and since the annuity (annual operating cash flows) is known, we can find the factor which satisfies the condition:

$$\text{Factor} = \frac{\text{Net investment}}{\text{annuity}}$$

For our investment example, we calculate the following results: $100,000 ÷ $25,000 = $4, and we can look for the closest
factor in the 8 percent column of Table 4–13. The answer lies
between years four and five (3.432 and 4.137) and an approximate interpolation indicates that the minimum life of the project
must be slightly under five years to achieve 8 percent. At 12 percent, the life is approximately five and a half years, the same result as before.

The test for present value payout or minimum life thus becomes one more step in assessing the margin for error in the
project estimates, and is a method of displaying the risk involved. It sharpens the understanding of the relationship of economic life and acceptable performance—a much improved version of the simple payback and a companion to the net present
value.

Annualized Net Present Value

The net present value calculation normally results in an excess or deficiency of present value benefits over the net investment. If positive, the amount can be viewed as a cushion against
estimating error in future cash inflows. Unless a project has
highly irregular annual flows, it is often useful to transform the
net present value cushion into an *equivalent annuity* over the
project's economic life. These annual equivalents representing a
margin of error can then be directly compared to the raw annual cash inflow estimates, since the net present value has in
effect been "reconstituted" into future cash flows. To illustrate,
we can transform the net present value in Table 4–4, $19,750,
into an annuity over the six-year life by simply again exploiting
the present value relationship:

$$\text{Present value} = \text{Factor} \times \text{annuity}$$

Since we are interested in finding the annuity represented by
the net present value, over a known economic life and a set discount rate (the opportunity rate employed in the present value

calculation in the first place), the annuity formula is transformed as follows:

$$\text{Annuity} = \frac{(\text{Net}) \text{ present value}}{\text{Factor}}$$

In our example the result is as follows:

$$\text{Annuity} = \frac{\$19,750}{4.790} = \$4,123$$

The annual operating cash inflows were originally estimated
at $25,000. The result above indicates that over the six-year life
the actual experience can be lower by about $4,000 per year (a
16 percent reduction) and the project will still meet the minimum return standard of 8 percent. Similar calculations can be
made for our other examples, and the reader is invited to do so.

There are two additional aspects to the process of annualization. As we shall see later, the process can be used to compare
the annual net benefits of alternatives with different lives. Moreover, in a general framework, the annualizing process is a very
practical and quick method to turn the investment analysis
process around. This is a useful way to find the approximate annual operating cash flow required to justify an investment if the
capital outlay itself is known (e.g., the cost of a machine) but
the operating benefits have not yet been established. Given an
economic life estimate and an opportunity rate of return, the
formula:

$$\text{Operating cash flow} = \frac{\text{Net investment}}{\text{Factor}}$$

can be employed to find a level annual *target cash flow*. Care
must be taken to modify this figure for the depreciation tax
shield adjustment to arrive at the minimal pretax operating improvement necessary. This simply involves working backward
through the analysis we employed earlier for the tax shield effect of depreciation in Table 4–3. The concept is a useful tool
for a first judgment of the chance of an investment's being "in
the ball park."

Yield (Discounted Cash Flow Return)

The concept of a true return on an investment over its economic life (often referred to as DCF return) has already appeared in the discussion of the previous measures. The yield of a project is simply that rate of discount which, when applied to cash outflows and inflows over the economic life, provides a zero net present value—that is, the present value of the inflows is sufficient to provide an exact trade-off with the present value of the outflows. Stated another way, the principal of the investment can be amortized over the economic life, earning the exact return implied by the discount rate. Naturally, the yield will vary with changes in economic life and cash flow patterns. While heretofore we had employed a specified opportunity rate to find present values, the yield analysis turns the problem around to find a rate of discount, given equality of inflows and outflows. Again we can employ our simple formula (Present value = Factor × annuity) if the project has one present investment outflow and level annual cash inflows. The formula can be turned around as follows:

$$(\text{Yield}) \text{ factor} = \frac{\text{Present value (investment)}}{\text{Annuity}}$$

This is the same approach employed earlier to find the present value payback (minimum life), and we again use the factor to check the result in Table 4–13. This time, however, the economic life is given and we look for the rate of discount indicated. Our investment example had a factor of 4 ($100,000 ÷ $25,000), and we find that on the six-year line the factor 4 lies between 15 percent (4.038) and 16 percent (3.948). Approximate interpolation indicates that the result is around 15.5 percent.

If a project has a more complex cash flow pattern, we must employ a trial-and-error approach to find the yield. Successive application of different discount rates to all cash flows over the economic life must be made until a close approximation to a zero net present value has been found. With some experience, usually no more than two trials are necessary, since the first result will indicate the direction of rate selection. A positive net present value indicates the need for a higher discount rate, and vice versa. We observed this process in Tables 4–4 and 4–5.

As a ranking device, the yield is reasonably accurate and much superior to the simple payback and return on investment. It is not without problems, however. Apart from the many conceptual and mathematical arguments possible, one should recognize that the use of yield alone is not necessarily accurate. For example, alternative projects of greatly different magnitudes may have yields inverse to the size of the investment. A $10,000 investment with a 50 percent yield cannot be directly compared to an outlay of $100,000 with a 30 percent yield, particularly if risks are similar and the company normally looks to 15 percent opportunity as acceptable. It may be better to employ the larger sum at 30 percent than the smaller sum at 50 percent, unless both projects can be undertaken.

Similarly, length of life is important here. It may be more advantageous to employ funds at the lower rate for a longer period of time than to have a short high yield, if a choice has to be made between the two investments. The problem with yield is that a unique rate is found for each project, which implies that the cash flows returned over time can be reinvested at that same rate—which may not be true at all. Net present value analysis, on the other hand, employs a long-run opportunity rate which represents a judgment as to the normal earnings power of funds in the enterprise. The reinvestment problem thus is not an issue. In addition, it is mathematically possible to have two or even more solutions for the yield in a complex project—which adds to the problem of interpretation. Increasingly there is a movement among practitioners to prefer the net present value as a concept of investment selection over the discounted cash flow return (yield), although the yield has had ready acceptance as a deceptively simple figure to understand. The reader is invited to turn to the references at the end of the chapter for a more exhaustive analysis of the theoretical and conceptual arguments.

SOME COMPLICATIONS

So far we have limited ourselves to simple examples with which to illustrate the methodology. Let us now turn to a more realistic and complex example and illustrate how the time-adjusted techniques can be applied to judge the desirability of the project. For the purpose we shall employ first the replacement example described on page 121, and second a generalized example with more aspects added.

We recall that the replacement involved a current net investment of $26,200 and operating cash flows of $4,880 per year for the five-year period of comparison. It was also indicated at the time that the analysis would have to consider the fact that after five years a new decision had to be made in any case, and that the most straightforward way of handling the problem of uneven lives was to cut off the analysis at the fifth year and to recognize the economic value of the new machine at that time. We shall assume that the economic value of the new machine will be equal to its book value of $20,000 ($40,000 less five years' depreciation at $4,000 per year) with no taxable gain or loss expected. This judgment would, of course, have to be modified if the circumstances indicated a different value to be expected due to technological change or other conditions.

With these data at hand, we can now lay out the problem for present value analysis, assuming a 10 percent return standard, as shown in Table 4–6. The result of the calculation is a sizable net present value of better than $5,500, which indicates that the replacement is desirable. Note that the analysis recognizes the recovery of the book value of the machine at the end of year five as an inflow even though there may be no intention of selling the machine in fact. This is a recognition of the economic value not chargeable to the current decision covering the five-year period ahead. The net investment in present value terms

Table 4–6

PRESENT VALUE ANALYSIS OF REPLACEMENT

Time Period	Investment	Operating Cash Inflows	P.V. Factors at 10 Percent*	P.V. of Net Investment	P.V. of Operating Inflows
0	−$26,200	....	1.000	−$26,200	....
1	....	+$ 4,880	.950	....	+$ 4,636
2	....	+ 4,880	.864	....	+ 4,216
3	....	+ 4,880	.785	....	+ 3,832
4	....	+ 4,880	.714	....	+ 3,484
5	....	+ 4,880	.649	....	+ 3,167
5 (end) ..	+ 20,000		.621†	+ 12,420	....
	−$ 6,200	+$24,400		−$13,780	+$19,335
				Net present value =	+$ 5,555

* For years one to five, we could use 3.962 from Table 4–13.
† From Table 4–10, since we assume recovery at the end of year five.

thus becomes a smaller figure, $13,780, representing the actual commitment of value to the proposition.

The present value index of the project is $19,335 ÷ $13,780 = 1.40, again an indication of a quite favorable project, given the validity of the estimates. Some analysts prefer to express the present value index by relating the present value of *all* inflows, including capital investment recoveries, to the original net investment at point zero. The result in this case would be $31,755 ÷ $26,200 = 1.21, again a favorable showing. While there are arguments for and against both methods, a consistent application of either will be satisfactory.

The present value payback (minimum life) must be found by cumulating the present values of the operating inflows until they approximate the net investment of $13,780. A quick addition shows that this will happen after about 3⅓ years, leaving a cushion of 1⅔ years against uncertainty. Now the question arises whether the recovery at the end of year five should be considered at an earlier point for a more correct answer. To do this, however, would involve a process of iteration, since not only would the present value of the recovery rise but so would the economic value itself in earlier years. Normally such a refinement is not called for, but it can certainly be handled, especially if a company employs a computer program for present value analysis.

The annualized net present value in this case is $5,555 ÷ 3.962, or approximately $1,400 per year. All other elements being equal, the project would still be acceptable if the annual operating cash inflows over the five years were only $3,480, a possible error of almost 30 percent!

Another way of looking at the net present value cushion would be, of course, to ask how much of a reduction in expected capital recovery would be tolerable. This can easily be found by reconstituting a dollar amount at the end of year five which has a present value of $5,555. We simply divide the present value by the Table 4–10 factor of .621 and find that the recovery could be reduced by about $9,000 and still leave the project acceptable.

The yield of the project has to be found by trial and error, since the cash flow pattern is complicated by the capital recovery at the end of year five. The problem can be handled as shown in Table 4–7. A trial at 15 percent indicates that the net

Table 4–7

PRESENT VALUE ANALYSIS TO FIND YIELD

Time Period	Cash Flows	P.V. Factors at 15 Percent	Present Values	P.V. Factors at 16 Percent	Present Values
0	−$26,200	1.000	−$26,200	1.000	−$26,200
1					
2					
3 }	+$ 4,880/yr	3.577	+ 17,456	3.508	+ 17,119
4					
5					
5 (end)	+$20,000	.497	+ 9,940	.476	+ 9,520
	+$18,200		+$ 1,196		+$ 439

present value is still a positive $1,200, which is reduced to about $400 at 16 percent. Thus the yield will be slightly in excess of 16 percent.

A more general cash flow pattern is represented by the next

illustration, which assumes not only an initial capital outlay for facilities and a terminal recovery, but also the commitment of working capital in the first two years of the project, and additional equipment outlays with recoveries assumed at the end of eight years. Furthermore, the operating cash flows vary considerably over the years. Nothing new in methodology is required to handle such a situation. Working capital (additional inventories and receivables less trade obligations) represents a commitment of capital just as definite as is the case with buildings and equipment, except that no depreciation is incurred. We can assume that commitments are made *during* a given time period instead of at the end, since the requirements for working capital build up in response to volume changes. If all inventories and receivables (less payables) can be expected to be liquidated at the end of the economic life, the capital will be fully recovered and can be shown as an inflow. If some losses are expected, a lower figure must be used.

Uneven operating cash flows present no problems. If partial annuities are encountered, the additive nature of Table 4–13 (or Table 4–11 for period-end incidence) can be exploited to reduce the chore of analysis somewhat (see below). Additional facilities expenditures during the life of the project are simply recognized as cash outflows when incurred, and care must be taken to reflect their depreciation patterns as additional tax shields in future operating periods.

A complex problem containing all of these elements would appear as shown in Table 4–8. The result is a positive net present value of about $9,000, which leaves little room for a margin of error, since on an annualized basis the operating cash inflows can be off by only $8,925 ÷ 5.235, or approximately $1,700 per year. The minimum life is about six and a half years, and the yield a little over 12 percent. (The reader is invited to check the yield by reworking the analysis at 14 percent.) The present value index is approximately 1.05 if we relate the present values of the investment in operating inflows. If we use the concept of relating only the present value of the outflows to the present value of all inflows, including recoveries, the present value index becomes about 1.39 ($203,860 ÷ $146,455).

Table 4-8

PRESENT VALUE ANALYSIS OF COMPLEX PROJECT

Time Period	Investments	Operating Cash Inflows	P.V. Factors at 12 Percent	Present Value of Investments	P.V. of Operating Inflows
0	−$140,000 (facilities)		1.000	−$140,000	.....
1	− 25,000 (working capital)	+$ 20,000	.941*	− 23,525	+$ 18,820
2	− 20,000 (working capital)	+ 40,000	.840*	− 16,800	.....
3	....	+ 40,000 ⎫	2.260†	.....	+ 90,400
4 (end) ..	....	+ 40,000 ⎭	....	.....	.....
4 (end) ..	− 15,000 (additional equipment)	.....	.636‡	− 9,540	.....
5	....	+ 50,000 ⎫	1.132†	.....	+ 56,600
6	....	+ 50,000 ⎭	....	.....	.....
6 (end) ..	− 10,000 (equipment overhaul)	.....	.507‡	− 5,070	.....
7	....	+ 20,000 ⎫	.477**	.....	+ 9,540
8	....	+ 10,000 ⎭	.426*	.....	+ 4,260
8 (end) ..	+ 25,000 (equipment recovery)	.....	.404‡	+ 24,240	.....
	+ 35,000 (working capital recovery)§	.....	....	.....	.....
	−$150,000	+$270,000		−$170,695	+$179,620
		(all tax adjustments made)		Net present value =	+$ 8,925

* From Table 4–12, to simulate receipt or disbursement during period.
† From Table 4–13, representing the difference between the annuity factors applicable: 3.201 − .941 and 4.333 − 3.201, respectively.
‡ From Table 4–10, to simulate disbursement or receipt at the end of the period.
§ Assume loss in liquidation of $10,000.

Additional complications are encountered in the use of *accelerated depreciation* for tax purposes. Since the various methods of fast depreciation write-offs invariably result in uneven declining amounts per year, the calculation of the tax shield effect year by year becomes tedious. Moreover, economic and depreciation lives often differ, adding to the complexity. Many users of present value analysis have found it useful to develop sets of tables for this particular need which provide factors to find the present value of all depreciation write-offs over the economic life in one lump, from which the total tax shield can be determined. A sample page of such tables (Table 4–14) is found at the end of the chapter, and the references contain publications with such tables.

The question of *uneven lives* among alternatives is often a problem. In our example, the approach of cutting off the analysis was taken. Another way of handling such problems is to annualize the relevant cash flows. In the case of replacement analysis, one can determine the annualized cost of going on as is and compare this amount with the annualized cost over the economic life of a new piece of equipment, including the net investment amortization. These methods raise additional detailed conceptual questions which are best dealt with in more specialized texts, such as are listed in the references.

Leasing. The increasing popularity of leasing as a means to obtain the use of a wide variety of capital assets has led to the need for a consistent framework of analysis. Leasing is a form of financing, and the charges levied against the user contain elements of interest, risk, obsolescence, maintenance charges and profit to the owner, all depending on the nature of the lease written, which can vary widely. Because of the complexity of the analysis required to deal with this form of financing, and because of its special nature, the reader is referred to the literature at the end of this chapter.

Inflation and its effect on present value analysis is often raised as an issue. If projections are made in constant dollars, the discount rate applied will not have to be adjusted. If a more normal projection method is used, with increases in prices and costs spelled out, it may be useful to raise the discount standard to compensate for the loss in purchasing power. The many issues connected with this problem go beyond the scope of our discussion.

A final word about the *accuracy* implied in the precise mathematical nature of the present value process and the tables of factors is in order. As pointed out before, the character of the cash flows analyzed is that of estimates, projections, forecasts, and sometimes guesses. It would therefore be spurious indeed to carry the analysis to the final precision possible. In our examples we have provided the analysis at greater levels of accuracy than probably is necessary, with the mere intention that the reader could check the data for complete understanding. In practice, liberal rounding of the various calculations, particularly of the final results, is desirable, to keep the process from overwhelming the realistic judgments required. This was at times implied in this chapter by the use we have made of approximate results in the discussion. The need for perspective is even greater when we realize that the power of discounting, particularly in more distant periods, is such that, through the reduction to present value, widely varying estimates will often not greatly affect the end result. A glance at the present value tables, which show the shrinkage of the factors in later periods and at higher discount rates, should drive this point home.

RISK ANALYSIS

As we have discussed the various present value tools for analysis, an informal methodology for risk adjustment has emerged: the determination of minimum life and the annualization of the net present value are in effect risk analyses, which serve to establish parameters within which the project remains acceptable. More formal methods are called for, however, to assess risk and the effect of uncertainty about key variables on the final results. We have referred before to "sensitivity analysis," which is a way of systematically working through the effects of assumed changes in revenues, operating savings, costs, size of outlays and recoveries, etc., on the final result. Often major projects are analyzed at three levels of assumptions—expected, optimistic, and pessimistic—to see if the project is acceptable under most conditions likely to be encountered.

An even more formal approach is found in the use of assigned probability weights to a variety of conditions and key variables, to determine the weighted average outcome as a measure of the project's attractiveness. The calculation of this "expectation," based on careful judgments by those in a company best qualified to make them, might take the form shown in Table 4–9. The

Table 4–9

RANGE OF LIKELY RESULTS AND
THEIR PROBABILITIES

Possible Levels of Annual Operating Cash Inflows	Probability (Weights)	Adjusted Results
$20,000	0.05	$ 1,000
25,000	0.10	2,500
30,000	0.15	4,500
40,000	0.25	10,000
50,000	0.15	7,500
55,000	0.10	5,500
60,000	0.10	6,000
65,000	0.10	6,500
	1.00	$43,500
		(Expectation)

calculated expectation will not necessarily come true as the specific result of the project, since the most likely estimated occurrence is $40,000 (25 percent probability). The weighted average, however, can be employed as a consistent input to present value analysis as the basis of comparison for various projects, similarly developed. Much more theoretical and conceptual background is necessary to develop these ideas further, and references for additional study are provided.

The most recent practical applications of risk analysis go beyond the mere probabilistic assessment of a calculated result, such as annual operating cash flows. The development of fairly sophisticated computer models has made it possible for decision makers to estimate, for each of a dozen or more key variables of major projects, ranges of possible outcomes and the probability distributions for these ranges. Distributions may be placed around unit volume, prices, key cost elements, cost of facilities, recoveries at the end of the project life, etc. The computer model then will simulate, based on the specified probabilities and relating the variables in a present value fashion, a series of outcomes of the project and summarize the results. This "Monte Carlo technique" is an application of probability theory receiving much attention in industry, since it is possible to simulate on paper hundreds and even thousands of trials of the proposition. The output of the computer model allows the following type of statement to be made: "There is a probability of 60 percent that the net present value of the project will be at least $0.5 million or better"; or, "Chances are 9 out of 10 that the project will meet the minimum standard of 10 percent." A "risk profile" can be drawn in the form of a cumulative probability distribution for competing projects which graphically displays the probability of reaching or exceeding any specified level of such measures as net present value, yield, or years of present value payback. A display such as Figure 4–4 provides management with a tool to match the riskiness of the project against their own risk preferences.

Figure 4–4

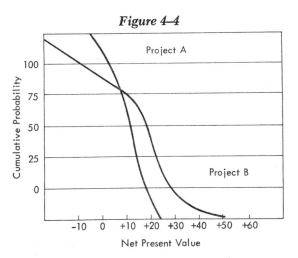

The use of such models is most attractive for major commitments with sizable uncertainties, such as new ventures, in contrast to fairly well understood routine requests for funds. Again, the required background for this type of analysis must be sought in literature beyond the scope of this book.

SUMMARY

In this chapter we have provided the highlights of the analytical framework for investment analysis in capital budgeting. The buildup of techniques reached from crude yardsticks to advanced present value concepts. Critical to the whole process, however, is the analysis preceding the application of the techniques. Here we refer to the statement of the problem, the development and selection of alternatives, and the careful preparation of relevant investment, revenue, and cost data. Once these inputs are satisfactorily developed, the application of the techniques for evaluation becomes relatively easy. Conceptual problems still surround the exact interpretation of the measures of economic desirability, but increasingly net present value, accompanied by several other related measures and at times supported by probabilistic analysis, has become accepted in practice. The results of these analyses then become an input to the broader strategic planning task of management—capital budgeting—as the matching long-range investment commitments with appropriate funds sources, in light of corporate objectives and goals.

Table 4-10

PRESENT VALUE OF $1

Periods until Payment	1%	2%	4%	6%	8%	10%	12%	14%	15%	16%	18%	20%	22%	24%	25%	26%	28%	30%	35%	40%	45%	50%
1	0.990	0.980	0.962	0.943	0.926	0.909	0.893	0.877	0.870	0.862	0.847	0.833	0.820	0.806	0.800	0.794	0.781	0.769	0.741	0.714	0.690	0.667
2	0.980	0.961	0.925	0.890	0.857	0.826	0.797	0.769	0.756	0.743	0.718	0.694	0.672	0.650	0.640	0.630	0.610	0.592	0.549	0.510	0.476	0.444
3	0.971	0.942	0.889	0.840	0.794	0.751	0.712	0.675	0.658	0.641	0.609	0.579	0.551	0.524	0.512	0.500	0.477	0.455	0.406	0.364	0.328	0.296
4	0.961	0.924	0.855	0.792	0.735	0.683	0.636	0.592	0.572	0.552	0.516	0.482	0.451	0.423	0.410	0.397	0.373	0.350	0.301	0.260	0.226	0.198
5	0.951	0.906	0.822	0.747	0.681	0.621	0.567	0.519	0.497	0.476	0.437	0.402	0.370	0.341	0.328	0.315	0.291	0.269	0.223	0.186	0.156	0.132
6	0.942	0.888	0.790	0.705	0.630	0.564	0.507	0.456	0.432	0.410	0.370	0.335	0.303	0.275	0.262	0.250	0.227	0.207	0.165	0.133	0.108	0.088
7	0.933	0.871	0.760	0.665	0.583	0.513	0.452	0.400	0.376	0.354	0.314	0.279	0.249	0.222	0.210	0.198	0.178	0.159	0.122	0.095	0.074	0.059
8	0.923	0.853	0.731	0.627	0.540	0.467	0.404	0.351	0.327	0.305	0.266	0.233	0.204	0.179	0.168	0.157	0.139	0.123	0.091	0.068	0.051	0.039
9	0.914	0.837	0.703	0.592	0.500	0.424	0.361	0.308	0.284	0.263	0.225	0.194	0.167	0.144	0.134	0.125	0.108	0.094	0.067	0.048	0.035	0.026
10	0.905	0.820	0.676	0.558	0.463	0.386	0.322	0.270	0.247	0.227	0.191	0.162	0.137	0.116	0.107	0.099	0.085	0.073	0.050	0.035	0.024	0.017
11	0.896	0.804	0.650	0.527	0.429	0.350	0.287	0.237	0.215	0.195	0.162	0.135	0.112	0.094	0.086	0.079	0.066	0.056	0.037	0.025	0.017	0.012
12	0.887	0.788	0.625	0.497	0.397	0.319	0.257	0.208	0.187	0.168	0.137	0.112	0.092	0.076	0.069	0.062	0.052	0.043	0.027	0.018	0.012	0.008
13	0.879	0.773	0.601	0.469	0.368	0.290	0.229	0.182	0.163	0.145	0.116	0.093	0.075	0.061	0.055	0.050	0.040	0.033	0.020	0.013	0.008	0.005
14	0.870	0.758	0.577	0.442	0.340	0.263	0.205	0.160	0.141	0.125	0.099	0.078	0.062	0.049	0.044	0.039	0.032	0.025	0.015	0.009	0.006	0.003
15	0.861	0.743	0.555	0.417	0.315	0.239	0.183	0.140	0.123	0.108	0.084	0.065	0.051	0.040	0.035	0.031	0.025	0.020	0.011	0.006	0.004	0.002
16	0.853	0.728	0.534	0.394	0.292	0.218	0.163	0.123	0.107	0.093	0.071	0.054	0.042	0.032	0.028	0.025	0.019	0.015	0.008	0.005	0.003	0.002
17	0.844	0.714	0.513	0.371	0.270	0.198	0.146	0.108	0.093	0.080	0.060	0.045	0.034	0.026	0.023	0.020	0.015	0.012	0.006	0.003	0.002	0.001
18	0.836	0.700	0.494	0.350	0.250	0.180	0.130	0.095	0.081	0.069	0.051	0.038	0.028	0.021	0.018	0.016	0.012	0.009	0.005	0.002	0.001	0.001
19	0.828	0.686	0.475	0.331	0.232	0.164	0.116	0.083	0.070	0.060	0.043	0.031	0.023	0.017	0.014	0.012	0.009	0.007	0.003	0.002	0.001	
20	0.820	0.673	0.456	0.312	0.215	0.149	0.104	0.073	0.061	0.051	0.037	0.026	0.019	0.014	0.012	0.010	0.007	0.005	0.002	0.001		
21	0.811	0.660	0.439	0.294	0.199	0.135	0.093	0.064	0.053	0.044	0.031	0.022	0.015	0.011	0.009	0.008	0.006	0.004	0.002	0.001		
22	0.803	0.647	0.422	0.278	0.184	0.123	0.083	0.056	0.046	0.038	0.026	0.018	0.013	0.009	0.007	0.006	0.004	0.003	0.001	0.001		
23	0.795	0.634	0.406	0.262	0.170	0.112	0.074	0.049	0.040	0.033	0.022	0.015	0.010	0.007	0.006	0.005	0.003	0.002	0.001			
24	0.788	0.622	0.390	0.247	0.158	0.102	0.066	0.043	0.035	0.028	0.019	0.013	0.008	0.006	0.005	0.004	0.003	0.002	0.001			
25	0.780	0.610	0.375	0.233	0.146	0.092	0.059	0.038	0.030	0.024	0.016	0.010	0.007	0.005	0.004	0.003	0.002	0.001	0.001			
26	0.772	0.598	0.361	0.220	0.135	0.084	0.053	0.033	0.026	0.021	0.014	0.009	0.006	0.004	0.003	0.002	0.002	0.001				
27	0.764	0.586	0.347	0.207	0.125	0.076	0.047	0.029	0.023	0.018	0.011	0.007	0.005	0.003	0.002	0.002	0.001	0.001				
28	0.757	0.574	0.333	0.196	0.116	0.069	0.042	0.026	0.020	0.016	0.010	0.006	0.004	0.002	0.002	0.002	0.001	0.001				
29	0.749	0.563	0.321	0.185	0.107	0.063	0.037	0.022	0.017	0.014	0.008	0.005	0.003	0.002	0.002	0.001	0.001					
30	0.742	0.552	0.308	0.174	0.099	0.057	0.033	0.020	0.015	0.012	0.007	0.004	0.003	0.002	0.001	0.001	0.001					
40	0.672	0.453	0.208	0.097	0.046	0.022	0.011	0.005	0.004	0.003	0.001	0.001										
50	0.608	0.372	0.141	0.054	0.021	0.009	0.003	0.001	0.001	0.001												

SOURCE: By permission, from Robert N. Anthony, *Management Accounting: Text and Cases*, rev. ed. (Homewood, Ill.: Richard D. Irwin, Inc., 1960), p. 656.

Table 4-11

PRESENT VALUE OF $1 RECEIVED ANNUALLY FOR N YEARS

Years (N)	1%	2%	4%	6%	8%	10%	12%	14%	15%	16%	18%	20%	22%	24%	25%	26%	28%	30%	35%	40%	45%	50%
1	0.990	0.980	0.962	0.943	0.926	0.909	0.893	0.877	0.870	0.862	0.847	0.833	0.820	0.806	0.800	0.794	0.781	0.769	0.741	0.714	0.690	0.667
2	1.970	1.942	1.886	1.833	1.783	1.736	1.690	1.647	1.626	1.605	1.566	1.528	1.492	1.457	1.440	1.424	1.392	1.361	1.289	1.224	1.165	1.111
3	2.941	2.884	2.775	2.673	2.577	2.487	2.402	2.322	2.283	2.246	2.174	2.106	2.042	1.981	1.952	1.923	1.868	1.816	1.696	1.589	1.493	1.407
4	3.902	3.808	3.630	3.465	3.312	3.170	3.037	2.914	2.855	2.798	2.690	2.589	2.494	2.404	2.362	2.320	2.241	2.166	1.997	1.849	1.720	1.605
5	4.853	4.713	4.452	4.212	3.993	3.791	3.605	3.433	3.352	3.274	3.127	2.991	2.864	2.745	2.689	2.635	2.532	2.436	2.220	2.035	1.876	1.737
6	5.795	5.601	5.242	4.917	4.623	4.355	4.111	3.889	3.784	3.685	3.498	3.326	3.167	3.020	2.951	2.885	2.759	2.643	2.385	2.168	1.983	1.824
7	6.728	6.472	6.002	5.582	5.206	4.868	4.564	4.288	4.160	4.039	3.812	3.605	3.416	3.242	3.161	3.083	2.937	2.802	2.508	2.263	2.057	1.883
8	7.652	7.325	6.733	6.210	5.747	5.335	4.968	4.639	4.487	4.344	4.078	3.837	3.619	3.421	3.329	3.241	3.076	2.925	2.598	2.331	2.108	1.922
9	8.566	8.162	7.435	6.802	6.247	5.759	5.328	4.946	4.772	4.607	4.303	4.031	3.786	3.566	3.463	3.366	3.184	3.019	2.665	2.379	2.144	1.948
10	9.471	8.983	8.111	7.360	6.710	6.145	5.650	5.216	5.019	4.833	4.494	4.192	3.923	3.682	3.571	3.465	3.269	3.092	2.715	2.414	2.168	1.965
11	10.168	9.787	8.760	7.887	7.139	6.495	5.937	5.453	5.234	5.029	4.656	4.327	4.035	3.776	3.656	3.544	3.335	3.147	2.757	2.438	2.185	1.977
12	11.255	10.575	9.385	8.384	7.536	6.814	6.194	5.660	5.421	5.197	4.793	4.439	4.127	3.851	3.725	3.606	3.387	3.190	2.779	2.456	2.196	1.985
13	12.134	11.343	9.986	8.853	7.904	7.103	6.424	5.842	5.583	5.342	4.910	4.533	4.203	3.912	3.780	3.656	3.427	3.223	2.799	2.468	2.204	1.990
14	13.004	12.106	10.563	9.295	8.244	7.367	6.628	6.002	5.724	5.468	5.008	4.611	4.265	3.962	3.824	3.695	3.459	3.249	2.814	2.477	2.210	1.993
15	13.865	12.849	11.118	9.712	8.559	7.606	6.811	6.142	5.847	5.575	5.092	4.675	4.315	4.001	3.859	3.726	3.483	3.268	2.825	2.484	2.214	1.995
16	14.718	13.578	11.652	10.106	8.851	7.824	6.974	6.265	5.954	5.669	5.162	4.730	4.357	4.033	3.887	3.751	3.503	3.283	2.834	2.489	2.216	1.997
17	15.562	14.292	12.166	10.477	9.122	8.022	7.120	6.373	6.047	5.749	5.222	4.775	4.391	4.059	3.910	3.771	3.518	3.295	2.840	2.492	2.218	1.998
18	16.398	14.992	12.659	10.828	9.372	8.201	7.250	6.467	6.128	5.818	5.273	4.812	4.419	4.080	3.928	3.786	3.529	3.304	2.844	2.494	2.219	1.999
19	17.226	15.678	13.134	11.158	9.604	8.365	7.366	6.550	6.198	5.877	5.316	4.844	4.442	4.097	3.942	3.799	3.539	3.311	2.848	2.496	2.220	1.999
20	18.046	16.351	13.590	11.470	9.818	8.514	7.469	6.623	6.259	5.929	5.353	4.870	4.460	4.110	3.954	3.808	3.546	3.316	2.850	2.497	2.221	1.999
21	18.857	17.011	14.029	11.764	10.017	8.649	7.562	6.687	6.312	5.973	5.384	4.891	4.476	4.121	3.963	3.816	3.551	3.320	2.852	2.498	2.221	2.000
22	19.660	17.658	14.451	12.042	10.201	8.772	7.645	6.743	6.359	6.011	5.410	4.909	4.488	4.130	3.970	3.822	3.556	3.323	2.853	2.498	2.222	2.000
23	20.456	18.292	14.857	12.303	10.371	8.883	7.718	6.792	6.399	6.044	5.432	4.925	4.499	4.137	3.976	3.827	3.559	3.325	2.854	2.499	2.222	2.000
24	21.243	18.914	15.247	12.550	10.529	8.985	7.784	6.835	6.434	6.073	5.451	4.937	4.507	4.143	3.981	3.831	3.562	3.327	2.855	2.499	2.222	2.000
25	22.023	19.523	15.622	12.783	10.675	9.077	7.843	6.873	6.464	6.097	5.467	4.948	4.514	4.147	3.985	3.834	3.564	3.329	2.856	2.499	2.222	2.000
26	22.795	20.121	15.983	13.003	10.810	9.161	7.896	6.906	6.491	6.118	5.480	4.956	4.520	4.151	3.988	3.837	3.566	3.330	2.856	2.500	2.222	2.000
27	23.560	20.707	16.330	13.211	10.935	9.237	7.943	6.935	6.514	6.136	5.492	4.964	4.524	4.154	3.990	3.839	3.567	3.331	2.856	2.500	2.222	2.000
28	24.316	21.281	16.663	13.406	11.051	9.307	7.984	6.961	6.534	6.152	5.502	4.970	4.528	4.157	3.992	3.840	3.568	3.331	2.857	2.500	2.222	2.000
29	25.066	21.844	16.984	13.591	11.158	9.370	8.022	6.983	6.551	6.166	5.510	4.975	4.531	4.159	3.994	3.841	3.569	3.332	2.857	2.500	2.222	2.000
30	25.808	22.396	17.292	13.765	11.258	9.427	8.055	7.003	6.566	6.177	5.517	4.979	4.534	4.160	3.995	3.842	3.569	3.332	2.857	2.500	2.222	2.000
40	32.835	27.355	19.793	15.046	11.925	9.779	8.244	7.105	6.642	6.234	5.548	4.997	4.544	4.166	3.999	3.846	3.571	3.333	2.857	2.500	2.222	2.000
50	39.196	31.424	21.482	15.762	12.234	9.915	8.304	7.133	6.661	6.246	5.554	4.999	4.545	4.167	4.000	3.846	3.571	3.333	2.857	2.500	2.222	2.000

SOURCE: By permission, from Robert N. Anthony, *Management Accounting: Text and Cases*, rev. ed. (Homewood, Ill.: Richard D. Irwin, Inc., 1960), p. 657.

Table 4-12

PRESENT VALUE OF $1/12 RECEIVED MONTHLY IN YEAR N

Year (N)	1%	2%	4%	6%	8%	10%	12%	14%	15%	16%	18%	20%	22%	24%	25%	26%	28%	30%	35%	40%	45%	50%
1	0.995	0.989	0.979	0.969	0.959	0.950	0.941	0.932	0.928	0.924	0.915	0.907	0.899	0.892	0.888	0.884	0.877	0.870	0.853	0.837	0.822	0.808
2	0.985	0.970	0.941	0.914	0.888	0.864	0.840	0.818	0.807	0.796	0.776	0.756	0.737	0.719	0.710	0.702	0.685	0.669	0.632	0.598	0.567	0.539
3	0.975	0.951	0.905	0.862	0.823	0.785	0.750	0.717	0.702	0.686	0.657	0.630	0.604	0.580	0.568	0.557	0.535	0.515	0.468	0.427	0.391	0.359
4	0.965	0.932	0.870	0.814	0.762	0.714	0.670	0.629	0.610	0.592	0.557	0.525	0.495	0.468	0.455	0.442	0.418	0.396	0.347	0.305	0.270	0.239
5	0.956	0.914	0.837	0.768	0.705	0.649	0.598	0.552	0.531	0.510	0.472	0.438	0.406	0.377	0.364	0.351	0.327	0.305	0.257	0.218	0.186	0.160
6	0.946	0.896	0.805	0.724	0.653	0.590	0.534	0.484	0.461	0.440	0.400	0.365	0.333	0.304	0.291	0.278	0.255	0.234	0.190	0.156	0.128	0.106
7	0.937	0.879	0.774	0.683	0.605	0.536	0.477	0.425	0.401	0.379	0.339	0.304	0.273	0.245	0.233	0.221	0.199	0.180	0.141	0.111	0.088	0.071
8	0.928	0.861	0.744	0.644	0.560	0.488	0.426	0.373	0.349	0.327	0.287	0.253	0.224	0.198	0.186	0.175	0.156	0.139	0.104	0.079	0.061	0.047
9	0.919	0.844	0.715	0.608	0.518	0.443	0.380	0.327	0.303	0.282	0.244	0.211	0.183	0.160	0.149	0.139	0.122	0.107	0.077	0.057	0.042	0.032
10	0.909	0.828	0.688	0.574	0.480	0.403	0.339	0.287	0.264	0.243	0.206	0.176	0.150	0.129	0.119	0.110	0.095	0.082	0.057	0.041	0.029	0.021
11	0.900	0.812	0.661	0.541	0.444	0.366	0.303	0.251	0.229	0.209	0.175	0.147	0.123	0.104	0.095	0.088	0.074	0.063	0.042	0.029	0.020	0.014
12	0.892	0.796	0.636	0.510	0.411	0.323	0.271	0.221	0.199	0.180	0.148	0.122	0.101	0.084	0.076	0.070	0.058	0.049	0.031	0.021	0.014	0.009
13	0.883	0.780	0.612	0.482	0.381	0.303	0.242	0.193	0.173	0.156	0.126	0.102	0.083	0.067	0.061	0.055	0.045	0.037	0.023	0.015	0.010	0.006
14	0.874	0.765	0.588	0.454	0.353	0.275	0.216	0.170	0.151	0.134	0.106	0.085	0.068	0.054	0.049	0.044	0.035	0.029	0.017	0.011	0.007	0.004
15	0.865	0.750	0.565	0.429	0.327	0.250	0.193	0.149	0.131	0.116	0.090	0.071	0.056	0.044	0.039	0.035	0.028	0.022	0.013	0.008	0.005	0.003
16	0.857	0.735	0.544	0.404	0.302	0.227	0.172	0.131	0.114	0.100	0.076	0.059	0.046	0.035	0.031	0.028	0.022	0.017	0.009	0.005	0.003	0.002
17	0.848	0.721	0.523	0.381	0.280	0.207	0.153	0.115	0.099	0.086	0.065	0.049	0.037	0.029	0.025	0.022	0.017	0.013	0.007	0.004	0.002	0.001
18	0.840	0.707	0.503	0.360	0.259	0.188	0.137	0.100	0.086	0.074	0.055	0.041	0.031	0.023	0.020	0.017	0.013	0.010	0.005	0.003	0.001	0.001
19	0.832	0.693	0.483	0.340	0.240	0.171	0.122	0.088	0.075	0.064	0.047	0.034	0.025	0.019	0.016	0.014	0.010	0.008	0.004	0.002	0.001	0.001
20	0.823	0.679	0.465	0.320	0.222	0.155	0.109	0.077	0.065	0.055	0.039	0.028	0.021	0.015	0.013	0.011	0.008	0.006	0.003	0.001	0.001	
21	0.815	0.666	0.447	0.302	0.206	0.141	0.098	0.068	0.057	0.047	0.033	0.024	0.017	0.012	0.010	0.009	0.006	0.005	0.002	0.001		
22	0.807	0.653	0.430	0.285	0.191	0.128	0.087	0.060	0.049	0.041	0.028	0.020	0.014	0.010	0.008	0.007	0.005	0.004	0.002	0.001		
23	0.799	0.640	0.413	0.269	0.176	0.117	0.078	0.052	0.043	0.035	0.024	0.016	0.011	0.008	0.007	0.005	0.004	0.003	0.001	0.001		
24	0.791	0.627	0.397	0.254	0.163	0.106	0.069	0.046	0.037	0.030	0.020	0.014	0.009	0.006	0.005	0.004	0.003	0.003	0.001			
25	0.783	0.615	0.382	0.239	0.151	0.096	0.062	0.040	0.032	0.026	0.017	0.011	0.008	0.005	0.004	0.003	0.002	0.002				
26	0.776	0.603	0.367	0.226	0.140	0.088	0.055	0.035	0.028	0.023	0.015	0.010	0.006	0.004	0.003	0.003	0.002	0.001				
27	0.768	0.591	0.353	0.213	0.130	0.080	0.049	0.031	0.025	0.019	0.012	0.008	0.005	0.003	0.003	0.002	0.001	0.001				
28	0.760	0.580	0.340	0.201	0.120	0.072	0.044	0.027	0.021	0.017	0.010	0.007	0.004	0.003	0.002	0.002	0.001	0.001				
29	0.753	0.568	0.326	0.190	0.111	0.066	0.039	0.024	0.019	0.014	0.009	0.006	0.003	0.002	0.002	0.001	0.001					
30	0.745	0.557	0.314	0.179	0.103	0.060	0.035	0.021	0.016	0.012	0.008	0.005	0.003	0.002	0.001	0.001						
40	0.675	0.457	0.212	0.100	0.048	0.023	0.011	0.006	0.004	0.003	0.001	0.001										
50	0.611	0.375	0.143	0.056	0.022	0.009	0.004	0.002	0.001	0.001												

Source: By permission, from Robert N. Anthony, *Management Accounting: Text and Cases*, rev. ed. (Homewood, Ill.: Richard D. Irwin, Inc., 1960), p. 658.

Table 4-13

PRESENT VALUE OF $1/12 RECEIVED MONTHLY FOR N YEARS

Years (N)	1%	2%	4%	6%	8%	10%	12%	14%	15%	16%	18%	20%	22%	24%	25%	26%	28%	30%	35%	40%	45%	50%
1	0.995	0.989	0.979	0.969	0.959	0.950	0.941	0.932	0.928	0.924	0.915	0.907	0.899	0.892	0.888	0.884	0.877	0.870	0.853	0.837	0.822	0.808
2	1.979	1.959	1.920	1.883	1.848	1.814	1.781	1.750	1.735	1.720	1.691	1.663	1.637	1.611	1.598	1.586	1.562	1.539	1.485	1.435	1.390	1.347
3	2.954	2.910	2.826	2.746	2.670	2.599	2.531	2.467	2.436	2.406	2.348	2.293	2.241	2.191	2.167	2.143	2.098	2.054	1.953	1.863	1.781	1.706
4	3.920	3.843	3.696	3.559	3.432	3.313	3.201	3.096	3.046	2.998	2.905	2.818	2.736	2.658	2.621	2.585	2.516	2.450	2.300	2.168	2.050	1.946
5	4.876	4.757	4.533	4.327	4.137	3.962	3.799	3.648	3.577	3.508	3.377	3.256	3.142	3.036	2.985	2.936	2.842	2.755	2.557	2.386	2.236	2.106
6	5.822	5.653	5.338	5.051	4.790	4.551	4.333	4.132	4.038	3.948	3.778	3.620	3.475	3.340	3.276	3.214	3.098	2.989	2.747	2.541	2.365	2.212
7	6.759	6.531	6.111	5.734	5.395	5.088	4.810	4.557	4.439	4.327	4.117	3.924	3.748	3.585	3.509	3.435	3.297	3.169	2.888	2.653	2.453	2.283
8	7.687	7.392	6.855	6.379	5.954	5.575	5.235	4.929	4.788	4.654	4.404	4.177	3.971	3.783	3.695	3.611	3.453	3.308	2.992	2.732	2.514	2.330
9	8.605	8.237	7.571	6.987	6.473	6.018	5.615	5.256	5.091	4.935	4.647	4.388	4.154	3.942	3.844	3.750	3.575	3.414	3.070	2.789	2.556	2.362
10	9.515	9.065	8.259	7.560	6.953	6.421	5.955	5.543	5.355	5.178	4.854	4.564	4.305	4.071	3.963	3.860	3.670	3.497	3.127	2.829	2.585	2.383
11	10.415	9.876	8.920	8.101	7.397	6.788	6.258	5.794	5.584	5.388	5.029	4.711	4.428	4.175	4.058	3.948	3.744	3.560	3.169	2.858	2.605	2.397
12	11.307	10.672	9.556	8.612	7.809	7.121	6.528	6.015	5.784	5.568	5.177	4.833	4.529	4.259	4.135	4.018	3.802	3.608	3.201	2.879	2.619	2.406
13	12.189	11.452	10.167	9.094	8.190	7.423	6.770	6.208	5.957	5.724	5.302	4.935	4.611	4.326	4.196	4.073	3.847	3.646	3.224	2.894	2.629	2.412
14	13.063	12.217	10.755	9.548	8.542	7.699	6.985	6.378	6.108	5.858	5.409	5.019	4.679	4.380	4.245	4.117	3.883	3.674	3.241	2.904	2.635	2.417
15	13.928	12.967	11.321	9.977	8.869	7.949	7.178	6.527	6.239	5.973	5.499	5.090	4.735	4.424	4.284	4.152	3.911	3.696	3.254	2.912	2.640	2.419
16	14.785	13.702	11.864	10.381	9.171	8.176	7.350	6.658	6.353	6.073	5.576	5.149	4.780	4.460	4.315	4.179	3.932	3.713	3.264	2.917	2.643	2.421
17	15.633	14.422	12.387	10.762	9.451	8.383	7.503	6.772	6.452	6.159	5.640	5.198	4.818	4.488	4.340	4.201	3.949	3.726	3.271	2.921	2.645	2.422
18	16.473	15.129	12.890	11.122	9.711	8.571	7.640	6.873	6.539	6.233	5.695	5.239	4.848	4.511	4.360	4.218	3.962	3.736	3.276	2.924	2.647	2.423
19	17.305	15.822	13.373	11.462	9.951	8.742	7.763	6.961	6.614	6.297	5.742	5.273	4.873	4.530	4.376	4.232	3.973	3.744	3.280	2.926	2.648	2.424
20	18.128	16.501	13.838	11.782	10.173	8.897	7.872	7.038	6.679	6.352	5.781	5.301	4.894	4.545	4.389	4.243	3.981	3.750	3.283	2.927	2.648	2.424
21	18.943	17.167	14.285	12.084	10.379	9.038	7.969	7.106	6.735	6.399	5.815	5.325	4.911	4.557	4.399	4.252	3.987	3.755	3.285	2.928	2.649	2.424
22	19.750	17.819	14.714	12.369	10.570	9.167	8.056	7.165	6.785	6.440	5.843	5.345	4.925	4.567	4.407	4.259	3.992	3.758	3.286	2.929	2.649	2.425
23	20.549	18.459	15.127	12.638	10.746	9.283	8.134	7.218	6.828	6.476	5.867	5.361	4.936	4.574	4.414	4.264	3.996	3.761	3.287	2.929	2.649	2.425
24	21.341	19.087	15.525	12.892	10.909	9.389	8.204	7.263	6.865	6.506	5.887	5.375	4.945	4.581	4.419	4.269	3.999	3.763	3.288	2.930	2.650	2.425
25	22.124	19.702	15.906	13.131	11.061	9.486	8.266	7.304	6.897	6.532	5.904	5.386	4.953	4.586	4.423	4.272	4.001	3.765	3.289	2.930	2.650	2.425
26	22.899	20.305	16.274	13.357	11.201	9.574	8.321	7.339	6.926	6.555	5.919	5.396	4.959	4.590	4.426	4.275	4.003	3.766	3.289	2.930	2.650	2.425
27	23.667	20.896	16.627	13.570	11.331	9.653	8.370	7.370	6.950	6.574	5.931	5.404	4.964	4.593	4.429	4.277	4.004	3.767	3.290	2.930	2.650	2.425
28	24.428	21.476	16.966	13.771	11.451	9.726	8.415	7.397	6.971	6.591	5.942	5.410	4.968	4.596	4.431	4.279	4.005	3.768	3.290	2.930	2.650	2.425
29	25.180	22.044	17.293	13.961	11.562	9.792	8.454	7.421	6.990	6.606	5.951	5.416	4.972	4.598	4.433	4.280	4.006	3.768	3.290	2.930	2.650	2.425
30	25.926	22.601	17.607	14.139	11.665	9.852	8.489	7.441	7.006	6.618	5.958	5.420	4.975	4.600	4.434	4.281	4.007	3.769	3.290	2.930	2.650	2.425
40	32.985	27.605	20.153	15.456	12.156	10.220	8.688	7.550	7.087	6.678	5.992	5.440	4.986	4.606	4.439	4.285	4.009	3.770	3.291	2.931	2.650	2.425
50	39.375	31.711	21.873	16.191	12.676	10.361	8.752	7.580	7.107	6.692	5.999	5.443	4.987	4.607	4.440	4.285	4.009	3.770	3.291	2.931	2.650	2.425

SOURCE: By permission, from Robert N. Anthony, *Management Accounting: Text and Cases*, rev. ed. (Homewood, Ill.: Richard D. Irwin, Inc., 1960), p. 659.

Annual discounting is assumed.   Formula: $\dfrac{1 - (1+i)^{-n}}{12[(1+i)^{1/12} - 1]}$.

Table 4-14

SAMPLE PRESENT VALUE TABLE FOR ACCELERATED DEPRECIATION

Present Value of Depreciation Write-Off Using
Double-Declining-Balance Method with Switch
to Straight-Line Method*

Opportunity Rate	Asset Tax Life	Analysis Life in Years							
		4	5	6	8	10	12	15	20
6%	3	.890	.890	.890	.890	.890	.890	.890	.890
	4	.823	.869	.869	.869	.869	.869	.869	.869
	6	.655	.728	.797	.830	.830	.830	.830	.830
	10	.465	.533	.584	.668	.742	.759	.759	.759
	12	.404	.469	.521	.596	.659	.715	.728	.728
	16	.319	.377	.425	.497	.548	.591	.646	.671
	20	.263	.315	.358	.426	.475	.511	.556	.616
	45	.125	.153	.179	.222	.257	.285	.318	.354
8%	3	.857	.857	.857	.857	.857	.857	.857	.857
	4	.789	.830	.830	.830	.830	.830	.830	.830
	6	.626	.692	.753	.781	.781	.781	.781	.781
	10	.443	.504	.550	.622	.683	.697	.697	.697
	12	.384	.444	.489	.554	.606	.650	.660	.660
	16	.303	.356	.398	.461	.502	.537	.579	.596
	20	.250	.297	.335	.394	.434	.463	.497	.539
	45	.119	.144	.167	.204	.233	.256	.280	.306
	3	.825	.825	.825	.825	.825	.825	.825	.825
	4	.756	.794	.794	.794	.794	.794	.794	.794
	6	.598	.658	.712	.737	.737	.737	.737	.737

Table 4-14 (continued)

Opportunity Rate	Asset Tax Life	Analysis Life in Years							
		4	5	6	8	10	12	15	20
10%	10	.422	.478	.518	.580	.631	.642	.642	.642
	12	.366	.420	.460	.516	.559	.594	.602	.602
	16	.289	.336	.374	.427	.462	.489	.521	.534
	20	.238	.280	.314	.365	.398	.421	.447	.476
	45	.113	.136	.156	.188	.212	.230	.249	.266
12%	3	.794	.794	.794	.794	.794	.794	.794	.794
	4	.725	.759	.759	.759	.759	.759	.759	.759
	6	.572	.626	.674	.696	.696	.696	.696	.696
	10	.402	.453	.488	.542	.584	.593	.593	.593
	12	.349	.397	.433	.481	.517	.545	.551	.551
	16	.275	.318	.351	.397	.426	.447	.472	.481
	20	.226	.264	.295	.338	.366	.384	.404	.424
	45	.107	.128	.146	.173	.193	.208	.222	.234

Example 1

To find the present value of all depreciation over a 10-year analysis life for a $10,000 asset with a tax life of 16 years, when the opportunity rate is 10%:

$$P.V. = f \times S = .462 \times \$10,000 = \$4,620$$

Example 2

To find the present value of the depreciation tax shield of the asset in Example 1 over an 8-year analysis life, when the opportunity rate is 12% and the income tax rate is 53%:

$$P.V. = f \times S \times Tx = .397 \times \$10,000 \times 0.53 = \$2,104$$

* The continuous method of discounting employed here differs slightly from Tables 4–10 through 4–13. Thus, these factors lead to lower than equivalent values, had the process of Tables 4–10 through 4–13 been employed.

SELECTED REFERENCES

Analytical Process

ANTHONY, ROBERT N. *Management Accounting, Text and Cases,* chaps. 18, 19. 4th ed. Homewood, Ill.: Richard D. Irwin, 1970.

BACKER, MORTON, and JACOBSEN, LYLE E. *Cost Accounting, A Managerial Approach,* chap. 18. New York: McGraw-Hill Book Co., 1964.

GRANT, EUGENE. *Principles of Engineering Analysis.* 3d ed. New York: Ronald Press Co., 1950.

HORNGREN, CHARLES T. *Cost Accounting, A Managerial Emphasis,* chaps. 13, 14. Englewood Cliffs, N.J.: Prentice-Hall, 1962.

MOORE, CARL D., and JAEDICKE, ROBERT K. *Managerial Accounting,* chap. 19. Cincinnati, Ohio: South-Western Publishing Co., 1963.

WESTON, J. FRED, and BRIGHAM, EUGENE F. *Managerial Finance,* chaps. 6, 7, 8. 3d ed. New York: Holt, Rinehart & Winston, 1971.

Broader Framework of Capital Budgeting

BIERMAN, HAROLD JR., and SMIDT, SEYMOUR. *The Capital Budgeting Decision.* 3d ed. New York: Macmillan Co., 1971.

HUNT, PEARSON; WILLIAMS, CHARLES M.; and DONALDSON, GORDON. *Basic Business Finance,* part VII. 3d ed. Homewood, Ill.: Richard D. Irwin, 1966.

JOHNSON, ROBERT W. *Capital Budgeting.* Belmont, Calif.: Wadsworth Publishing Co., 1970.

PORTERFIELD, JAMES T. S. *Investment Decisions and Capital Costs.* Englewood Cliffs, N.J.: Prentice-Hall, 1965.

Specialized Areas

Present Value Tables

GUSHEE, CHARLES H. (ed.). *Financial Compound Interest and Annuity Tables.* 5th ed. Boston: Financial Publishing Co., 1970.

HARLAN, NEIL E.; CHRISTENSON, CHARLES J.; and VANCIL, RICHARD F. *Managerial Economics.* Homewood, Ill.: Richard D. Irwin, 1962. (See Appendix.)

MAPI Method

TERBORGH, GEORGE. *Business Investment Management.* Washington, D.C.: Machinery and Allied Products Institute, 1967.

Probability Analysis

HERTZ, DAVID B.   *New Power for Management, Computer Systems and Management Science.* New York: McGraw-Hill Book Co., 1969.

SCHLAIFER, ROBERT O.   *Probability And Statistics For Business Decisions.* New York: McGraw-Hill Book Co., 1959.

Leasing

HUNT, PEARSON; WILLIAMS, CHARLES M.; and DONALDSON, GORDON.   *Basic Business Finance,* chap. 33. 3d ed. Homewood, Ill.: Richard D. Irwin, 1966.

VANCIL, RICHARD F. (ed.).   *Financial Executive's Handbook,* chap. 20. Homewood, Ill.: Dow Jones-Irwin, 1970.

VANCIL, RICHARD F. (ed.).   *Leasing of Industrial Equipment.* New York: McGraw-Hill Book Co., 1963.

CHAPTER

5

ANALYSIS OF FINANCIAL FUNDS SOURCES

After our discussion of operational analysis and projection and the key elements of capital investment decisions, it is now time to turn to the third element of the management picture—the analysis of financial funds sources, which are the fuel of business activity.

This chapter will deal with two main considerations in reviewing the financing options open to management: (1) the *cost* of different funds sources from the point of view of the enterprise, and (2) the *value* of different financing devices to the provider of the funds, the investor. It is necessary to distinguish clearly between these viewpoints in looking at funds sources, as the techniques to be applied will differ. In keeping with the purpose of this book, the main emphasis will be on the viewpoint of the management of the business and only a few of the concepts of valuation will be given from the investor's standpoint, enough to provide a flavor of the concerns and desires of the funds providers. The concept of cost of capital has been paid increasing attention in recent years, especially as it affects the proper economic choices among investment opportunities, but there has also been considerable discussion on the proper measurement of the cost of capital itself, and how the circumstances around such an analysis affect the methods chosen. There is, of course, no such thing as *the* cost of capital, applicable to all problems, since the concept is part of the dynamic and ever-changing financial and operational environment of the corporate enterprise. The interested student is directed to the references listed at the end of the chapter.

Sources of funds for a going enterprise are numerous and varied, and the types of contracts, understandings, and arrangements can be suited in a tailor-made fashion to almost any conceivable set of circumstances. This variety is introduced, however, largely through modifications of two basic choices: debt on the one hand, and equity on the other; with a third choice, preferred equity, representing a middle ground. Debt, of course, is created through a contract which calls for eventual repayment of value committed, usually at interest; while equity is an ownership commitment, generally without termination and carrying all the risks of ownership. Preferred equity has elements of both, even though it basically is an ownership involvement. The choice of appropriate financing sources is part of the planning task of management, and is inextricably connected with the nature of the operations, the projected conditions, the industry, and the style of management. As we already expressed in the earlier chapters, this planning task involves a matching of appropriate funds sources to the current and expected future operations and investments.

The alternative funds sources available to management involve varying degrees of risk exposure, since the proportion of debt and equity (see Chapter 2) to a large extent determines the ability of a company to fulfill its obligations in periods of high and low earnings. Management, responsible to the stockholders for a fair return on their investment, must therefore spend much thought and care to determine the right mix of debt and equity in a company's capital structure—enough low-cost debt to boost the owner's return by applying debt to projects earning more than the cost of borrowing the necessary funds, and not too much debt to endanger the stockholders' return and even the company's solvency in low earnings periods. The latter point relates to the fact that fixed debt obligations must be met regardless of circumstances.

Our discussion of techniques of funds source analysis will be built around a common example of these options, without going into detail on the many institutional, legal, and organizational concepts. These represent a vast body of knowledge and practice and are best found in works on corporate finance and investment management. Not covered will be the question of new enterprises, whose more limited choice of funds is a special case, and we shall assume a going enterprise in our discussion. Moreover, the stress will be on incremental financing, although the consideration of existing funds sources is part of the total picture and will be covered when necessary.

The point of view of the investor will similarly be taken on the basis of commonly encountered examples, and valuation techniques will be demonstrated. The reader will be referred to relevant literature at the end of the chapter for fuller study of the background of all these questions.

In the preceding chapter we discussed the techniques of the proper selection of investment opportunities for a business. In analyzing the funds sources to provide the basis for these investments, we shall now assume that management has planned and fully thought out the intended use of the funds. We shall only concern ourselves with the problem of obtaining the funds. In this we shall be discussing the cost and obligations assumed by choosing among different funds sources and the key principles of choice involved. In the case of the investor, we shall discuss the concepts of income yield, risk, and value considerations. As will become clear, many of the techniques to be discussed tie directly to our past chapters on ratio analysis and financial projection—as we would expect, since they are part of the total operating picture. With this background we shall now turn to the first portion of the chapter, the discussion of the cost of alternative funds choices open to management.

THE COST OF DIFFERENT FUNDS

Throughout the existence of a corporation, the management makes financing decisions which result in changes in the funds sources used and quite often in changes of the capital structure itself. These range from minor modifications to possible recapitalization. Each increment of change involves an increment or decrement of cost, as well as having an effect on the cost of the total capital structure. For the time being, let us concentrate on the increments of funds involved when a corporation incurs additional debt or raises funds through issuing additional preferred or common stock. Techniques for measuring the cost of the many alternatives open to management are an important part of the decision process.

The Cost of Debt

In the course of business an enterprise commonly employs many forms of debt, which range from trade obligations (accounts payable) to long-term mortgage loans or debenture (bond) issues, and which include simple notes payable to banks or individuals, tax payments owed to various governmental agencies, wages due, payments due on installment purchases, and even lease obligations. All types of debt, which include many others not mentioned, can be analyzed relatively easily as a first step by deriving the *explicit cost* involved for the company. Normally, debt arrangements carry specific interest provisions payable either during the debt period, at its end, or deducted in advance from principal (called discounting). The explicit cost of debt in those cases is simply the cost of this interest commitment.

Before we take up specific examples of debt and the analysis of the cost of these forms of debt, it should be remembered that interest is tax-deductible for corporations and that, therefore, the cost to a corporation (at least those with sufficient profits to pay taxes or able to apply tax-averaging provisions) will be the fraction of the annual interest payment multiplied by a factor of one minus the applicable tax rate. For example, if a corporation pays 6 percent per year on the principal of a note payable and its effective tax rate for incremental revenue or cost is 48 percent, the net annual effective interest cost of this note will be:

$$1 - 0.48 = 0.52$$
$$0.52 \times 6\% = 3.12\% \text{ (after taxes)}$$

The effect of tax deductibility is a reduction of the cost of debt to corporations (and to individuals under many circumstances) to a net amount after applying the prevailing tax rate. This is in contrast to situations involving other forms of capital, as will be shown later.

Operating Debt. First, a few comments should be made about operating debt, which is defined as short-term or revolving obligations incurred in the ordinary everyday operations of most businesses. Some of these debt funds are in fact provided free of any explicit cost, under trade terms generally accepted in the type of industry in which the company operates. Foremost in this category are accounts payable, which are incurred under terms such as 2/10, n/30; or 3/15, n/45; or many variations thereof. Up to 10 or 15 days, therefore, or even as long as 45 days, the company being billed for goods or services can hold off payment and, without cost, can make use of the values received on credit. We recall from Chapter 1 that trade credit is in fact a significant funds source.

In most cases of trade credit, when payment is made within a specified period, it is possible to earn a discount of 2 percent if paid within 10 days (2/10), or 3 percent if paid within 15 days (3/15) from the date of the invoice. This practice allows the customer to reduce, in effect, the cost of the goods or services by the specified amount. The purpose of this inducement is to help the vendor collect his funds faster and thus to reduce his own funds tied up in accounts receivable. If the discount period is missed, however, the net amount is due by the end of the credit period specified (n/30, n/45, etc.). If the debtor company makes use of this option, a very definite cost is incurred for prolonging the time during which it can make use of the funds. This is an *opportunity cost* in the form of cash discounts lost. For instance, if the credit terms are 2/10, n/30, the cost of using the funds for an extra 20 days amounts to 2 percent in cash discount lost, or an annual rate of:

$$\frac{360 \text{ days}}{20 \text{ days}} \times 2\% = 36\% \text{ (before taxes)}$$

In this case, however, the corporation loses as taxable income the cash discount it would have otherwise earned, and the explicit net cost must be reduced by the taxes saved. If taxes are assumed to be 48 percent of income, the net cost for the extra 20 days' use of the creditor's funds amounts to:

$$1 - 0.48 = 0.52$$
$$0.52 \times 2\% = 1.04\% \text{ (after taxes)}$$

This cost remains a fairly sizable figure on an annual basis, as compared to the prime interest rate (between 5 and 8 percent) generally charged large corporations of impeccable credit rating:

$$\frac{360 \text{ days}}{20 \text{ days}} \times 1.04\% = 18.72\% \text{ (after taxes)}$$

Some companies, especially small and rapidly growing enterprises, make it a practice to use accounts payable as a convenient source of credit, often unilaterally exceeding the outside limits of credit terms by sizable periods. The longer the funds are kept, of course, the lower becomes the explicit cost of accounts payable, since normally no interest charges are levied by the trade creditor. In extreme cases, unpaid accounts may be converted to notes payable, with or without interest, upon the request of the trade creditor who wishes to establish a somewhat stronger claim. From the standpoint of credit-worthiness and company reputation, it is clearly a poor practice to go beyond the stipulated credit period, since other prospective creditors will take such tardy performance into account when they evaluate further credit extension. This aspect is part of the *implicit* cost of credit and other forms of capital, which will be discussed later.

Another form of operating debt is the short-term note and the installment contract, in which interest is either charged ahead of time or is added to the amount of principal stated in the contract. For example, a $1,000 note which carries 6 percent interest will provide the debtor with only $940 if the time period is one year and the note is discounted by deducting the interest in advance. The effective cost before taxes now becomes higher than the stated interest, since the company is paying $60 for the privilege of borrowing $940 for one year:

$$\frac{\$\ 60}{\$940} = 6.38\% \ (\text{before taxes})$$

The adjustment for income taxes is made exactly as shown previously. In the case of an installment contract for, say, $1,000 payable in four quarterly installments, with interest of 5 percent on the original balance, the effective cost of interest is much higher than stated, since over the term of the contract decreasing amounts of principal are outstanding and used by the borrowing company.

For a quick method of calculating the approximate effective cost we can argue that over the term of the contract the principal amount dropped from $1,000 to zero, with the average amount outstanding being roughly half of the principal, or $500. The contractual interest was 5 percent on $1,000, or $50, which became part of each of the four payments. When the interest paid is related to the average amount of capital in the hands of the borrowing company over the period of the loan, the following doubling of cost is the result:

$$\frac{\$\ 50}{\$500} = 10\% \ (\text{before taxes})$$

Again, the adjustment for income taxes is the same as before. If the contract runs over more than one year, care must be taken to *annualize* the interest cost, that is, to relate the interest amount to the specific time period involved in order to arrive at a true cost per year, which is the normal period of comparison.

If more precision is required, we can refine the approximate results achieved with the calculations presented above through the use of present value techniques (time discounting) described in Chapter 4. Such an approach is useful where exactness is important and where the incidence of the funds flows covers considerable time periods and a variety of patterns. Banks and other lending institutions use tables based on present value techniques to calculate with precision the charges and payments connected with contracts of this sort. It should be added, however, that the simple averaging technique is useful in many circumstances, including personal finance, to obtain for decision purposes a fair approximation of the true (effective), or explicit, cost of contracts of this type.

The preceeding discussion has shown ways to ascertain the cost of common operational debt obligations, whose explicit cost may range from zero to quite substantial rates of interest. This explicit cost is not the only aspect of debt, however. As already mentioned, repayment schedules have to be met, and while there is no specific cost connected with the repayment of principal, the obligation to do so in a timely fashion forces the financial manager to forecast and plan cash receipts and disbursements with care. Chapter 2 has shown the basic techniques of such cash projection. Another element of the debt burden, and one that will be important in the ensuing discussion, is the implicit impact of various forms of debt obligations in the creditworthiness of a company contemplating future capital needs. In other words, the balance between debt and equity may become precarious and forestall further borrowing for some time, until the company has worked itself from under its debt obligations. Having "closed off the top," as debt-heavy operations are often characterized, can be a costly endeavor, both in terms of the risk of not meeting obligations as they fall due and in having to turn to much costlier sources of credit or equity funds as additional needs arise. More detail will be given on this later.

Debt in the Long-Term Capital Structure. So far we have concentrated on operating debt and its cost, represented by essentially short-term obligations. More important for a company in the long run, however, is the cost and proportion of debt in its more permanent form—debt as part of the long-term capital structure of the corporation. Here management must make well-planned decisions which involve the cost and amount of debt relative to investments in expanded or diversified activities. Commitments made here are by their very nature bound to have a much more lasting impact than short-term working capital decisions. At times refinancing or even recapitalization may be involved, with significant and far-reaching changes in a company's capital structure. We shall, therefore, turn our attention to the cost of debt in the long-term capital structure, focusing our discussion on incremental amounts of debt added to an existing situation. Later we shall expand the discussion to include the broad role of debt as one of the several options open to management.

Since the basic objective and obligation of management normally is to provide adequate and growing earnings to the stockholders, and to at least maintain and hopefully enhance the value of their investment, we shall incorporate these characteristics in the analysis of a hypothetical company, the ABC Corporation, whose balance sheet (abbreviated) appears as shown in Figure 5–1. The corporation has one million shares of common stock outstanding, with a par value of $10 per share. Most recently, ABC Corporation has earned $11 million before taxes on sales of $115 million. Income taxes paid amounted to $5.3 million. We begin our appraisal of the current position of ABC Corporation and its stockholders by calculating the earnings

Figure 5–1

ABC CORPORATION

Balance Sheet

(millions of dollars)

Assets		Liabilities and Net Worth	
Current assets	$15	Current liabilities	$ 7
Fixed assets (net)	29	Common stock	10
Other assets	1	Retained earnings	28
Total	$45	Total	$45

per share of common stock (EPS), using a format which will be applied throughout this chapter. The format is based on a step-by-step development of the earnings impact of obligations in order of their normal priority.

We first state the earnings before interest and taxes (EBIT) and subtract from that figure a variety of charges applicable to different obligations. The first of these is interest charges on long-term debt; normally we ignore short-term interest unless it is a significant amount. The assumption is that because of the temporary nature of such obligations, as part of normal operations, these charges have been deducted properly in arriving at the EBIT figure quoted. The data will be arranged as in Figure 5–2.

Figure 5–2

ABC CORPORATION

Earnings per Share Calculation
(thousands of dollars, except per share)

Earnings before interest and taxes (EBIT)	$11,000
Less interest charges on long-term debt	–0–
Earnings before income taxes	$11,000
Federal income taxes at 48 percent	5,280
Earnings after income taxes	$ 5,720
Less preferred dividends	–0–
Earnings available for common stock	$ 5,720
Common shares outstanding (number)	1 million
Earnings per share (EPS)	$ 5.72
Less common dividends per share	2.50
Retained earnings per share	$ 3.22
Retained earnings in total	$ 3,220

The analysis format has made provision for interest and preferred dividends, but no amounts are shown since our hypothetical ABC Corporation has at this point neither long-term debt nor preferred stock outstanding. The result of the calculations in Figure 5–2 shows a residual earnings available to common stockholders of $5.72 per share, from which a dividend of $2.50 per share has been voted as a cash distribution by the board of directors. We assume that this dividend payout (between 40 and 50 percent of earnings) has been maintained for many years, and that earnings have steadily grown by about 6 percent over the years. Let us further assume that the stock is widely held and traded, and that it commands a price of about $60 to $65 in the stock market, roughly 11 times current earnings. Such is the present condition of ABC Corporation.

The introduction of debt to this capital structure and the earnings position of the company will again demonstrate the concept of explicit cost discussed earlier in this chapter. Let us assume that the corporation is planning to borrow $10 million in order to exploit a new product it has developed. There is the possibility of issuing bonds, which are not secured by assets of the company but are based on the general corporate credit standing. Such debenture bonds will carry an interest rate of 6 percent, will become due 20 years from date of issue, and will carry a sinking fund provision of $400,000 per year beginning with the fifth year. The balance outstanding at the end of 20 years will become payable as a "balloon" payment of $4 million. After the new product has been introduced, the company hopes for incremental earnings of at least $1.5 million before taxes, and expects little risk of obsolescence or competitive inroads for the next 10 to 15 years.

We can now trace the impact of debt on the current corporate situation, both in terms of earnings and dividends, and in terms of the explicit cost of the newly created debt. Two conditions will be analyzed: first, the immediate impact of the debt without any offsetting benefits of profitable investment; and second, the picture presented once the investment has become operative and the incremental earnings from the new product have been brought about.

The results of the calculations are shown in Figure 5–3. The effect of adding debt is a reduction of the stockholders' earnings, an immediate dilution caused by the interest cost entering the earnings pattern of ABC Corporation. Earnings after interest and taxes dropped $312,000, which is, of course, 52 percent $(1 - 0.48)$ of the pretax interest cost of $600,000. Earnings per share dropped about 31 cents, a reduction of 5.4 percent from the prior level, purely because of the additional interest burden,

Figure 5–3

ABC CORPORATION

Earnings per Share with New Bond Issue

(thousands of dollars, except per share)

	Current	With New Product
Earnings before interest and taxes (EBIT)	$11,000	$12,500
Less interest charges on long-term debt	600	600
Earnings before income taxes	$10,400	$11,900
Federal income taxes at 48 percent	4,992	5,712
Earnings after income taxes	$ 5,408	$ 6,188
Less preferred dividends	–0–	–0–
Earnings available for common stock	$ 5,408	$ 6,188
Common shares outstanding (number)	1 million	1 million
Earnings per share (EPS) .... $	5.41	$ 6.19
Less common dividends per share	2.50	2.50
Retained earnings per share .... $	2.91	$ 3.69
Retained earnings in total	$ 2,908	$ 3,688
Original EPS (Figure 5–2) .... $	5.72	$ 5.72
Change in EPS .... $	–0.31	$ +0.47
Percent change in EPS	–5.4%	+8.2%

which on a per share basis amounts to about 31 cents ($312,000 ÷ 1 million shares).

The explicit cost of the incremental funds is therefore 52 percent of 6 percent, or 3.12 percent per year, given a tax rate of 48 percent. Another way of figuring this cost is, of course, the relationship of the annual after-tax interest cost to the amount provided, which is $312,000 for $10 million, or 3.12 percent. Finally, we can also argue that the explicit cost is the specific change in earnings to the stockholders, as pointed out before. If earnings are not disturbed by any other factor, as we have assumed, the earnings drop represents the explicit cost. If earnings on the new investment are sufficient just to offset the earnings drop from interest, leaving earnings unchanged, the investment would earn (yield) precisely the explicit cost of the capital required.

This thinking is reflected in the second column of Figure 5–3, where we observe that as soon as the new product has been successfully brought out the additional earnings generated have more than offset the explicit cost of the debentures. The after-tax earnings jumped to $6,188,000, a net increase of $468,000 over the original $5,720,000. As a consequence, earnings per share rose 47 cents above the original amount of $5.72, an increase of about 8 percent. The successful investment of the funds provided by the debentures has more than offset their explicit cost, and thereby boosted common earnings. Incremental earnings exceed incremental cost, and the investment— if our earnings assumption proves true—has made possible a true increment of value.

This condition raises the following questions: Would it not have been sufficient for the investment to earn only $312,000 after taxes, since this would leave the stockholders as well off as before? By earning more, ABC Corporation has used financial leverage (Chapter 6) and given the equity owners a "free ride" —or has it? At first glance, it might be reasonable to believe so. Nevertheless a number of points must be raised to be developed more fully later. First of all, no mention has been made so far of the sinking fund obligations which will begin five years hence and which call for a cash outlay of $400,000 per year. Even though this amount is not tax deductible and must be paid out of the cash flows generated by the company, are we justified in ascribing no "cost" to this obligation? In fact, this debt service amounts to 40 cents per share per year which is no longer available for dividends or other corporate purposes, since it is committed to the repayment of principal. If the investment were just to earn the interest cost on the debt, how would we repay this principal? Chapter 4 has dealt with the concept of how to calculate an appropriate payout of such an investment.

Another question addresses the implicit cost of risk: What if the earnings of the investment turned out to be much worse than expected? Should such a risk be expressed as part of the cost considerations? Is the payment obligation pattern of interest and principal an appropriate concern to current and future creditors, stockholders, and other interested parties? Finally, should the explicit after-tax cost of 3.12 percent per year be used as a criterion for judging the return or yield of the investment, or is a broader, more overall cost of capital applicable here? Will there always be an opportunity to borrow at this cost, and will it not be necessary to raise funds in some form other than debt next time? Could the investment project stand up under such conditions? In other words, is it possible to look at capital costs in small increments, depending on the type of capital raised?

These significant questions and many more lead toward the economic framework of capital budgeting. Clearly, the debt service burden implicitly costs the company some of its flexibility. The risk of earnings fluctuations impairing the fulfillment of the contract for fixed debt service payments is real, and must be carefully appraised. Some of the ratios discussed in Chapter 2 are helpful here, and clues as to the reasonableness of "earnings coverage" of the obligations can be gained. The investment must be judged in broader terms; incremental debt cost is not a sufficient criterion, as was seen in Chapter 4. In short, we are only at the beginning of the full analysis of the funds source decision and are limited by the scope of this book from considering all aspects. Yet we have established the need to relate the cost and other effects of different types of capital sources to operational and investment strategy, and we shall return to this broader subject in later sections of this chapter as well as in Chapter 6.

The Cost of Preferred Stock

When considering the cost of adding preferred stock to a capital structure, we must consider that this type of equity holds a middle ground between debt and common stock. Subordinated to the various creditors of the corporation, the preferred stockholder has a prior claim to corporate earnings up to the amount of the preferred dividend. In liquidation, his claims are satisfied prior to the residual claims of the common stockholders. Because of the near-equity nature of preferred stock, preferred dividends are not considered tax deductible by the Internal Revenue Service. Such dividends therefore represent an outflow of after-tax funds from the corporation. For instance, a share of 7 percent preferred stock, par value $100, costs the issuing corporation $7 in after-tax earnings. For each dollar of dividends to be provided, the corporation must therefore earn $1.92 before taxes. Where the 6 percent bond discussed before had an after-tax cost of 3.12 percent, the 7 percent preferred has an after-tax cost of 7 percent. Thus, the stated dividend rate on a preferred stock is directly comparable to the *tax-adjusted* interest rate on a bond.

All along we have assumed, of course, that in the examples shown the bonds or preferreds were issued at such prices as to yield proceeds exactly equal to the par or face value—in other words, that the corporation receives $100 for a share of $100 preferred after expenses of issuing the shares. Where there is a difference—where proceeds are either greater or smaller than the par value of a bond or preferred, as often happens because of market conditions—it is necessary first to calculate an *effective* interest or dividend rate based on the proceeds, and then to develop the tax adjustments to arrive at comparable figures.

To illustrate further the effect of introducing preferred stock to a corporate capital structure, we return to the example of the ABC Corporation. This time the $10 million in capital to be added is raised via 7 percent preferred stock (100,000 shares) at $100 per share net proceeds to the corporation after legal and issuing expenses.

The results of the calculations in Figure 5–4 reflect a sizable drop in the earnings from those of the initial condition—a much more serious effect than in the case of the 6 percent bonds. A small increase in earnings is achieved after the investment becomes operative, which again is much different from the bond alternative. The cause for this is the stated 7 percent dividend rate, which, while only slightly higher than the bond interest, has a much costlier effect because it is not tax deductible. This time the annual cost is shown as a deduction from after-tax earnings, and the immediate dilution amounts to 70 cents per share, or 12.2 percent. With the new earnings, the eventual earnings increase is only 8 cents per share or 1.4 percent. The corporation is committed to a total of $700,000 of after-tax funds, which leaves very little room for a net gain from the

Figure 5–4

ABC CORPORATION

Earnings per Share with New Preferred Issue
(thousands of dollars, except per share)

	Current	With New Product
Earnings before interest and taxes (EBIT)	$11,000	$12,500
Less interest charges on long-term debt	–0–	–0–
Earnings before income taxes	$11,000	$12,500
Federal income taxes at 48 percent	5,280	6,000
Earnings after income taxes	$ 5,720	$ 6,500
Less preferred dividends	700	700
Earnings available for common stock	$ 5,020	$ 5,800
Common shares outstanding (number)	1 million	1 million
Earnings per share (EPS)	$ 5.02	$ 5.80
Less common dividends per share	2.50	2.50
Retained earnings per share	$ 2.52	$ 3.30
Retained earnings in total	$ 2,520	$ 3,300
Original EPS (Figure 5–2)	$ 5.72	$ 5.72
Change in EPS	$ –0.70	$ +0.08
Percent change in EPS	–12.2%	+1.4%

earnings generated by the investment, which are $1.5 million
before taxes and $780,000 after taxes.

In this situation the assumed conditions provide very limited
financial leverage. Only a little more than a 1 percent rise in
common earnings over prior levels is achieved, since the fixed
costs imposed have risen to $700,000. Were the investment in
the new product to earn precisely $\frac{\$700,000}{0.52} = \$1,346,154$ before
taxes, we would observe no change in earnings per share—incremental cost would offset incremental earnings, for a break-even
situation. Note that this sizable earnings requirement compares
with only $600,000 required by the bonds.

Questions similar to those of the first case arise: What about
the repayment of the principal? Even though preferred stock
is generally a very long-term proposition, many preferreds contain a call provision, and a sinking fund may be established to
retire the stock eventually. Such potential actions, even though
not necessarily contractual obligations, can cause future funds
drains. There is also the risk of defaulting on the dividend,
which would block payment of the common dividends. Again,

such risks must be evaluated in terms of the likely range of earnings to be encountered and the uncertainties in the corporate and industry picture. While the explicit cost of the preferred was established as the effective dividend rate, what impact is there of preferred stock on future financing? Is it fair to assess the merits of the investment proposal against this specific cost only? Only a broader analysis can answer these and other questions.

The Cost of Common Stock

Generally, management is obligated to provide a threefold benefit to its common stockholders: first, the earnings performance of the company; second, the payment of dividends to pass part of the earnings on to the stockholder; and third, the appreciation of the value of the shares of stock in the market in response to growing earnings or dividends or both. As discussed earlier, it is desirable to have a fairly stable long-term growth trend in any or all of these aspects. Any action, especially in the form of a long-term commitment, which jeopardizes or materially changes the stockholder's expectations about a particular company should be deemed harmful or at least worthy of serious reappraisal. More will be said on these points later in the chapter.

How are these considerations related to calculating a cost of common stock? In the case of common stock we do not have a directly measurable element as was the case with interest for bonds and dividends for preferred. Common dividends are declared at the discretion of the corporate board of directors, and while many companies strive for a stable and consistent policy (e.g., American Telephone and Telegraph Company), others pay very erratic dividends or none at all. In fact, many small "growth situations" of the space age variety or capital gains—oriented conglomerates would not even consider paying a cash dividend, since stockholders of this type of company prefer to see earnings reinvested in order to achieve maximum acceleration of growth and, they hope, a corresponding rise of market value. Yet one cannot argue that an issue of stock with no intention of paying dividends means that this stock has no cost to the issuing company and the existing stockholders!

In the previous examples, we calculated earnings per share and discussed the effect of the cost of incremental capital in terms of the immediate dilution of earnings. We shall use the same approach for common stock. ABC Corporation, we assume, will issue $10 million worth of new common stock at a net price of $50 per share to the Corporation after underwriters' fees and legal expenses. Such a discount from the current market price of $60 should ensure the success of the issue. Under these conditions, a total of $200,000 shares have to be issued, an increase of 20 percent in the number of shares outstanding. A calculation of the earnings picture is shown in Figure 5–5.

Figure 5–5

ABC CORPORATION

Earnings per Share with New Common Stock Issue
(thousands of dollars, except per share)

	Current	*With New Product*
Earnings before interest and taxes (EBIT)	$11,000	$12,500
Less interest charges on long-term debt	–0–	–0–
Earnings before income taxes	$11,000	$12,500
Federal income taxes at 48 percent	5,280	6,000
Earnings after income taxes	$ 5,720	$ 6,500
Less preferred dividends	–0–	–0–
Earnings available for common stock	$ 5,720	$ 6,500
Common shares outstanding (number)	1.2 million	1.2 million
Earnings per share (EPS)	$ 4.77	$ 5.42
Less common dividends per share	2.50	2.50
Retained earnings per share	$ 2.27	$ 2.92
Retained earnings in total	$ 2,720	$ 3,500
Original EPS (Figure 5–2)	$ 5.72	$ 5.72
Change in EPS	$ –0.95	$ –0.30
Percent change in EPS	–16.6%	–5.3%

We observe that the initial dilution under current conditions is a full 95 cents per share, a drop of 16.6 percent, which is the most severe among the three examples analyzed. Common stock, when viewed in this light, must surely be the costliest type of capital, since it causes the greatest dilution in the stockholders' position. Moreover, an annual funds drain of at least $500,000 in after-tax earnings is imposed in the form of dividends, assuming that the corporation will continue its policy of paying regular cash dividends. The funds drain amounts to a pretax earnings requirement of:

$$2.50 \times 200,000 \text{ shares} = \$500,000 \text{ (after taxes)}$$

$$\frac{\$500,000}{0.52} = \$961,538 \text{ (before taxes)}$$

We can directly compare this requirement of almost $1 million to $600,000 for the bonds and $1,346,154 for the preferred.

Not only is there the effect of immediate dilution, but dilution will continue, since (in contrast to the other two types of capital, which had fixed interest and dividend provisions) the new shares we have created are on an equal footing with the old shares in participating in any increase (or decrease) in corporate earnings. Growth in earnings per share will thus tend to be retarded because of the additional new shares outstanding.

When we turn to the second column of Figure 5–5 to study the effect of the increased earnings from the new product, it is quite apparent that there remains a net dilution of earnings per share of 30 cents or 5.3 percent. The contribution from the new investment was not sufficient to offset the earnings claims of the new stockholders and at the same time to maintain the old per-share earnings level. The explicit cost of the stock is thus greater than the earnings from the capital raised. As a rule, the explicit cost of the common stock can be calculated by relating the earnings required to maintain the old EPS level to the amount of funds provided by the stock. This is done most easily on a per-share basis, where the earnings required for each new share are precisely $5.72 (the old level). The proceeds to the company were assumed to be $50, and the result of the calculation can be shown as follows:

$$\frac{\$5.72}{\$50} = 11.44\% \text{ (after taxes)}$$

It should be noted that this result must be compared with the 3.12 percent for the bonds and 7 percent for the preferred.

We can arrive at the same answer by making the analysis on

a total basis. The $10 million provided is represented by 200,000 shares, for each of which earnings of $5.72 must be provided to leave the old stockholders' earnings position unchanged. A total of $1,144,000 in earnings after taxes ($2,200,000 before taxes) must therefore be achieved by the investment to maintain the break-even situation. This works out to 11.44 percent after taxes, or a full 22 percent before taxes. One look at the investment proposition shows that projected earnings are not sufficient to provide this offsetting effect. Were the expected earnings from the new product higher than $2.2 million before taxes, the investment would, of course, boost the earnings per share of both old and new stockholders.

Our discussion of explicit cost has so far not touched a key expectation of stockholders, namely growth in the market value of their shares. This growth is related, although not exclusively, to the performance of corporate earnings over the long run, and the static picture shown so far is not flexible enough to deal with this aspect. We also recall that earlier, with two of the alternatives, some questions were raised regarding earnings fluctuations and their effect upon the fixed obligations incurred by the corporation. Since it would be quite laborious to calculate earnings per share and other data for a great number of earnings levels and assumptions, we can exploit the linear relationships between the factors analyzed and use a graphic approach to compare the alternate sources of financing and to gauge the relative impact of fluctuations in EBIT as part of the measurement of cost and relative desirability. Such a model is quite a helpful device, short of a computerized analysis.

GRAPHIC ANALYSIS OF EARNINGS FLUCTUATIONS

First, Figure 5–6 will be used to recap the data developed up to this point, for the original situation as well as for the three alternatives of financing the new product. The EPS data will be recorded as points on a graph, often called an EBIT chart, on which we show earnings per share in dollars on the horizontal axis. Straight lines can be drawn once two points have been de-

Figure 5–6

ABC CORPORATION

Recap of EPS Analyses

(thousands of dollars, except per share)

	Original	Debt	Preferred	Common
EBIT	$11,000	$12,500	$12,500	$12,500
Less interest	–0–	600	–0–	–0–
Earnings before taxes	$11,000	$11,900	$12,500	$12,500
Taxes at 48 percent	5,280	5,712	6,000	6,000
Earnings after taxes	$ 5,720	$ 6,188	$ 6,500	$ 6,500
Preferred dividends	–0–	–0–	700	–0–
Earnings to common	$ 5,720	$ 6,188	$ 5,800	$ 6,500
Common shares	1 million	1 million	1 million	1.2 million
EPS	$ 5.72	$ 6.19	$ 5.80	$ 5.42
Common dividends	2.50	2.50	2.50	2.50
Retained earnings	$ 3.22	$ 3.69	$ 3.30	$ 2.92
Total retained	$ 3,220	$ 3,688	$ 3,300	$ 3,500
Original dilution	–0–	–5.4%	–12.2%	–16.6%
Final EPS change	–0–	+8.2%	+1.4%	–5.3%
Explicit cost	–0–	3.12%	7.0%	11.44%

termined for each alternative, and it is common to use as one of the points the intersection of each line with the horizontal axis, where EPS are zero. These points can easily be found by working our framework of analysis backward, that is, starting with EPS of zero and building up to an EBIT which just provides for this condition. This calculation, for each of the alternatives and the original situation, is shown in Figure 5–7.

Figure 5–7

ABC CORPORATION

Zero EPS Calculation

(thousands of dollars)

	Original	Debt	Preferred	Common
EPS	–0–	–0–	–0–	–0–
Common shares	1 million	1 million	1 million	1.2 million
Earnings to common	–0–	–0–	–0–	–0–
Preferred dividends	–0–	–0–	$ 700	–0–
Earnings after taxes	–0–	–0–	700	–0–
Taxes at 48 percent	–0–	–0–	646	–0–
Earnings before taxes	–0–	–0–	$1346	–0–
Interest	–0–	$600	–0–	–0–
EBIT	–0–	$600	$1346	–0–

The two sets of calculations provide us with sufficient data to draw the linear functions of EPS and EBIT for the various situations, as shown in Figure 5–8. We can quickly observe visually that the conclusions drawn from the two previously analyzed EBIT levels hold true over the fairly wide range of earnings presented. There is one difference, however, and that is the behav-

Figure 5–8

ABC CORPORATION

Range of EBIT and EPS Chart

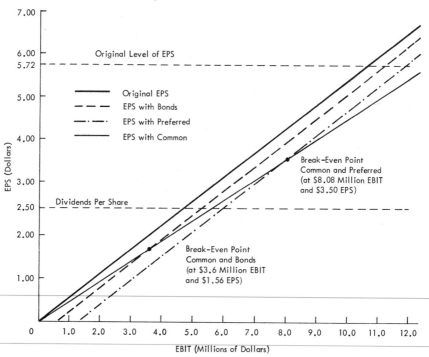

ior of EPS under the common stock alternative, which has a slope different from all others and in fact intersects the debt and preferred EPS lines. The latter two alternatives are represented by parallel lines which are also parallel to the line representing the original situation. This phenomenon is easily explained, since the parallel shift to the right is caused by the superimposition of fixed interest or dividend charges on earnings available to the common stockholders, whose number of shares does not change over the whole range of EBIT studied. The use of common stock, on the other hand, represents a proportional dilution of earnings for the common stockholders at all levels, and the imposition of additional shares causes earnings per share for everyone to rise less rapidly with EBIT. The lesser slope of the common stock line is the result.

The significance of the intersection should now become clear: it is not possible to speak of a cost of capital for incremental common stock without referring to the "normal" earnings level which the existing stockholders have come to expect—if we accept the framework of analysis used here. There are EBIT levels in the lower ranges where the imposition of additional common stock can have a lesser effect upon EPS than one or the other alternatives or both.

This has a bearing upon the analysis of the choice to be made, since it is possible to tell the effects on EPS if EBIT should fluctuate rapidly in the future. If future EBIT levels are expected to move fairly well within the range bounded by the two break-even points, common stock looks more attractive than preferred stock from the standpoint of diluting EPS. If EBIT can be expected to grow and move fairly well to the right of the second break-even point, the issuance of common stock is the least desirable alternative in terms of EPS dilution. All these considerations are based, of course, on unchanging assumptions about the terms under which the three forms of capital can be issued. If any terms, such as the issue price of common stock, can be expected to change significantly, a new chart must be drawn up.

We can quite easily calculate the intersections between the EPS lines, which represent the break-even points among the alternatives. For this purpose we express the assumptions about any pair of lines in the form of simple equations. EPS are then considered equal for the pair, and we solve the equations for EBIT. To illustrate, let us use the following conditions:

E = EBIT level for break-even among alternatives.

i = annual interest on bonds, in dollars (before taxes).

t = tax rate applicable.

p = annual preferred dividends, in dollars.
n = number of common shares outstanding.

The equation for any particular line can be found by substituting known facts in the following expression:

$$EPS = \frac{(E - i)(1 - t) - p}{n}$$

We can now find the EBIT break-even level for bonds and common stock. For this purpose, we write the two expressions and consider them as equal:

$$\underbrace{\frac{(E - 600,000)0.52 - 0}{1,000,000}}_{Bonds} = \underbrace{\frac{(E - 0)0.52 - 0}{1,200,000}}_{Common}$$

Solving for E, we obtain the following result:

$$0.52\,E - 312,000 = \frac{0.52\,E}{1.2}$$

$$0.624\,E - 374,400 = 0.52\,E$$

$$E = \$3,600,000$$

This result can easily be verified on the EBIT chart in Figure 5–8. When the same approach is applied to the preferred and common stock alternatives, the following result emerges:

$$\underbrace{\frac{(E - 0)0.52 - 700,000}{1,000,000}}_{Preferred} = \underbrace{\frac{(E - 0)0.52 - 0}{1,200,000}}_{Common}$$

$$0.52\,E - 700,000 = \frac{0.52\,E}{1.2}$$

$$0.624\,E - 840,000 = 0.52\,E$$

$$E = \$8,076,920$$

Again, the chart can be used for verification of this result.

It is also possible to use the EBIT chart to display the impact of any dividend requirement for common stock on the three alternatives. The horizontal line at EPS of $2.50 in the chart represents the current annual dividend, and where this line intersects any alternative EPS line we can read off the minimum level of EBIT required to supply this dividend. Similarly, it is possible to reflect on the chart the burden of sinking funds or other regular repayment provisions, by carrying the calculations one step further and arriving at "uncommitted earnings per share" (UEPS) for each alternative. This is done by simply subtracting the after-tax cost of such repayments on a per-share basis from the EPS of those alternatives where they apply, and drawing lines on the chart, which will fall to the right of the EPS lines.

By now the usefulness of this framework for the analysis of the various alternatives should be clear, and the reader is invited to think through the implications of the variety of tests that can be applied. It is possible, for instance, to check the EBIT level under each alternative which would endanger the $2.50 per share dividend, assuming a variety of payout ratios, such as 50 percent. In this case, a line could be drawn at the $5 EPS level extending horizontally, and the intersections would represent the minimal EBIT levels required to support a $2.50 dividend under a 50 percent payout assumption. The decision maker would have to assess the likelihood of the EBIT's reaching this level and the risk this represents to the stockholders. Again it must be emphasized, however, that the chart works only under the fixed assumptions about proceeds received and unchanging interest and preferred dividend rates. If one can reasonably assume that these will change, the positions of the EPS lines on the graph must be changed.

An additional word about the significance of changes in the issuing conditions: as the spread between the alternatives increases, that is, as the differences among the explicit costs of the alternatives widen, the distance between the parallel lines will increase. This is simply a reflection of the depressant effect on EPS which the imposition of fixed obligations brings about. A similar effect is achieved by increasing the relative size of the incremental capital issue. The slope of the lines is governed by the degree of leverage in the existing capital structure. In other words, if there had already been debt or preferred stock in the original capital structure, the original EPS would have risen and fallen much more sharply, and with them the EPS of the fixed-cost alternatives. The slope of the EPS line for the common stock alternative is, of course, governed by the relative number of shares issued, which in turn is related to the explicit cost of common stock as we have defined it—normal EPS compared to the issue proceeds. As we have mentioned in earlier chapters, a computerized analysis with the help of a financial planning model can be quite revealing, since it is possible to make changes in a greater number of variables and to calculate the effect of these on the earnings pattern.

THE CHOICE AMONG THE ALTERNATIVES

So far we have limited the incremental analysis of the several alternatives essentially to finding the explicit cost of each and making some comparisons in the process. At this point, it will be helpful to summarize the total framework in which the decision maker must consider the choice among the three alternatives. During the discussion of explicit cost it became clear that cost is only one factor in this choice, that there are implicit costs involved, and that the problem must be seen in the perspective of time and under changing conditions. There are at least four major areas of consideration involved, and the discussion of incremental analysis would not be complete without the highlights of each of these.

The first area is, of course, the question of the *explicit cost* of the alternatives, which we have discussed in detail. This aspect increases in importance with the spread between the alternatives and the risk of earnings fluctuations which could cause default. Clearly, the decision maker will wish to minimize the cost he has to pay for funds in the interest of enhancing the stockholders' earnings.

The second area is the question of *flexibility*, which has been mentioned before. As an increment of capital is added, the choice among alternatives may be more limited on the next round. The current choice may have imposed fixed obligations, restrictive covenants, and other constraints. This problem is important in considering future capital needs, and the deliberations must include long-range plans and corporate policies with regard to expansion and diversification. The flexibility question arises also with the problem of the funds flows required to service each alternative. Again, long-range planning is required to forecast the impact of these burdens on the corporate treasury.

The third element in the decision is *timing* in relation to the movements of prices in the securities markets. There is a direct relationship to relative explicit cost, since price and cost are inseparable. The timing aspect will therefore influence the spread between the alternatives and at times preclude or favor particular alternatives. For instance, in times of depressed stock prices, bonds may prove to be the most suitable alternative from both a cost and a demand standpoint. Since the proceeds from an issue depend on the success of the placement—public or private —of the securities involved, the conditions at the time can seriously affect the choice.

Finally, there is the element of *control*, that is, the relative dilution of ownership and control of the enterprise suffered by the existing stockholders. This issue is most important in the case of the common stock alternative, since the only direct dilution can come from issuing additional shares. In the other alternatives, the control of existing stockholders may indirectly be endangered by restrictive provisions and covenants necessary to obtain bond financing, or by the prior and more senior rights of preferred stockholders. The degree of dilution of ownership will be a very important problem in closely held corporations, as it may affect the immediate control certain majority stockholders exercise over the company. The dilution of earnings and the possible retardation of earnings growth connected with dilution of ownership is, of course, a generally applicable phenomenon.

It is clear from this brief résumé of considerations that the decision among the alternative sources of incremental capital is one that cannot simply be made on cost alone, even though cost is a most important first consideration. There are no hard and fast rules as to precisely how such decisions can be made, since they depend so much on the circumstances, points of view, and negotiating skills of the decision makers. The techniques presented earlier can assist in specifically calculating quantifiable results, which then must be entered in the decision process.

COST OF CAPITAL IN COMPOSITES

At the beginning of this chapter we stated that our emphasis would be on incremental reasoning. We have done this and wound up with an overall framework of analysis. In order to have a better perspective of cost of capital, it is necessary to cover briefly the most difficult area in this economic analysis—the problem of an overall composite cost of capital in an existing capital structure as one guide in judging the desirability of existing and new investment projects. Here a variety of problems converge: the reliability and meaning of recorded values carried on the balance sheet, the reliability and meaning of earnings in the measurement process, and the reliability and meaning of market values for stock involved, to name just the most important ones.

To keep the discussion manageable within the framework of this book, we shall assume from the start that a weighted cost of capital is the proper concept to use and that common equity consists of two parts, stated stock values and retained earnings. Furthermore, we shall not deal with the problem of funds flow from depreciation and its cost, since some aspects of this were covered in Chapters 1 and 4. The interested reader is referred to the bibliography at the end of this chapter for further materials on these aspects, as well as on the ones briefly covered here.

From the outset we shall stipulate that any source of funds to a corporation has a cost, either explicit or implicit, at times in the form of an opportunity cost. The composite of funds corporate management can employ contains many types, the relative importance of which usually is determined by corporate policy, but whose amounts may fluctuate from time to time as conditions change. Therefore, no one particular funds source can be used as a cost standard to gauge the desirability of investments;

rather, over the long run it is the mixture of funds sources that will determine the economic cutoff point for investment propositions.

A common attempt to arrive at such a measure, namely, the minimum acceptable return from an investment in the interest of the stockholders, is the *weighted cost of the capital structure*. In order to calculate one example, we return to our ABC Corporation, which we now assume has undergone a few changes over the years, and presently has a capital structure which in the view of its management closely represents relationships they would like to see perpetuated. An abbreviated balance sheet is shown in Figure 5–9.

Figure 5–9

ABC CORPORATION

Condensed Balance Sheet

(thousands of dollars)

Assets		Liabilities and Net Worth	
Current assets	$27,500	Current liabilities	$ 9,500
Fixed assets (net)	35,000	Bonds (6 percent)	12,000
Other assets	1,500	Preferred stock ($7)	6,000
Total	$64,000	Common stock	10,000
		Retained earnings	26,500
		Total	$64,000

We further assume that the market price of the common stock currently fluctuates between $70 and $75, and that most recent EPS were $6.25. Overall company prospects are assumed to be satisfactory, with a normal growth in earnings per share forecasted by financial analysts. Management is faced with the problem of having to decide among a variety of capital investments, both of a replacement and minor expansion nature, and wishes to set a minimum floor in the form of a weighted cost of capital below which the yield of future investments should not fall.

The first step will be to determine the proportions of capital types in the long-term capital structure; the second will be to attach a relevant explicit cost to each; and finally the combined cost will be calculated. In the first step we take each of the long-term forms of capital and make a judgment about its relative value. The obvious initial reaction will be to take the book value of each funds class as recorded on the balance sheet. Upon some reflection, however, doubts arise. For instance, the bonds of the corporation, if traded publicly, may currently be quoted above or below par and thus represent a value quite different from the balance sheet figure. Similarly, preferred stock may be traded at market values different from what is recorded on the books. The most critical difference of this sort is likely to exist in the case of common stock, whose value in the market rarely corresponds with the recorded owner's equity: stated value plus retained earnings and any unspecified surplus reserves. We observe that in the case of ABC Corporation there is such a differential; while the one million shares on the books of the corporation are represented by a book value of $36.50 per share, the current market is trading these shares between $70 and $75—about twice the stated value.

Those arguing for taking the book value of each type of capital will say that the assets recorded on the other side of the balance sheet are represented in the same terms (original cost), and that this would preserve consistency of approach. Others argue, however, that the increase in the market value of the stock in fact represents an increase in the economic value of the corporation's assets. It represents a market judgment about the earning power of these assets in the framework of the company and its industry. In this view, the balance sheet is no longer an indicator of economic facts, and must be adjusted to reflect the realities of valuation with which the common stockholder is faced. (Some valuation concepts will be discussed later in this chapter.) A counterargument is that the vagaries of the market-place are not a reliable judgment of value, as witnessed, for instance, by the great slide in the stock market in 1969–70, when within a few months the stock market averages dropped by one third from the record highs achieved.

Without going into the many fine points, it should be obvious that a satisfactory answer to the first step will lie neither in the

precise book value proportions (although many financial analysts will start from here) nor in current market value proportions, but somewhere between these values. In some cases, neither measure may provide any satisfaction, and a judgmental
valuation must be used. In keeping with the basic nature of the
book, we shall present two of the approaches mentioned while
cautioning that many more considerations call for utmost care
in the application of the results.

The *book value* approach will result in the following proportions of capital sources:

Bonds	$12,000	22.02%
Preferred	6,000	11.01
Common stock	36,500	66.97
Totals	$54,500	100.00%

The *market value* approach will bring the following results if
we assume that common stock has a fair market value of $72.50
per share and that preferred stock is traded at $110 per share,
with bonds at par:

Bonds	$12,000	13.18%
Preferred	6,600	7.24
Common stock	72,500	79.58
Totals	$91,100	100.00%

The second step is to determine the cost of the individual
components. The simplest of these is the cost of the bonds,
whose explicit cost based on the interest charges is 3.12 percent
after taxes, as calculated earlier. The next item, preferred stock,
can differ depending on whether we take the book value or the
market value into our calculations. In the first instance, the after-
tax cost is simply the $7 dividend rate, or 7 percent; while in the
other, we must adjust for the premium at which the stock is
trading in the market by relating the $7 dividend to the $110
market price per share. This works out to an effective cost of
$7 ÷ $110 or 6.36 percent. Finally, the explicit cost of the common stock was established earlier as the normal earnings per
share related to the normal market value. In the case of ABC
Corporation, this works out to EPS of $6.25 related to a price of

$72.50, or 8.62 percent. The completed calculations will now appear as shown in Table 5–1.

Table 5–1

	Book Value Approach			Market Value Approach		
	Cost	Weight	Composite	Cost	Weight	Composite
Bonds	3.12%	0.220	0.6864	3.12%	0.132	0.4118
Preferred	7.00	0.110	0.7700	6.36	0.072	0.0460
Common stock	8.62	0.670	5.7754	8.62	0.796	6.8615
Totals		1.000	7.2318%		1.000	7.3193%

The results under the two approaches do not differ materially, yet under other circumstances there could be sizable differences in the two cost of capital figures. These could be due to varying spreads among the types of capital provided; the relative proportions of capital in the company's structure; and, in the case of common stock, the size, stability, and nature of earnings and their valuation in the marketplace. The reader is invited to make calculations on his own to observe the differences under varying assumptions. One example would be to calculate the results for the ABC Corporation in the earlier sections of this chapter, by assuming acceptance of the different incremental capital proposals.

This brief discussion of cost of capital has served to demonstrate the complexity of the problem and the need to analyze carefully the many economic issues involved. The concept of cost of capital cannot be separated from the particular application intended; otherwise the results are meaningless. As stated before, the point of view of any analysis must be carefully spelled out. Yet, as applications and points of view differ, so do the results of the calculations, and assumptions even within a specified framework for analysis can become tenuous. One way to help minimize the problem of uncertainty about the results is to figure out the range within which variables can be reasonably expected to fluctuate, and then to establish the limits or extremes for the results as the basis for deliberation. Such an approach to sensitivity analysis is sound under most problem-solving conditions, and cost of capital considerations are no exception.

THE VALUE OF DIFFERENT FUNDS TO THE INVESTOR

So far we have taken the point of view of the user of the funds, the business enterprise, in discussing the impact of funds selection decisions. While these questions are of critical importance, corporate management must not overlook the point of view of the provider of the funds. Moreover, the concepts of evaluating the economic and other values of the key legal instruments by which funds sources are opened to business enterprise are by themselves a vast subject of considerable complexity. We shall discuss only the highlights and the key techniques, to provide the full perspective of funds source analysis.

The provider of funds, ranging from the holder of long-term notes and bonds to the preferred stockholder and common stockholder (subject to myriad variations in terms), looks upon his investment in two main ways. First, he is interested in the value of his stake, which depends on the operational performance of the company in which he has invested as well as on the value of the assets backing up the various claims. Of interest to him will also be the assessment of value in the securities markets, if the issue is traded. Second, he is interested in the compensation he receives for the risk undertaken in providing funds to the enterprise. The two aspects are, of course, interwoven, and their priorities will shift, depending on the interests of the investor and the type of security he holds. All calculations shall be made on a *pre-tax* basis, in contrast to our earlier analyses, since the tax considerations of individual investors vary so widely that assumptions about them would be tenous at best.

We shall discuss valuation from the point of view of the holder of each of the three types of securities we used earlier in the chapter to demonstrate the cost of different funds sources to the company—namely, straight bonds, preferred stock, and common stock, with some comments on convertible stocks and stock rights. It should also be pointed out that in the course of this discussion we shall deal with several types of value, which must be recognized as part of a whole series of concepts, the most important of which are briefly defined as follows:

Market value is the value placed at any one time on a security traded in a stock exchange or over the counter, or even between private parties in an unencumbered transaction without duress. There is nothing absolute in market value, since it represents a momentary consensus of two or more parties to a trading proposition, and this value is therefore subject to the whims of the individuals involved, the psychology of the stock market in general, economic conditions, industry developments, political conditions, and so forth. Moreover, the degree of trading taking place in any one security will influence the value at any one time. Still, market value is generally a more valid concept than *book value*, which is the stated value of a debt or equity security based on the accounting concepts of recorded value as reflected in the balance sheet. This concept is subject to all the limitations of historical accounting, which is not designed to reflect economic values at any one time. *Economic value* has been used before in the earlier chapters, and we refer to the value of an asset or claim as reflected by its current and future earnings power plus any potential recovery of all or part of the investment. Other value concepts include *liquidation value*, which expresses the cash value to be received from disposal of all assets of an operation being dissolved (normally relatively low values, since liquidation takes place under stress). *Reproduction value* is the replacement cost of an asset which had been acquired in the past, while *collateral value* is the amount of value ascribed to an asset when pledged as a security. *Assessed value* is, of course, the value ascribed to property for the basis of taxation, while *appraised value* refers to the value ascribed to assets by an impartial expert in the absence of clearly defined market values. Finally, *going-concern value* represents the economic value of an operation as a cohesive, functioning unit, which may exceed the individual values of the parts which comprise it. With this background we shall now turn to the specific discussion of the three security types and their values.

Bond Values

The bondholder's contract with the issuing company normally presents a fairly straightforward valuation problem. The corporate bond, without complicating aspects such as convertibility, participation, etc., is a simple debt instrument which generally provides for semiannual interest payments based on a stated par (nominal) value, usually $1,000 per bond, and which promises repayment at a specific maturity date a number of years hence. In this sense the bond is representative of most normal debt arrangements.

We recall that from a company's point of view we recognized an explicit cost and a future repayment obligation when analyzing the impact of bond financing. The bondholder in turn looks to a specific promise for interest income and the eventual return of the face value (principal) at a fixed date. One can choose to keep the bond until maturity or trade the contract to others at any one time. The value of the bond contract to the investor must therefore be based on his own assessment of the attractiveness of this stream of future receipts and the quality of the promise for eventual return of this principal at maturity. Risk and uncertainty play a role here, since the investor must judge the quality of the enterprise and its future ability to generate sufficient cash to pay interest and principal. We recognize also that this proposition is an exact analogy to the investment problems we dealt with in Chapter 4. The valuation of bonds is readily achievable through present value analysis, using the type of tables presented at the end of Chapter 4.

To determine the value of a bond at any one time, therefore, we must find the present value of the interest payments to maturity and the present value of the final principal payment. A discount rate to be applied will, just as in the previous investment analysis, be the opportunity rate which represents the investor's own standard of alternative earnings possibilities, with the type of risks and rewards attractive to him. For example, an investor with an 8 percent annual return standard (4 percent per six-month period) will value a 6 percent bond as shown in

Table 5–2. The value derived in this fashion is $832.89, which is the maximum amount our investor should be willing to pay (or the minimum price for which he should be willing to sell), if he normally expects a return (yield) of 8 percent from this type of investment. He would thus acquire the bond only at a considerable discount from par, if it were offered to him. Note that the stated interest rate on the bond is relevant only in determining the semiannual cash receipts in absolute terms; it is the investor's own opportunity rate which is used as the valuation yardstick. This very same principle applies to the market quotation for publicly traded bonds—the price (value) quoted is a function of the desired return of the parties to the transaction.

Table 5–2

Date of analysis: July 1, 1972
Face value (par) of bond: $1,000
Maturity date: July 1, 1986
Bond interest (coupon rate):   6% per year
Interest receipts: $30 semiannually

	Total Cash Flow	Present Value Factors, 4 Percent*	Present Value
28 receipts of $30 over 14 years (28 periods) ....$	840	16.663 (× $30)	$499.89
Receipt of principal 14 years hence (28 periods)	1,000	0.333	333.00
Totals ....$	1,840		$832.89

* From Tables 4–11 and 4–10, respectively.

If our investor were satisfied with a low yield of only 4 percent on the same bond (2 percent per six-month period), the value to him would rise considerably above par, as shown in Table 5–3. Under these conditions he should be willing to pay up to a $212.43 premium for the bond, since his own return standard is lower than the stated interest rate. If his own standard and the stated interest rate coincided precisely, the value of the bond would, of course, be exactly $1,000. In fact, the market price of a bond will approach $1,000 as it reaches maturity, since the only remaining value will be the imminent principal repayment—assuming the company is able to pay.

Table 5–3

	Total Cash Flow	Present Value Factors, 2 Percent*	Present Value
28 receipts of $30 over 14 years (28 periods) $1,120		21.281 (× $30)	$ 638.43
Receipt of principal 14 years hence (28 periods) 1,000		0.574	574.00
Totals $2,120			$1,212.43

* From Tables 4–11 and 4–10, respectively.

Bond Yields

A more common problem for the investor is to determine the yields represented by the quoted prices for various bonds in the securities markets. The relationship of value and yield discussed above is the key to this analysis, which again uses present value concepts. Just as we were able to find the yield of an investment project in Chapter 4, we can use a trial-and-error approach on a bond cash flow pattern to find the exact discount rate at which the present value of the interest and principal receipts will equal the quoted price. Quite clearly, the tables provided in Chapter 4 are not of sufficient detail to handle the precision of analysis required. Not only must we deal with semiannual periods, but bond prices are quoted in a very specific manner as a percentage of par (for example, a bond quoted at 103⅜ has a price of $1,033.75). Also, yields are calculated rather precisely, normally two places beyond the decimal point (for instance, 6.95 percent). To ease this task, therefore, "yield tables" are in use (see reference at end of the chapter) which provide the fine gradation required to answer the problems with sufficient accuracy. The principle of the tables is exactly the same as that of the tables in Chapter 4; only the details and format differ. A small section of such a table is shown as Table 5–4; it relates the stated interest rate, the yield to maturity, and the time period remaining to the current price. Note that the answer to our example of the 6 percent bond in the previous section can be found quickly on the 4 percent line and in the 28-period column.

Should yield tables be unavailable, it is possible to use a

Table 5–4

SAMPLE OF BOND TABLE
6 Percent Bond

Maturity: Yield	13 Years (26 Periods)	13½ Years (27 Periods)	14 Years (28 Periods)	14½ Years (29 Periods)	15 Years (30 Periods)	15½ Years (31 Periods)
3.80%	1.224 043	1.230 661	1.237 155	1.243 528	1.249 782	1.255 919
3.85	1.218 284	1.224 709	1.231 012	1.237 196	1.243 263	1.249 215
3.90	1.212 559	1.218 793	1.224 907	1.230 904	1.236 787	1.242 557
3.95	1.206 868	1.212 913	1.218 841	1.224 654	1.230 354	1.235 944
4.00	1.201 210	1.207 068	1.212 812*	1.218 443	1.223 964	1.229 377
4.05	1.195 585	1.201 260	1.206 821	1.212 273	1.217 616	1.222 853
4.10	1.189 993	1.195 486	1.200 868	1.206 142	1.211 310	1.216 375
4.15	1.184 434	1.189 747	1.194 952	1.200 051	1.205 046	1.209 940
4.20	1.178 908	1.184 043	1.189 073	1.193 999	1.198 823	1.203 549
4.25	1.173 414	1.178 374	1.183 230	1.187 985	1.192 642	1.197 201

* Example used in previous section (slight difference due to rounding of present value factors).

quick shortcut to derive an approximate yield from a price quotation. If we assume that our 6 percent bond was quoted at $832.89 on July 1, 1972 (the result of our earlier calculation), we note that the discount from par is $167.11. The investor will thus not only receive interest of $30 for 28 periods each, but will also earn the $167.11 if he holds the bond to maturity and receives the $1,000 par value. The shortcut method involves an amortization of the $167.11 discount over the 28 interest periods (which is commonly done for accounting purposes), which results in a periodic value increment of $5.97 ($167.11 divided by 28 periods). This increment is added to the periodic interest of $30, resulting in a six-month earnings pattern of $35.97.

The next step is to relate the periodic earnings to the average investment outstanding over the 28 periods. The current quote is \$832.89, while the value at maturity is \$1,000, an average of \$916.45. The periodic yield then is:

$$\frac{\$\ 35.97}{\$916.45} = 3.925\% \text{ or } 7.85\% \text{ per year}$$

This result is slightly below the precise yield of 8 percent per year on which the original calculation was built. As yield rates and time periods increase, larger errors result; yet, the rough calculation provides satisfactory initial results for most purposes.

If a premium had been involved, the shortcut calculation would call for a reduction of the periodic interest amount by the amortization of the premium. The second example in the previous section involved such a condition, and the results would be as follows, again a close approximation of the 4 percent solution:

$$\frac{\$22.41}{\$1,106.22} = 2.026\% \text{ or } 4.05\% \text{ per year}$$

The reader is invited to check the details of this calculation.

Bond Complications

The simple value relationships discussed earlier are affected by specific conditions surrounding the company and its industry, and by additional elements in the character of the bond instrument itself. The quality of the promise to pay must be assessed through careful analysis of the earnings pattern and projections of the company. Techniques of Chapters 2, 3, and 4 are helpful in this process. The ability to pay is a function of projected cash flows and the coverage by these cash flows of debt service, both interest and principal. Sensitivity analysis based on high and low estimates in performance may be useful here.

Variations in the bond instrument will affect value and yield. *Mortgage bonds* are secured by the specific assets acquired with their proceeds, and they provide a cushion against the risk of default on the principal. *Income bonds* are on the other extreme of the risk scale, since they are unsecured and will pay interest only if earned. The attractiveness of participating in the future appreciation of the market value of common stock is built into the increasingly popular device of *convertible bonds,* which can be converted into a specified number of common shares during a stipulated time span. Normally, the conversion price of common stock will be below the current market value of common, to build in an expectation for future growth. With convertibility, the bond acquires some aspects of ownership in its original form, and the bond can be turned into full ownership at the investor's option. This potential has an effect on value and yield, since value will no longer be determined purely on the future cash flows of the contract. In fact, convertible bonds quotations are increasingly affected by the market values of the common shares they represent, especially if these common shares trade near or above the conversion price.

The variation in bond provisions calls for careful judgments beyond the simple analysis tools displayed earlier, since these tools are only the starting point of analysis. No hard and fast techniques and rules exist to weigh all aspects of the problem mechanically. In the final analysis, adjustments in value and yield must be made within the individual's scheme of economic and risk preferences and the specific objectives of ownership of debt instruments. The reader is referred to literature which covers these aspects in more detail.

Preferred Stock Values

Preferred stock, by its nature, is a middle ground between debt and outright common stock ownership. The investor looks to a series of dividend payments as compensation, but has normally no specific contract for these or for the repayment of the par value of the stock. While he enjoys a preferential position regarding dividends and proceeds in case of liquidation of the enterprise, he is an owner to the extent that he may have to forgo dividends if performance is poor and may suffer impairment of his capital. Dividends are declared at the discretion of the board of directors and may not be made up if missed, unless there are specific legal provisions to the contrary.

The valuation problem thus is less definite than in the case of bonds, since the only reasonably certain element is the stipulated dividend based on a percentage of par value. For example, an 8 percent preferred stock usually refers to a $100 share of stock which pays a dividend of $8 per year. The investor is faced with the valuation of this stream of prospective dividends. If he paid $100 for the stock and intended to hold it indefinitely, the yield on this stock would be 8 percent, assuming that the company is likely to be able to pay the dividend regularly. If he paid more or less than the $100, the yield could be found by relating the amount of the dividend to the actual investment per share, based on this formula:

$$\text{Preferred yield} = \frac{\text{Dividend per share}}{\text{Price paid per share}}$$

If the investor could expect to sell the stock at $110 five years hence, one could determine the precise yield through the present value techniques or the shortcut methods discussed earlier. The problem of determining value at a future time is one of speculation, however, unless the issuing company had a mandatory call provision at a specific price.

If we look at preferred stock values from the point of view of the investor's own return (yield) standards, we can use the following simple rule to arrive at the maximum price the investor should be willing to pay or the minimum price at which he should be willing to sell. We must relate the stipulated dividend rate to the required opportunity rate of our investor to arrive at this answer. If our investor had a 9 percent standard against which to analyze the 8 percent preferred, he would arrive at a value as follows (stated dividend rate based on $100 par):

$$\text{Value per share} = \frac{\text{Stated dividend rate}}{\text{Required return}} = \frac{0.08}{0.09} = \$88.89$$

If he were satisfied to achieve only a 7 percent return, the value would be:

$$\text{Value per share} = \frac{0.08}{0.07} = \$114.28$$

The main judgments remaining would be, of course, the uncertainty of the dividend pattern and any material change in the future value of the stock, through either changing market conditions or a call provision at a usually higher-than-par price.

Preferred Stock Complications

As in the case of bonds, preferred stock can have many modifications. An added attraction is at times provided through a *participation* feature, which enables the preferred holder to share (in the form of higher dividends) in earnings above a set level. This feature can favorably affect the yield, and a judgment must be made as to the likelihood of such an improvement taking place. A more common feature is *convertibility,* which adds the attraction of changing the preferred position into full ownership if favorable operating and stock market conditions come about. The value of this feature cannot be calculated precisely, as was true in the case of bonds. Again, convertible preferred stock will tend to reflect the market value of the equivalent number of shares of common as the common reaches and exceeds the conversion price, while it will be valued largely as a regular preferred in advance of this situation. Normally, convertibility is accompanied by a *call provision,* at a price somewhat above par, to enable the company to bring about conversion when conditions are right.

The challenge of preferred stock valuation thus lies in the judgments beyond the simple techniques shown, and in a careful assessment of the relative attractiveness of the features of the specific issue.

Common Stock Values

The most complex problem of valuation is found in the case of common stock, since the full ownership aspects of this type of security remove all relative certainty about earnings potential and principal recovery. Common stock investment is a sharing of the risks and rewards of the performance of the enterprise, and measurement techniques can be applied only to highly judgmental variables. Moreover, the rewards of successful common stock ownership are severalfold: there may be cash dividends or additional stock distributions, and there may be a sharing of growing earnings which are partly reinvested by management. Finally, there is a potential appreciation of the market price of the stock, if the issue is traded with reasonable volume and frequency. The subject of stock values contains so many theoretical and practical issues that we must limit ourselves here to only a few selected highlights. The basic problem is to develop some approximation of share value, and also to find an expression for the yield an investor is deriving from an investment.

Earnings Approaches to Common Stock Value

The most obvious way to arrive at a value for a share of common stock is to make a judgment about the likely future level of earnings and to capitalize these earnings at an appropriate rate which represents the relative desirability of the earnings stream —the investor's opportunity rate or a rate applicable to the industry in question. The approach will appear as follows:

$$\text{Value per share} = \frac{\text{Earnings per share (projected)}}{\text{Rate of capitalization}}$$

While the concept is attractive, the practical problem remains one of finding both an appropriate earnings level expected for the future and the proper rate of capitalization. The former is made more difficult by the need to project total performance of the enterprise and by all the problems of accounting and reporting. Some of these have appeared in the earlier chapters. The latter is to a large extent a question of individual preference. There is a relationship between required earnings and the relative uncertainty and risk surrounding the enterprise. The greater the uncertainty, the greater will be the required rate of earnings, which will decrease the value of the stock.

A similar concept can be employed to find the yield of a share of stock. Here we can employ the current market price or the original investment and relate them to the projected earnings per share:

$$\text{Earnings yield} = \frac{\text{Earnings per share (projected)}}{\text{Market price per share}}$$

or:

$$\text{Earnings yield} = \frac{\text{Earnings per share (projected)}}{\text{Original price paid}}$$

The inverse of the above formulations is, of course, the familiar price-earnings ratio, which is used quite frequently in securities analysis. Reference was made to this ratio in Chapter 3, but for purposes of completeness we shall restate it here:

$$\text{Price-earnings ratio} = \frac{\text{Market price per share}}{\text{Earnings per share (projected or current)}}$$

This measure reflects the estimate of value the marketplace is willing to assign to per share earnings. The market price is normally a reflection of the projected earnings although the concept can be applied to past and current earnings as well. The earnings multiple typical for the company or its industry can at times be applied to projected earnings levels to derive estimated future market values.

Upon closer examination, however, these simple measures of value and yield are not sufficiently precise to allow for two important aspects of normal common stock ownership. First, no allowance is made for the fact that many stockholders look to cash *dividends* as a way of participating in the success of the business. The size, regularity, and trend in dividend payout to the stockholders can be quite important in affecting the value of a share of stock, depending on the stockholders' objectives. There is some uncertainty surrounding dividends, not only with regard to the ability of the company to pay, but also due to the fact that dividends are declared at the option of the corporate board of directors. No general rule is followed by companies; dividend policies can range from no or only token dividends to regular payment of 75 percent or more of current earnings. The only rule one can apply with some degree of confidence is that many boards of directors see value in the consistency with which dividends are paid, and major changes in payout, up or down, are made only with extreme reluctance. Regardless of the policies of an individual company, one can certainly not be indifferent to the impact of various levels of dividend payments on common stock values.

The second critical aspect ignored so far is the relative rate of *earnings growth* achieved by a company. The use of a single projected earnings figure as part of the formula represents a static viewpoint which may not do justice to a company's prospects to grow in earnings at 5, 10, or even 15 percent per year or more. There certainly must be economic attractiveness in such performance, particularly when backed up by an historic record of growth, when contrasted with static or even declining earnings.

Without going into the many ramifications of theory and practice, we shall present briefly some approaches which attempt to take into account either dividends alone or dividends and growth together. So far no universal and generally applicable rule or method of analysis is available, although much advanced research has gone into the problem. A simplistic way of looking at dividends would be to capitalize the estimated dividend stream at an appropriate discount rate, quite like the approach used for earnings earlier. The only difference would be the focus on dividends as a cash flow received by the stockholder, in contrast to the economic claim provided from earnings, part or all of which are reinvested for him by company management.

A more promising approach for valuing common stock is the following growth model, which is one of many concepts which can be employed here. The formula relates dividends per share to a net capitalization rate, which is composed of the difference between the investor's own opportunity rate and the rate of earnings growth of the company. The argument here is that the company growth is a stimulant which has a proportional effect on value. Also, the higher the dividend per share, the greater should be the value:

$$\text{Value per share} = \frac{\text{Dividend per share}}{\begin{array}{c}\text{Investor's opportunity rate minus}\\ \text{company growth rate}\end{array}}$$

An alternative calculation is the attempt to find the price-earnings ratio from a relationship of the percentage payout of dividends to the difference between the opportunity rate and the growth rate. The result can then be used to derive a per-share value from earnings estimates for future years:

$$\text{Price-earnings ratio} = \frac{\text{Percent dividend payout}}{\begin{array}{c}\text{Investor's opportunity rate minus}\\ \text{company growth rate}\end{array}}$$

While these formulas represent an intriguing attempt to relate dividends, growth, and stockholder expectations, there are some obvious problems in their use. Theoretically, the company growth rate might exceed the investor's opportunity rate, which would result in a negative value and would be obviously non-functional, unless one interpreted this result to mean simply that the investor's expectations do not match the characteristics of the company. One could, of course, argue that investment in a very fast-growing company would also call for high return expectations. In the second formula, a high payout of dividends is likely to be coupled with a low growth rate and vice versa, although this is not necessarily so. We shall discuss more aspects of this in the next chapter.

While not conclusive, the approaches shown nevertheless illustrate the type of analysis which is possible. There are many more sophisticated ways of dealing with the valuation problem for which we do not have sufficient space.

Other Common Stock Values

One value often quoted for common stock is *book value* per share. This value represents the residual recorded claims on the balance sheet and does not take into account earnings or dividends. Only under unusual conditions will book value per share be reasonably representative of anything approximating the economic value of a share of common stock. If a company has just started or is about to be liquidated, the book value may be close to an economic value. Under normal conditions, however, book value per share becomes increasingly remote from current values, since changes in economic values of existing assets and the going-concern values of the various parts of an organization are rarely, if ever, reflected in an adjustment of the books of account. In a stagnant company it is possible to find that book value exceeds market value, which is one signal which acquisition-minded conglomerates are using to find potential candidates for acquisition.

The question of *market values* for common stocks is being treated very lightly in this chapter. It is the subject of much learned analysis and speculation, and this book of techniques is not the place in which to go into detail. Suffice it to say that several attributes will make the market value of the share of common stock reasonably representative of economic value. First, a stock should be traded frequently and in fairly sizable volume to ensure that transactions take place between parties at arm's length. Second, the share ownership ideally should be fairly widespread, to avoid the movement of blocks of stock between narrowly concerned parties. Third, stock should be traded on one or more exchanges, or be part of the increasingly important over-the-counter market. Even under all of these conditions, however, the market value of a share of stock at any one point in time could still be subject to a great deal of psychological, economic, and other pressures and thus not necessarily reflect the potential of the corporation. Normally it is best to analyze the range within which market values have moved, preferably over at least one full year, and to chart the movement of prices and weekly or monthly ranges relative to the movement of the stock market as a whole. It is against this complex background, however, that corporate management must often make the decision to issue additional shares of equity, as we discussed earlier in the chapter.

One valuation issue of occasional importance is the question of *rights values*. Rights represent the privilege of purchasing additional securities, based on the number of shares currently held by existing stockholders of the corporation. There is usually a time limit on this right, which allows the purchase of new shares at a price below the current market. Such rights protect the current stockholders' proportionate share in the total earnings of the corporation, since the exercise of the right will prevent any dilution in ownership on their part. Normally detachable and salable separately, rights assume a value and are traded as they represent a potential discount in buying new shares.

The value of such a right (R), prior to its expiration, depends on the current market price (M) of a share of common stock, the number of old shares (N) required to acquire one new share, and the subscription price (S) at which the new share can be acquired. The formula relates these magnitudes to each other to determine the value of an individual right as follows:

$$R = \frac{M - S}{N + 1}$$

We can illustrate the value of rights by using the following example. If a stock with rights attached (cum rights) were trading at $95, the issue price were $80, and 15 rights are required to buy a new share, the theoretical value of the right derived through our formula would be as follows:

$$R = \frac{\$95 - \$80}{15 + 1} = \frac{\$15}{16} = \$0.94$$

The value per right of slightly under $1 in effect represents the proportionate discount from market value provided by the ability to buy a new share advantageously. We can demonstrate the calculation in a different way:

```
Investment in old shares (cum rights), 15 × $95 .......... $1,425
Additional investment to acquire 1 share ...............      80
    Total investment (16 shares)  ....................... $1,505
```

The 16 shares now owned represent an investment of $1,505, or $94.06 per share, which is a drop in value per share of $0.94. This must be the value of the right to protect the existing holder from this dilution. In fact, the actual drop in quoted market value per share encountered from the cum rights to the ex-rights position (after rights are traded separately from the old stock), is normally very close to that range.

SUMMARY

This chapter has shown the major techniques of analyzing the implications to corporate management of choosing among major sources of funds, and the major considerations the holders of various forms of securities have in investing their funds. Many aspects of this analysis are judgmental beyond the specific tools of analysis, since the complexities of the marketplace and the difficulty of dealing with future projections subject many of the variables to considerable uncertainty. Moreover, the theoretical questions behind some of these concepts are knotty and not fully resolved. Nevertheless, the development of the appropriate funds sources and the formation of an appropriate balance between debt, preferred, and equity is one of the critical planning tasks of management. It must be undertaken with full knowledge of the implications to the enterprise as a whole and the types of obligations undertaken vis-à-vis current and potential investors and their objectives.

SELECTED REFERENCES

BONBRIGHT, J. C. *The Valuation of Property*, 2 vols. New York: McGraw-Hill Book Co., 1937.

DONALDSON, GORDON. *Corporate Debt Capacity*. Boston: Division of Research, Graduate School of Business Administration, Harvard University, 1961.

GRAHAM, B.; DODD, D. L.; and COTTLE, S. *Security Analysis*, part IV. 4th ed. New York: McGraw-Hill Book Co., 1962.

GUTHMANN, H. G., and DOUGALL, H. E. *Corporate Financial Policy*. 4th ed. Englewood Cliffs, N.J.: Prentice-Hall, 1962.

HELFERT, ERICH A. *Valuation; Concepts and Practice*. Belmont, Calif.: Wadsworth Publishing Co., 1966.

HUNT, PEARSON; WILLIAMS, CHARLES M.; and DONALDSON, GORDON. *Basic Business Finance*. 3d ed. Homewood, Ill.: Richard D. Irwin, 1966.

JOHNSON, R. W. *Financial Management*; chaps. 18, 19. 2d ed. Boston: Allyn & Bacon, 1962.

KENT, RAYMOND P. *Corporate Financial Management,* parts V to VIII. 3d ed. Homewood, Ill.: Richard D. Irwin, 1969.

VAN HORNE, JAMES C. *Financial Management and Policy,* chaps. 6, 7, part IV. Englewood Cliffs, N.J.: Prentice-Hall, 1968.

WESTON, J. FRED, and BRIGHAM, EUGENE F. *Managerial Finance,* chaps. 9, 11, 17–20. 3d ed. New York: Holt, Rinehart & Winston, 1971.

CHAPTER

6

BUSINESS AS
A DYNAMIC SYSTEM

In the previous five chapters we mentioned frequently the need
to view a business operation as a system of interconnected conditions, objectives, and policies. It was necessary, however, to
discuss key aspects of financial analysis separately in order to
highlight and explain the concepts involved, and we have done
this under the several headings of the earlier chapters. This final
chapter on techniques will provide an overview, not so much of
all the detailed and specialized aspects of financial analysis, but
of the use of selected approaches toward broad financial and
operational planning. We have continually distinguished between investment, operations, and financing, and the ensuing
pages will provide a format by which to test the key decisions
in these areas as they affect each other. The overview provided
will be that of a dynamic closed system, rather than a static
look at any one set of conditions.

Among the specific dynamic elements of the system to be discussed will be a closer analysis of the concepts of operating and
financial leverage which were mentioned in Chapters 2, 3, and
5. Furthermore, a deeper insight will be provided into the effect of the disposition of profits on financial plans, and into the
capability to make investments as affected by retained earnings

and the debt-equity balance. In addition, we shall test the constraints under which specific financial objectives, such as growth in equity or earnings, must be planned. The thrust of the discussion will be that of financial planning, and the analytical framework will display the effect of financial objectives and goals as constrained by specific policies decided upon by management.

THE BUSINESS SYSTEM: AN OVERVIEW

It will be useful to visualize the concept of a closed business system with the help of a diagram on which to display the ideas and measures discussed earlier in the book. Figure 6–1 represents such a business model, which is separated into four areas of management interest and strategy: (1) the conduct of operations, (2) the disposition of profits, (3) financing strategy, and (4) investment strategy. Note that disposition of profits has been added to our previous three areas, since it merits special attention due to its impact on future growth.

The key strategies for the *conduct of operations* involve the appropriate deployment of assets for serving selected markets, and the use of appropriate price and service strategies to do so effectively. At the same time, care must be taken to operate with good cost efficiency, which will depend to a large extent both on the proportion of fixed (period) costs not changed by volume fluctuations, and the level of variable costs incurred in manufacturing, service, or trade. It is this interplay of forces which brings about the operating profit for the period: the effect of market selection on pricing, the price-volume trade-off in the competitive environment, and the operating efficiency based on good management and leverage conditions. The deployment of existing and new investments—whether they be plant and machinery, various physical resources, manpower development, working capital, or promotional investments—is the action trigger for almost any kind of business operation, and it permits the other operating decisions to take place.

The key measures in this area, of course, include the rate of

Figure 6–1

THE BUSINESS SYSTEM: AN OVERVIEW

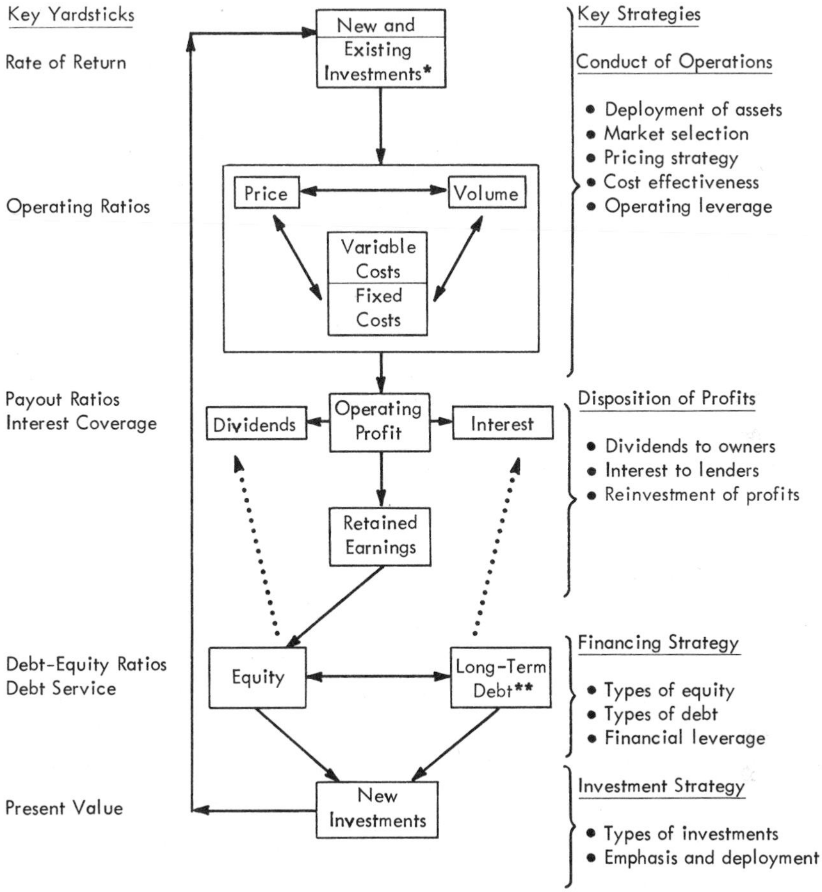

° Assumes an amount equal to depreciation reinvested here.
°° Assumes continuous rollover, with no reduction through repayments.

return on net assets (capitalization) before interest, as an over-all judgment of the effectiveness of capital deployment. Furthermore, we encounter the great variety of operating ratios, ranging from gross margins to specific expense and profit ratios, discussed in Chapter 2. We shall return shortly to the impact of operating leverage on these results.

The *disposition of profits* amounts essentially to a three-way split, each part of which is subject to current or prior management decisions and policies. The payment of dividends to owners, as observed before, is a matter of discretion by the board of directors. The degree of payout, however, influences the possible use of profit dollars for reinvestment and growth. The payment of interest is a matter of contractual obligation, but the relative amount is a function of the financial policies toward the use of debt—the higher the debt proportion of the capital structure, the greater the demand on profit dollars for use as interest payments, given a normal return on assets. Furthermore, high debt proportions will generally require higher interest rates to compensate for potential risk to the holders. Finally, earnings retained will be the residual amount of profit available to fuel additional investment and growth, together with new capital provided by investors and lenders. Payout ratios and coverage of interest are key measures in this area.

Financing strategy represents the selection and balancing of the relative proportions of ownership and debt funds to bring about an acceptable level of profitability with due regard to business risks and the obligations of debt service. The types of equity which can be employed are numerous, as already observed in Chapter 5, and the same is true of the choice of debt instruments. Here the key concept is the impact of financial leverage, to be taken up in more detail later. This refers to the prudent use of fixed-cost debt obligations and the investment of such funds in opportunities with potentially higher earnings than the interest obligation itself. Key measures include the ratio of debt to equity, debt service coverage, and return on equity.

Investment strategy covers the whole area of capital budgeting, that is, the selection of investments to match both the operational characteristics and the objectives of the business and the financial policies it deems acceptable. Various types of outlays must be analyzed and matched with plans, and market selection and emphasis will govern the deployment of these investments. Present value techniques and economic analysis, as described in Chapter 4, are applicable yardsticks here.

Our simplified model of the business system contains two key assumptions worth spelling out. First, depreciation is not recognized as such, since it is assumed that an amount equal to depreciation each year will have to be invested to maintain the productive capacity of the business without providing any incremental profits. Consequently, we show operating profit instead of cash flow as one of the bases for new investment. Second, the amount of long-term debt outstanding is assumed to be unchanged by any repayments, since only a continuous rollover of expiring debt through new borrowing can provide a steady debt-equity ratio. As the equity balance grows, management will likely want to match this with an appropriate incremental amount of debt, unless a change in policy is desired.

It should now be obvious that this picture of the business system forces us to the recognition of interrelationships. For example, it would be ineffective for a company to have the conduct of operations governed by a set of venturesome objectives unrelated to its conservative financing and investment strategies. Similarly, high payout of profit in the form of dividends together with very restricted use of debt would not match an objective of fast growth of the business, since adequate funds for new investments would simply not be available under these conditions. A consistent set of objectives, goals, and strategies must be the basis on which proper financial analysis and planning can take place, and this systems approach shows these interconnections.

We shall now turn to a more detailed analysis of the importance of operating and financial leverage, and then combine all concepts into a simplified version of a financial long-term plan.

OPERATING LEVERAGE

Leverage, as mentioned before, refers to the often favorable condition of having a stable element of cost (fixed or period cost) support a wide range of operating volume. This condition tends to magnify the profitability of the higher levels of operations, as each unit of additional output contributes a sizable margin of profit based on strictly variable costs only. Once all fixed (period) costs have been recovered by a minimum level of operations, profits rise proportionately faster than the rate of increase in volume itself. Unfortunately, a similar condition holds for declining operations, with acceleration of losses out of proportion to the rate of volume reduction.

The concept of separating fixed and variable costs, i.e., costs that vary with time and costs that vary with level of operations, is an old idea and the basis of break-even point analysis. We are particularly interested in this idea, both for a better understanding of the operational aspects of a business for better financial projections and planning, and in a broader sense to make us aware of the distorting effect significant operating leverage can have on the ratios, comparisons, and other tools employed in financial analysis.

Figure 6–2 is a representation of a simple business with relatively high fixed costs of $200,000 in relation to the volume of output and the variable costs per unit. The company has a maximum level of production of 1,000 units, and for simplicity we assume that there is no lag between production and sales. Units sell for $750 each, and variable costs of materials, labor, and supplies amount to $250 per unit. As a consequence, each unit provides a contribution of $500 towards fixed costs and profit.

The break-even chart is a simple representation of the condition just outlined. At zero volume, fixed costs amount to $200,000 and remain level until full capacity is reached. Variable costs, on the other hand, accumulate at $250 per unit as volume increases until a level of $250,000 has been reached at capacity, for a total cost of $450,000. Revenue rises from zero, in increments of $750, until the total revenue has reached $750,000 at capacity.

Where the revenue and variable cost lines cross (at 400 units of output), a break-even condition of no profit and no loss has been reached, since the total cumulative revenue of $300,000 at that point is just sufficient to offset the fixed costs of $200,000 and the total variable costs of 400 units at $250 each ($100,000). If operations exceed this point, profit begins to appear; while at volumes less than 400 units, losses are incurred. The break-even point can be found numerically, of course, by simply divid-

Figure 6–2

ABC CORPORATION

Simple Operating Break-Even Chart No. 1
Basic Conditions

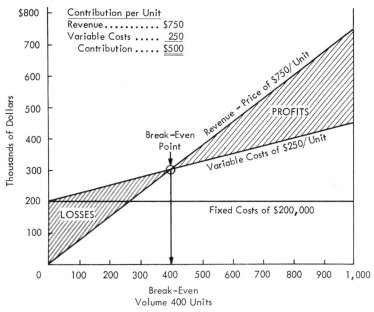

Break-Even
Volume 400 Units

Profits and Losses as a Function of Volume

Volume	Increase	Profits	Increase
400	...	–0–	...
500	25%	$ 50,000	infinite
625	25	112,500	125%
781	25	190,500	69
976	25	288,000	51

Volume	Decrease	Losses	Increase
400	...	–0–	...
300	25%	$ 50,000	infinite
225	25	87,500	75%
169	25	115,500	32
127	25	136,500	18

ing the unit contribution of $500 into the total fixed costs of $200,000, which results in 400 units, as we expected:

$$\text{Break-even point} = \frac{\text{Fixed costs}}{\text{Unit contribution}} = \text{Unit volume}$$

The most interesting aspect of the break-even chart, however, is the introduction of proportionality. A series of 25 percent increases in volume above the break-even point will result in much larger percentage jumps in profit growth. The results applicable to our example are displayed in the table under the chart, and show a gradual decline in the profit growth rate from infinite to 51 percent. Similarly, as volume decreases below the break-even point in 25 percent decrements, the loss rate declines from infinite to a modest 18 percent, as volume approaches zero. Thus changes in operations close to the break-even point, whether up or down, are likely to produce sizable swings in earnings. Changes in operations well above or below the break-even point will cause lesser fluctuations.

We must be careful in interpreting these changes, however, as in any percentage analysis the specific results depend on the starting point and the relative magnitudes. Nevertheless, the concept should be clear—the closer a firm is to its break-even point, the more dramatic will be the profit results of volume changes. This can be serious and must not be overlooked in operational or financial analysis, since financial projections should reasonably represent the expected operating characteristics of the business. Furthermore, the greater the relative level of fixed costs, the more powerful leverage becomes, and with it the need to understand this operating condition. Capital-intensive industries, such as steel, mining, and heavy manufacturing are all subject to highly leveraged operations. Most of the costs of production, including some of the labor costs, will be fixed for a wide range of volumes, and this condition will tend to accentuate profit swings as such companies move away from break-even operations. Another example is the airline industry, which very recently added a sizable increment of capacity to its flight equipment. This has caused most major airlines to suffer sharp drops in profit. As business and private travel rise to approach the new level of capacity, many airlines should experience dramatic profit improvements. On the other hand, service industries, such as professional advisers, can usually influence their major cost, manpower, by adjusting the number of employees as demand changes, and thus are much less subject to the operating leverage condition.

What are the key elements management can affect in operations and what is the impact of such decisions on leverage? There are three main items in the leverage relationship: fixed costs, variable costs, and price, all of which are in one way or another related to volume. We shall demonstrate the effect of changes in all three by varying the basic conditions in our example.

If management is able to lower the level of *fixed costs* through energetic reduction in overhead elements, the effect can be a significant lowering of the break-even point. As a consequence, the profit boost effect is moved to a lower level of operations. This is shown in Figure 6–3. Note that a lowering of fixed costs by one eighth has led to a similar reduction in break-even volume, since it will take one-eighth fewer units at $500 contribu-

Figure 6–3

ABC CORPORATION

Simple Operating Break-Even Chart No. 2
Reduced Fixed Costs by $25,000

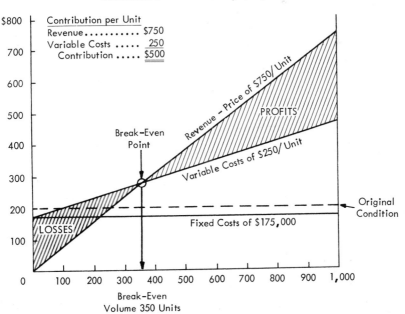

Figure 6–3 (continued)

Profits and Losses as a Function of Volume

Volume	Increase	Profits	Increase
350	...	–0–	...
438	25%	$ 44,000	infinite
547	25	98,500	125%
684	25	167,000	69
855	25	252,500	51

Volume	Decrease	Losses	Increase
350	...	–0–	...
262	25%	$ 44,000	infinite
196	25	77,000	75%
147	25	101,500	32
110	25	120,000	18

tion each to cover the lower fixed costs. Starting from the reduced break-even point of 350 units, 25 percent increments or
decrements in volume will lead to profit or loss increases similar
to the earlier example, as shown in our illustration. The reduction of fixed cost, therefore, is a very direct and effective way to
lower the break-even point for an improved profit position.

Any effort expended at reducing *variable costs* (and thereby
increasing the unit contribution) can similarly have a salutary
effect on profits at current levels as well as on the movement of
the break-even point itself. In Figure 6–4 we have shown the
resulting change in the slope of the variable cost line, which in
effect widens the profit. This is indicated graphically in the
shaded area. Loss conditions are similarly reduced. The change
in break-even volume resulting from a 10 percent change in
variable costs is not as dramatic as we found when fixed costs
were lowered earlier by one eighth. The reason for this is that the
reduction applies only to a small part of the total cost picture,
since variable costs are relatively low in this example. Only at
the full capacity of 1,000 units does the profit impact of $25,000
correspond to the amount of reduction in fixed costs in the earlier example. At lower levels of operations, reduction in unit
volume and the low importance of variable costs combine to
minimize the effect of this change. Nevertheless, the result is
clearly an improvement in the break-even condition and the

Figure 6–4

ABC CORPORATION

Simple Operating Break-Even Chart No. 3
Reduced Variable Costs by $25 per Unit

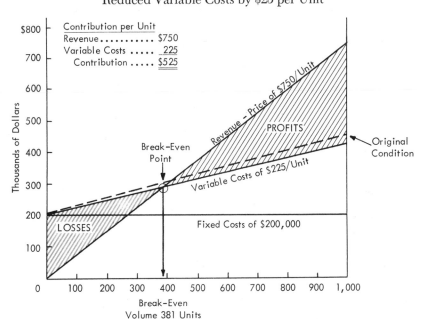

Break-Even
Volume 381 Units

Profits and Losses as a Function of Volume

Volume	Increase	Profits	Increase
381	...	–0–	...
476	25%	$ 49,900°	infinite
595	25	112,375	125%
744	25	190,600	69
930	25	288,250	51

Volume	Decrease	Losses	Increase
381	...	–0–	...
286	25%	$ 50,150°	infinite
215	25	87,125	75%
161	25	115,475	32
121	25	136,475	18

° First 25 percent change not exactly equal due to rounding.

achievement of a profit boost earlier on the volume scale. Again, 25 percent incremental changes are tabulated to show the specific conditions.

Price changes are perhaps the most complex adjustment to

analyze, since heretofore we have concentrated on the cost effects which are strictly under the control of management. A change in price normally has an effect on the competitive equilibrium and will directly influence the volume a business is able to sell. Thus it is not enough to trace the effect of high or low prices on the break-even chart, but an attempt must be made to interpret the likely change in volume resulting from the price change. In other words, raising the price may more than proportionally affect the volume which can be sold and thus actually lower the total profit achieved. Conversely, lowering the price may more than recoup the lost contribution on all units by boosting the total unit volume which can be sold against competition.

The chart in Figure 6–5 demonstrates the effect of lowering the price by $50 per unit, a 6.7 percent reduction. Note that this

Figure 6–5

ABC CORPORATION

Simple Operating Break-Even Chart No. 4

Reduced Price by $50 per Unit

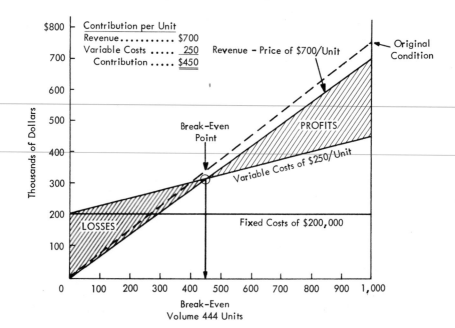

Break-Even
Volume 444 Units

Figure 6–5 (continued)

Profits and Losses as a Function of Volume

Volume	Increase	Profits	Increase
444	. . .	–0–	. . .
555	25%	$ 49,750*	infinite
694	25	112,300	125%
867	25	190,150	69
1084	25	287,800	51

Volume	Decrease	Losses	Increase
444	. . .	–0–	. . .
333	25%	$ 50,150*	infinite
249	25	87,950	75%
187	25	115,850	32
140	25	137,000	18

* First 25 percent change not exactly equal due to rounding.

action raises the required break-even volume by about 11 percent, to 444 units—which indicates the need to sell 44 additional units to recoup the loss in contribution on the sale of each unit. For example, if current volume had been 800 units, with a contribution of $400,000 and a profit of $200,000, the price drop of $50 would require the sale of enough additional units to recover 800 times $50 or $40,000. This must be done through the lower unit contribution of $450, and the result is 89 units, an increase of 11 percent, which is a more than proportional change in unit volume versus unit price.

Price changes affect the internal operating results but may have an even more pronounced and lasting impact on the competitive environment. If a more than proportionate volume advantage can be obtained for some time by price reductions, it may be wise to do so. On the other hand, if price reductions can be expected to be met quickly by others in the business, the final effect may simply be a drop in profit for all concerned, since no shift in market share would come about. This is not the place to discuss the many strategic issues involved in price policy; the intent is merely to show the effect of this important element on the operating system and to provide a way of analyzing likely conditions.

In the foregoing analysis, cost, volume, and price implications and their impact on profit were analyzed separately. In practice, the many conditions and pressures encountered by a business often affect these variables simultaneously. Cost, volume, and price for a single product may all be changing at the same time in subtle and often unmeasurable ways. The analysis is further complicated when several products are involved in a business, as is true of all major corporations. In such cases, changes in the sales mix can introduce many complexities to the analysis. Moreover, our simplifying assumption about simultaneous production and sales does not hold true in practice, and this lag effect must be introduced. In a manufacturing company, sales and production can be widely out of phase, with inventories absorbing differences. Some of these complications were indicated in our examples in Chapter 3, where of necessity the cash budget and the accounting statements had to be analyzed with these elements in mind.

Up to this point we have used very simplifying conditions to demonstrate essentially *linear* operating conditions for leverage and break-even analysis. A more realistic framework is sketched out in Figure 6–6. This chart shows the changes in both period costs and variable costs which may be encountered over the full range of operations. Furthermore, changed price-revenue possibilities are reflected. While only illustrative, the chart indicates that the simple straight-line relationships used in Figures 6–2 through 6–5 are normally only approximations of the "step functions" and gradual shifts in cost and price behavior often encountered under realistic circumstances. A few of the possible changes in conditions and sample reasons for these are described below the chart.

With the concept of operating leverage in mind, we can now turn to the application of the fixed-variable relationship to the financial structure of a company.

FINANCIAL LEVERAGE

A similarity exists between operating leverage and financial leverage, since in both cases there is an opportunity to profit

Figure 6–6

GENERALIZED BREAK-EVEN CHART

Allowance for Changing Cost and Revenue Conditions

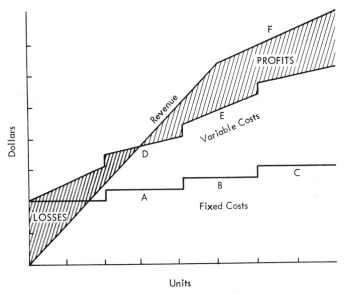

Units

A. A new layer of fixed costs is triggered by growing volume.
B. A new shift is added, with additional requirements for overhead costs.
C. A final small increment of overhead is incurred as some operations need overtime.
D. Efficiencies in operations provide a lesser slope for variable unit costs.
E. The new shift causes inefficiencies and lower output, with more spoilage.
F. The last increments of output must be sold on contract at lower prices.

from the fixed nature of certain costs relative to increments of profit. In financial leverage, as already mentioned in Chapter 5, the advantage arises from the simple notion that funds borrowed at a fixed contractual interest rate can often be employed at an opportunity rate of return higher than the interest paid. Given a company's ability to make investments which provide returns consistently above the going rate of interest, it will be to its advantage to "trade on equity." This means borrowing as much as prudent management will permit and thereby boosting the return on ownership equity by the difference between the rate of return and the interest paid.

Chapter 5 contained a visual display of the effect of financial leverage in the EBIT chart (Figure 5–8) based on the choice between different types of capital. In the context of this chapter, we shall employ another form of graphic analysis to display the boosting impact of leverage on return on equity, one of our key measures. We shall also use a formula approach to express the basics of leverage, as it affects both return on equity and minimum investment standards.

In Figure 6–7, the leverage effect on return on equity is

Figure 6–7

RETURN ON EQUITY AS AFFECTED
BY FINANCIAL LEVERAGE
(after-tax interest on debt is 4 percent)

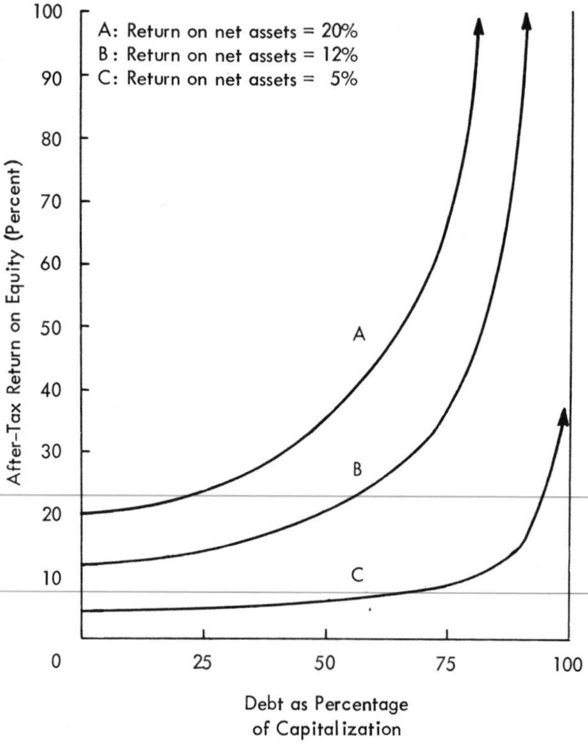

A: Return on net assets = 20%
B: Return on net assets = 12%
C: Return on net assets = 5%

Debt as Percentage
of Capitalization

graphed for three sample conditions, all under the assumption that funds can be borrowed at 4 percent per year after taxes. If the normal return on capitalization (before interest, after taxes) is 20 percent (*A*), the introduction of increasing proportions of debt causes a dramatic rise in return on equity, which jumps to infinity as debt approaches 100 percent. Lines *B* and *C* show the leverage effect under more modest earnings conditions. While dampened somewhat, the return on equity still shows sharp increases as the debt proportion rises. As we observed before, one should not forget that leverage works in reverse circumstances also. This condition is demonstrated by the widening space between the lines at higher debt levels: should earnings drop, the plunge in return on equity can be massive.

The same conditions are expressed in the formulas of Figure 6–8, which demonstrates the effect of leverage on return on

Figure 6–8

EFFECT OF FINANCIAL LEVERAGE ON
RETURN ON EQUITY AND INVESTMENT STANDARDS

D = Debt
E = Equity
R = Return on equity

i = Rate of interest after taxes
r = Return on net assets after taxes

A. Return on Equity (R):

$$R = \frac{(D+E)\,r - Di}{E}$$

If (1) $D = 0, E = 100$ and $i = 4\%$
   (2) $D = 25, E = 75$ $r = 12\%$
   (3) $D = 50, E = 50$
   (4) $D = 75, E = 25$

then return on equity R equals:

   (1) 12.0%
   (2) 14.7
   (3) 20.0
   (4) 36.0

B. Return on Net Assets (r):

$$r = \frac{ER + Di}{D + E} \quad \text{(from formula in A)}$$

If the same four debt–equity conditions hold as under A and $i = 4\%$ with R (required return on equity) $= 12\%$, then minimum return r equals:

   (1) 12%
   (2) 10
   (3) 8
   (4) 6

equity (A) and the impact on required earnings standards (B). The formula for return on equity is a simple expression of the ratios we discussed in Chapter 2; that is, the return is calculated from the after-tax profit for the period earned (less the after-tax interest) related to the capitalization. The net amount is then related to the amount of equity outstanding. We observe four different sample conditions for debt-equity ratios, ranging from no debt in the first case to a 3:1 debt-equity relationship in the fourth case. Given an after-tax cost of interest of 4 percent and the normal ability to earn 12 percent after taxes on net assets invested, the return on equity in the first case must also be 12 percent after taxes, since no debt exists and the total capitalization is represented by equity. As increasing amounts of debt are introduced to the capital structure, the return on equity is boosted considerably, since in each case the assumption is made that the effectiveness with which investments are made far exceeds the cost of interest paid to the debt holders. This was, of course, shown in the graph of Figure 6–7. The reader is invited to work through the opposite effect, that is, interest charges in excess of the ability to earn a return on investments.

Part B of Figure 6–8 develops the minimum return on net assets (capitalization) which has to be achieved to provide a given return on equity, a useful concept for the investment analysis process. This approach simply turns the calculation around, by fixing the return on equity standard and letting the opportunity rate of investment vary. The formula was developed from the relationship under A and the calculation is straightforward, given an after-tax interest cost of 4 percent and a required return on equity of 12 percent. Note that the required amount of earnings on net assets (capitalization) drops sharply as leverage is introduced, until it begins to approach the 4 percent interest cost after taxes. It will never quite reach this figure, however, since some small amount of equity must be maintained in the capitalization to keep the problem realistic.

While it is simple to work out the mathematical relationships, the translation of these conditions into the appropriate financial strategy is much more complex. No business is completely free to vary its capital structure at will, and there are realistic constraints on the managements of all types of companies to keep some "normalcy" in their financial structures. While no absolute rules exist, the various tests employed by lenders of funds run the gamut of the ratios we discussed in Chapter 2, and with enlightened self-interest in mind they will impose upper limits on the amount of debt capital to be employed. Manufacturing companies will normally range between zero and 50 percent debt in the capitalization, while public utilities will vary between 30 and 60 percent. Trading companies with highly liquid assets can reach debt proportions of even greater magnitude.

As stated before, we are interested in the effects of financial leverage to assist us in the broader financial planning for a company. As such, it is only one of several aspects affecting the performance of an operation, and we shall now turn to a more integrated look at financial planning based on the interrelationships discussed earlier.

FINANCIAL GROWTH PLANS

Management can set a variety of possible objectives of a financial nature in planning for its operational and financial future. Foremost among these are growth in earnings per share, market value appreciation, growth in dividends, growth in ownership equity, and growth in sales volume. None of these can be singly chosen as an overall standard, as we observed before. It will be useful, nevertheless, to select one of these objectives to work through an integrated financial plan for illustrative purposes. One of the simplest objectives on which to demonstrate such integrated modeling is growth in ownership equity. Not only is this magnitude relatively easy to calculate but it also is one of the key elements through which earnings growth and stock value are directly or indirectly affected.

The next exhibit, Table 6–1, is an illustration of such a simplified financial growth model which shows the several aspects of a corporation's growth, that is, capitalization, profitability, earnings disposition, and financing. With the results we can demon-

Table 6–1

FINANCIAL GROWTH MODEL

Three Different Sets of Policies

(dollars in thousands)

	Case I	Case II	Case III
Capitalization:			
Debt-equity ratio	0:1	1:1	1:1
Debt	–0–	$250	$250
Equity	$500	250	250
Net assets	$500	$500	$500
Profitability (after taxes):			
Gross return on net assets*	10%	10%	10%
Amount of profit	$50	$50	$50
Interest at 4 percent	–0–	10	10
Profit after interest	$50	$40	$40
Earnings disposition:			
Dividend payout	0%	0%	50%
Dividends paid	–0–	–0–	$20
Reinvestment	$50	$40	$20
Financing:			
Additional debt	–0–	40	20
New investment possible	$50	$80	$40
Results (in percent):			
Net return on net assets†	10	8	8
Return on equity	10	16	16
Growth in equity‡	10	16	8

* Profits *before* interest, *after* taxes related to net assets (capitalization) as a measure of operational return on assets.

† Profits *after* interest and taxes related to net assets, as often shown in financial reports.

‡ The growth in recorded equity due to earnings reinvested after payment of dividends.

strate the effect of different financial policies. Three cases are worked out, the first showing an unleveraged company with $500,000 in equity which pays no dividends and reinvests all of its profits in operations similar to the ones now carried out. The second case shows the same company in a leveraged condition, with a 1:1 debt-equity ratio. In the third case we take the conditions of Case II, but assume a dividend payout of 50 percent of earnings. As we discussed in our earlier overview of the business system, we shall assume that the financial strategy chosen will be maintained unchanged in each case.

Let us trace through the data for Case I. Given a gross return on net assets after taxes of 10 percent, the amount of profit generated for the year is $50,000, all of which can be reinvested as new investment in the company's activities. As we assumed in our business system overview, the annual depreciation is considered to be necessary to maintain the current facilities in operating condition, and these funds therefore do not represent investments in new profit opportunities. The results of Case I are a net return on capitalization of 10 percent, a return on equity of 10 percent, and a growth in equity of 10 percent, since all of the profits for the period are assumed to be reinvested in the business. The reader is invited to calculate one or more additional periods for the operations of this particular business, without changing the assumptions. He will observe quickly that given stable policies and conditions, equity growth will indeed continue at 10 percent per year.

The second case differs only with regard to the use of debt financing. Since $250,000 has been borrowed at 4 percent after taxes, $10,000 must be deducted from profit on net assets, which reduces the amount available for reinvestment to $40,000. If management desires to maintain its policy of a 1:1 debt-equity ratio, an additional $40,000 of debt can be borrowed. This raises the funds available for new investment to $80,000. The results have changed in several ways compared to Case I. Net return on capitalization has dropped to 8 percent since interest charges were introduced. As we expected, return on equity at the same time has been boosted to 16 percent from the introduction of leverage. Similarly, under these conditions, growth in equity can be maintained at 16 percent as long as all of the internally generated funds are reinvested and matching additional borrowings are made for new investments.

In the third case, the introduction of dividends is the only change involved. A 50 percent profit payout reduces the internal funds available for reinvestment to $20,000 and also reduces the additional debt to $20,000 under a 1:1 debt-equity ratio. Total funds available for new investment have thus been reduced to $40,000. This action seriously affects growth in equity, which now has been cut in half.

This very simple model illustrates the combination of investment, operations, earnings disposition, and financing strategy in a very easy manner. Clearly the conditions have been oversimplified, but refinements regarding such items as return on net assets, dividend payout ratios, and increments of additional borrowing, to name but a few, will only be variations on the basic theme expressed here.

If growth in ownership equity indeed is considered to be the chief objective in our illustrative company, it may be useful to express the relationships on the basis of formulas, along the lines of our earlier examples.

In Case I, when no debt was employed and no dividends were paid, the following conditions held:

$$g = r$$

where g is growth in equity and r is rate of return on capitalization. This formula simply expresses the fact that, under these basic conditions, earnings on capitalization are equal to earnings on equity, and growth is equal to earnings.

In Case II, debt is introduced to the capital structure, and the leverage effect is added to the formula as follows:

$$g = r + \frac{D}{E}(r - i)$$

where D is debt, E is equity, and i the interest rate. Leverage, as we discussed earlier, is a direct function of the proportion of debt in the total capital structure and the size of the margin between the return on investment and the interest cost of the funds, both after taxes. This condition is observed in the formula.

In Case III, the introduction of dividends causes a slowing of the growth in equity, since only the earnings retained can be reinvested. We have to factor each of the two return aspects to reflect this change, and p stands for the proportion of earnings retained as a percentage of total earnings. The resulting formula is shown below:

$$g = rp + \frac{D}{E}(r - i)p$$

We now have the generalized formula for the rate of growth

in equity which can be maintained by a business if stable conditions and policies hold. If the business, over the long run, is able to invest its funds at the return indicated; if management maintains the debt-equity ratio as indicated; and if interest costs and payout ratios do not change: then the growth in equity obtained will stabilize as expressed in the formula.

Similar models can be developed for the conditions surrounding earnings per share, dividends per share, debt service, or any other aspect of the financial area of the business. We shall not attempt to go into detail on these, but rather let the example of growth in equity stand as a representation of this type of thinking.

We can now turn to an illustration of an integrated financial plan over a sample five-year period for XYZ Corporation, which we assume is considering a number of changes in the policies governing its financial behavior. This integrated financial plan is shown in Table 6–2. Changes are introduced over the five-year span in the following areas: debt-equity proportions, return on net assets achieved, interest cost (as debt proportions rise), and dividend payout proportion. While almost any type of assumption can be played through on a model of this sort, one of the benefits of displaying the key relationships is that obviously inconsistent conditions will show up in the results. As these appear, the analyst has the possibility of correcting them with more tenable assumptions and calculating the effect of these changes.

XYZ Corporation starts with a debt-equity ratio of 5:1 in a total capitalization of $900,000. Current return on net assets after taxes but before interest is 8 percent, which provides a profit of $72,000. Interest after taxes requires $12,000, which leaves a profit after interest of $60,000. Under a dividend payout of 60 percent, cash dividends of $36,000 are required, which leaves $24,000 for reinvestment. Since the debt-equity ratio is to be maintained at 0.5:1, new debt of $12,000 can be introduced, supported by the increased equity.

Looking ahead to the second year, management has decided to raise its debt-equity ratio to 0.75:1, which would call for ad-

Table 6–2

XYZ CORPORATION

Integrated Financial Plan
Sample Five-Year Projection of Effect of Policy Changes
(dollars in thousands)

	Year 1	Year 2	Year 3	Year 4	Year 5
Capitalization:					
Debt-equity ratio	0.5:1	0.75:1	0.75:1	1:1	1:1
Debt	$300	$ 468	$ 489	$ 688	$ 728
Equity	600	624	652	688	728
Net assets	$900	$1,092	$1,141	$1,376	$1,456
Profitability (after taxes):					
Return on net assets	8%	7%	8%	8%	9%
Amount of profit	$ 72	$76	$ 91	$110	$131
Interest after taxes	4%	4%	4%	4.5%	4.5%
Amount of interest	$ 12	$19	$ 20	$ 31	$ 33
Profit after interest	$ 60	$57	$ 71	$ 79	$ 98
Earnings disposition:					
Dividend payout	60%	50%	50%	50%	40%
Dividends paid	$ 36	$29	$ 35	$ 39	$ 39
Reinvestment	$ 24	$28	$ 36	$ 40	$ 59
Financing and investment:					
New debt, old ratio	12	21	27	40	59
New debt, revised ratio ...	156	...	172	...	...
New investment	$192	$49	$235	$ 80	$118
Results:					
Net return* on					
net assets	6.7%	5.2%	6.2%	5.7%	6.7%
Return on equity	10.0%	9.1%	10.9%	11.5%	13.4%
Growth in equity	4.0%	4.6%	5.5%	5.8%	8.1%
Earnings per share					
(100,000 shares)	$0.60	$0.57	$0.71	$0.79	$0.98
Dividends per share	$0.36	$0.29	$0.35	$0.39	$0.39

* Return after taxes and interest.

ditional borrowing of $156,000 at the end of the first year. For
simplicity, we have assumed that all changes take place at year-
end.

The results for the first year show a net return on capitalization of 6.7 percent, a return on equity of 10 percent and a
growth in equity of 4 percent. Earnings per share are $0.60 and

dividends $0.36. The influx of new funds at the beginning of year two raises the capitalization to well over $1 million.

For the second year, the assumption about returns earned is lowered to reflect some inefficiencies as the new funds are invested; the overall return on net assets thus is dropped to 7 percent. After proper allowance for interest, profits available for equity are $57,000. A change in dividend payout to 50 percent calls for only $29,000 in dividends, leaving $28,000 for reinvestment. This is matched with $21,000 of new debt. These funds are added to the investment base of the third year.

The process is repetitive, as changes in policies are anticipated at the end of the year's operations. For example, we find a new influx of capital into year four, as debt-equity proportions are changed to 1:1. Some additional interest cost is assumed as the capital structure becomes more leveraged and thus more risky. At the same time, however, the effectiveness of employing capital has been left at 8 percent in years three and four, and raised to 9 percent in year five.

The results at the bottom of the exhibit indicate some fluctuations in net return on capitalization over the years, as either profitability or interest cost is changed. The return on equity, however, after dropping in year two, rises steadily to a sizable 13.4 percent in year five. Growth in equity jumps, after some intermediate boosts, to about double the original 4 percent rate in year five, that is, 8.1 percent. Earnings per share show a similarly encouraging growth, while dividends per share fluctuate somewhat.

The results of such a model run raise some realistic questions. For example, it may not be prudent to change the dividend *payout* ratio in sizable steps as was done. We observe that there was a drop in dividends *per share* of almost 20 percent in the second year. In the absence of general economic problems, the directors might be very reluctant to do this, since a consistent dividend pattern is generally considered desirable. It would therefore be possible to adjust the dividend payout for the second year back to the original level and to lower the dividend payout only as earnings rise sufficiently to avoid a sharp drop in dividends per share. At the same time, it might be useful to refine the assumptions about return on net assets. So far we have shown an overall percentage, which could be made more realistic by splitting the analysis into existing assets and additional assets. Such a practice might be particularly useful if a company were embarking on diversification in its operations, with highly different return expectations from some of these activities. More attention might also be paid to the assumption that depreciation will be reinvested without additional profits. A company contracting some of its ongoing operations to redeploy its funds in diversified lines might in fact not be willing to reinvest comparable amounts in old product lines.

The main purpose of this illustration is to show the usefulness of financial planning in an overall sense. By observing the key result areas of interest to management, the analyst can arrive at a set of assumptions and recommendations which fairly reflect the desires and capabilities of the management involved. Many more refined formats are possible, a process greatly enhanced by the construction of computerized models, as discussed briefly in Chapter 3. Computerized financial models are nothing more than representations of financial and operational conditions like those indicated in the simple approaches used here, but with a great number of additional details and complications.

SUMMARY

In this chapter, we have attempted to integrate some of the key concepts discussed in the earlier parts of this book. Through the use of a simplified overview of the business as a system and the development of a basic financial planning model, we have demonstrated the need to provide a consistent set of strategies in order to develop creditable plans. In the end, the key test of financial analysis is the viability of the methods and results as predictors of future activity, which was a major point we made in the earlier chapters. The optimal approach is the use of quite detailed and sensitive models of all conditions of the business.

Yet the outside analyst, and even inside management, will often have to get by with simplified yardsticks and modeling efforts which can approximate the solution sufficiently for broad planning needs. It is for this perspective that the chapter was provided, as a capstone to the various techniques of this book.

SELECTED REFERENCES

Break-Even and Leverage Concepts

ANTHONY, ROBERT N. *Management Accounting, Text and Cases*, chap. 15. 4th ed. Homewood, Ill.: Richard D. Irwin, 1970.

BACKER, MORTON, and JACOBSEN, LYLE E. *Cost Accounting, A Managerial Approach*, chap. 12. New York: McGraw-Hill Book Co., 1964.

HORNGREN, CHARLES T. *Cost Accounting, A Managerial Emphasis*, chap. 3. Englewood Cliffs, N.J.: Prentice-Hall, 1962.

VAN HORNE, JAMES C. *Financial Management and Policy*, chap. 26. Englewood Cliffs, N.J.: Prentice-Hall, 1968.

WESTON, J. FRED, and BRIGHAM, EUGENE F. *Managerial Finance*, chaps. 23, 24. 3d ed. New York: Holt, Rinehart & Winston, 1971.

Financial Strategy and Planning

BOSTON CONSULTING GROUP, INC. *Perspectives on Corporate Strategy*. Boston, 1968.

———. *Growth and Financial Strategies*. Boston, 1971.

CHILDS, JOHN F. *Long Term Finance*. Englewood Cliffs, N.J.: Prentice-Hall, 1961.

DONALDSON, GORDON. *Strategy of Financial Mobility*. Boston: Division of Research, Graduate School of Business Administration, Harvard University, 1969.

STEINER, GEORGE A. *Top Management Planning*. New York: Columbia University Graduate School of Business and Macmillan Co., 1969.

CHAPTER

7

SOURCES OF
FINANCIAL INFORMATION

While the orientation of this book has been the presentation and discussion of financial analysis techniques, we have all along assumed that a great deal of information of a financial and economic nature was readily available to us. The student, analyst, or businessman should be quite familiar with the various main sources which provide this information, in order to obtain the desired input for the analysis. For this reason, the final chapter in this book is devoted to a brief review of common data sources, and where required guidelines are given for the interpretation of financial data presentations. Familiarity with this type of background will permit more informed decisions about company performance, new financing, temporary borrowing, investments, credits, capital budgeting, etc.

Again in keeping with the nature of this book, the treatment of the subject cannot be exhaustive, and the chapter only introduces the form, extent, and character of financial information which is published daily, weekly, or monthly in current media or is collected and interpreted annually in reference works and investor services of a large variety. The information will be discussed in the following segments:

Current Financial Information

Periodic Financial Information
Background Company and Business Information

CURRENT FINANCIAL INFORMATION

The most common and convenient way to keep abreast of the financial developments is the review of the daily financial pages of metropolitan and regional newspapers. Among these newspapers, the most complete and widely read financial news coverage is found in the pages of the *Wall Street Journal* and the *New York Times,* which contain detailed information on securities and commodity markets; news, feature articles, and statistics on economic and business conditions; individual company news and earnings reports; dividend announcements; currency, commodity, and trading data; and a great deal of international business and economic coverage. The major dailies in the United States and Canada also carry key financial and economic data, but the coverage and emphasis vary greatly. Smaller and regional papers will often provide only selected highlights tailored to the area and the readership.

Securities transactions and current financial data represent the bulk of the materials shown in the financial pages. Since the display of this information is not entirely self-explanatory, we shall describe some of the details and give examples of the way in which the *Wall Street Journal* carries data on stock transactions (traded on exchanges and over-the-counter), bond transactions, and other key financial data. Other newspapers generally present data in a fairly comparable fashion, only in less detail.

Stock Quotations

Exchange Quotations. The transactions of the organized stock exchanges (New York Stock Exchange, American Stock Exchange, and several regional exchanges) appear in total or in part in daily and weekly papers generally in the same form. Figure 7–1, as an example, shows the day's transactions in 8 stocks

Figure 7-1

NEW YORK STOCK EXCHANGE STOCK TRANSACTIONS

Monday, August 23, 1971

Volume: 13,040,000 shares

1971 High	1971 Low	Stocks	Div.	Sales in 100S	Open	High	Low	Close	Net Change
18	12⅛	Avco Corp	...	153	13½	14⅜	13¼	14⅜	+ ¾
277	174½	Cor Gl Wks	2.50a	76	246	246	243	243	−2½
38	29¼	Crwn Zell	1.20	114	31	31⅜	31	31¼	+ ¼
44⅝	35⅛	Dart Ind	.30b	25	41¾	42	41½	41¾	+ ¼
62½	53⅝	Gen Mot pf	3.75	9	56¾	56⅞	56½	56¾	...
28⅞	22¾	Mass Mut	.63g	70	26⅞	27	26½	27	...
39	32½	Tex Gas T	1.52	x52	33	33	32¼	32½	− ¼
95	83	Un El pf	6.40	z20	84	84	84	84	+ ⅝

out of the 1,655 stocks traded on the New York Exchange on Monday, August 23, 1971, as reported in the *Wall Street Journal* of Tuesday, August 24. The total share volume for the day was about 13 million, a little above average in a year in which days with over 20 million shares became quite common and in which volume under 10 million shares came to be considered a "slow day."

The first stock in the listing, Avco Corporation, is recorded as having had, during 1971, a high value of $18 and a low of $12.125, noting the range in which actual transactions took place in the last eight months. The quotations are made in dollars and fractions of a point not smaller than one eighth ($0.125). The stock did not pay a dividend during 1971, as there is no entry in the dividend column. If a dividend had been paid, as was true in the other seven sample stocks, the normal annual rate of dividend based on current quarterly payments would be shown. Extra dividends, stock dividends, or passed dividends are noted through special symbols, as we shall see later.

The day's transactions in Avco stock totaled 15,300 shares as indicated in the fifth column, where sales are given in hundreds of shares. The custom of listing sales in hundreds arises from the practice of considering one hundred shares a round lot for trading, as contrasted with less than one hundred shares, considered an odd lot. Brokerage fee structures allow for somewhat higher commissions for the odd lots.

The next five columns indicate the day's price movements of the stock, based on actual transactions during August 23. The stock opened at $13.50, but successive trades reached a high for the day of $14.375 and a low of $13.25. Apparently there was a rising tendency in the stock's value during the day, since it opened near its low and closed at the high. The net change in the last column indicates the difference between the day's closing price and the close of the previous trading day.

Unless otherwise indicated, transactions listed in this fashion represent common stocks. If a preferred stock was traded, the symbol "pf" is added right after the abbreviated name of the company. In our example, General Motors and Union Electric stocks are preferred stocks. The dividend quoted for preferred stock is the annual rate, as was the case with common stocks. Thus, the General Motors stock has a dividend rate of $3.75, while Union Electric pays $6.40 per year.

A number of additional symbols and abbreviations are in common use, all of which are explained briefly in the footnotes of the financial pages. A number of these apply in the cases cited in our brief listing. For example, the *a* next to the Corning Glass dividend of $2.50 indicates that the company has paid extra dividends in addition to the annual rate shown. The *b* after the Dart Industries dividend shows that a stock dividend was paid in addition to the $0.30 annual cash dividend, while the *g* with Massachusetts Mutual indicates the amount of dividends paid thus far this year. The latter notation implies an irregular dividend pattern. Other symbols are used for issues with dividends in arrears (*k*), liquidation dividends (*c*), and so on.

Apart from notations for dividend exceptions, symbols are also used to show such occurrences as new issues (*n*), calls (*cld*), various conditions of rights and warrants, quotations on a when-issued basis, etc. In our example, two symbols help define the price level and the volume of trading. The Texas Gas Transmission stock was traded ex-dividend (*x*), which has affected the price for the day; while the total sales volume for the day in Union Electric stock was only 20 shares (*z* indicates sales in full), not 2,000 as we would have assumed without this notation.

The individual listings are supplemented in the *Wall Street Journal* financial pages by various summaries. One of these is the list of the day's most active stocks. On August 23, 1971, the stock with the highest turnover of shares among the ten stocks listed was Bristol Myers (150,700 shares), closing at $64.25, off one eighth. Another summary, the "market diary" for the last five days showed that August 23, 1971, had a trading volume of 1,655 issues with 917 advances, 474 declines, and 264 unchanged listings. New highs achieved were 72, and new lows were 37. Also shown in a listing are the various closing stock price averages (for example, the Dow-Jones Industrial average, which closed at 892.38), as well as a four-month chart of the Dow-Jones averages, by day, showing the range and closing position. All of these summary data and others not mentioned here provide an indication of the mood and direction of the market.

Stock quotations representing the transactions of the American Stock Exchange are generally presented along the same lines, if the newspaper is carrying this information. Transactions from regional exchanges, such as the Pacific Stock Exchange in San Francisco and the Midwest Stock Exchange in Chicago, are often found, together with the most important selections from the trading activity on the major Canadian stock exchanges in Toronto and Montreal. Less detail is provided on these quotations: normally, only the number of shares traded, the high and low prices achieved, and the closing prices with changes from the previous close. At times, the quotations are limited to volume and closing prices only.

Reference was made earlier to the various stock price averages, which are popular and important clues to the behavior of the stock market in general. Several of these averages are calculated daily and in some cases continuously, with the help of computers. The averages are followed closely by analysts, investors, and financial managers to interpret market movements in view of their plans for recommendations or actions on investing or selling of securities, or for issues of new securities to raise additional funds. Since the various averages, which will be discussed shortly, are averages of a selected and relatively small number of stocks, the upward or downward movement over time is not necessarily a predictor of the likely movement of any particular stock.

As discussed in the earlier chapters of the book, there are many factors underlying the value and market position of a particular security, the most important of which are the current and prospective operating circumstances of the company. The atmosphere of the market and general economic conditions will certainly influence the behavior of a particular stock, but one must caution against the adage that a "rising tide lifts all ships in the harbor," which is a gross oversimplification of the behavior of the stock market. The limitations of the stock indices are those of averages in general, which can only be broad indicators of a likely trend against which all particulars of a security have to be compared.

The most commonly quoted and publicized stock price averages are the Dow-Jones averages of 30 industrial, 20 railroad, and 15 utility stocks, and the composite average of all of these 65 securities. The Dow-Jones Industrial Average contains most of the well-known companies in American business, such as General Motors, General Electric, U.S. Steel, DuPont, Procter and Gamble, etc. Being heavily weighted toward "blue-chip" securities, the Dow-Jones average becomes less applicable as one analyzes the securities of lesser known companies, specialized "growth situations," or conglomerate corporations.

A newer indicator is the *New York Times* average of 50 stocks, which includes 25 railroad and 25 industrial stocks. This average is also weighted somewhat in favor of the blue-chip stock variety. A broader index is found in Standard & Poor's averages (an industrial composite index of 425 stock, 50 utility, and 25 railroad averages, and the combination of all these into the "Standard 500"). The Standard and Poor's averages more closely approximate the average price level of all stocks listed on the New York Stock Exchange, representing somewhat less than one third of the issues traded there.

As pointed out before, the various stock averages are plotted and charted daily, including the daily ranges and the average price levels; and with the advent of computers the current level of these averages has become available almost instantaneously during the trading period. Continuous adjustments are made for stock splits, stock dividends, and many other changes of the corporate structures of the companies in the index to maintain continuity. Some references are provided at the end of the chapter for those interested in more details about the way the indices are calculated.

Over-the-Counter Transactions. A huge volume of securities is traded without the medium of the organized exchanges in an "auction market" consisting of hundreds of security dealers and individuals in all parts of the country who are connected by telephone and wire. This over-the-counter market is an amazingly flexible trading arrangement which serves to put in touch with each other prospective buyers and sellers of such securities as government bonds, state and municipal bonds, stocks and bonds of corporations (particularly smaller and newer companies), bank stocks, mutual funds, insurance companies, small issues, and companies whose stocks have relatively infrequent demand or are held very closely. In contrast to the organized exchanges, individual transactions are not recorded and broadcast on the stock ticker. Instead, representative quotations are provided by either the National Association of Securities Dealers, Inc. or by individual dealers who specialize in particular securities, i.e. "maintain a market." The important distinction is that the quotations provided by the over-the-counter traders and listed in the financial pages are only indicative of the prices an individual or a dealer would have been willing to pay for a particular security, and at what price an individual or dealer would have been willing to sell during the trading period. The quotations are given in terms of bid and asked prices, the bid price representing the interest of the potential buyer and the asked price representing the position of a potential seller. A dealer specializing in the security and handling both sides of the transactions thus has a "spread" with which to cover his expenses and profit.

In the financial pages we find over-the-counter quotations by geographic regions or by types of company, such as the Eastern market, the National Funds market, and the National market, or listed in categories such as industrials, bank stocks and insurance stocks. Only a limited number of stocks are shown on a daily basis, while less active issues can be followed on a weekly basis. Again, Figure 7–2, from the *Wall Street Journal* of August 24, 1971, provides a sample listing of over-the-counter quotations encountered in the trading period of August 23, 1971.

The format is similar to the one shown for exchange transac-

Figure 7–2

OVER-THE-COUNTER MARKET STOCK QUOTATIONS

Monday, August 23, 1971

Stocks and Dividends		Bid	Asked	Bid Change
Barnes Hind	...	43¾	44½	−¼
Booz-Allen	.09*b*	14¾	15¼	+¼
Contl Capital	*k*	7½	7⅞	+¼
Dewey Elec	3*i*	3	3½	−¼
Samsonite	.30	*x*13⅛	13½	+¼
Bank Hawaii	2.60	65½	66½	...
1st Bankcorptn	...	(*z*)	(*z*)	(*z*)
Pref Risk	.15*e*	29¾	30½	...

tions, with the stocks and the annual dividend rate listed first, and the price levels represented by bid and asked quotations. The last column contains the change in the bids, which, as in the case of stock exchange transactions, represents the change from the quoted bid of the earlier trading period. We note that the bid quotations are normally below the asked quotations, as we would expect in an auction market.

In our sample listing we again encounter a series of symbols which are quite comparable to the symbols of stock exchange listings. For example, the *b* with the Booz-Allen stock indicates that the dividends shown are only those declared or paid this year, with no regular rate implied. The letter *k* with Continental Capital indicates the percentage of stock dividend paid in 1971, which in our case would be none, while the *i* with Dewey Electric refers to the percentage of stock dividend paid in 1970. The symbol *e* with Preferred Risk denotes dividends paid in 1971 plus additional stock dividends, while the *x* with Samsonite refers to an ex-dividend quotation and *z* indicates that no representative bid-asked data was available for the trading period. References are provided at the end of the chapter for those interested in more detail on the activities of the over-the-counter market.

Other Exchange Quotations. Some of the larger newspapers carry limited and selected quotations from major foreign stock exchanges. Trading of internationally recognized securities on the Paris, London, Tokyo, or Frankfurt stock exchanges are reported in the currency of the country involved. At times, the financial pages may contain current stock averages of foreign countries, supplemented by accounts of major activities there.

Bond Quotations

The three major types of bonds—corporate bonds, state and municipal debt, and federal government obligations—represent a huge financial market which extends to both the organized exchanges and the over-the-counter market. In fact, the overwhelming majority of governmental bonds are traded in the over-the-counter market, while the majority of corporate bond issues are traded on the stock exchanges.

It will be useful to discuss briefly a listing of bond transactions on the New York Stock Exchange, to demonstrate the type of reporting of bonds practiced, which is applicable to the bonds traded on the American Stock Exchange and other regional exchanges as well. Figure 7–3 again uses the trading day of Au-

Figure 7–3

NEW YORK STOCK EXCHANGE BOND TRANSACTIONS

Monday, August 23, 1971

Volume: $21,680,000 (All Issues)

| 1971 | | | Sales in | | | | Net |
High	Low	Bonds	$1,000s	High	Low	Close	Change
111¾	106	Am T&T 8¾ 2000 xw	381	108⅜	107¾	108⅛	...
109½	97⅞	Chrysler Cp 8⅞s 95	38	103½	103	103½	...
97⅜	97⅜	Firestone 2⅝s 72	5	97½	97½	97½	+⅛
71⅞	69⅛	Inland Stl 3½s 81	5	70½	70½	70½	−½
...	...	Jamaica fn 6¾s 81	2	80⅛	80⅛	80⅛	...
108⅝	95	Pillsbury cv 4¾s 89	5	102½	102½	102½	...
15⅝	11	vj NY Centr 5s 2013 f	7	12¾	12¼	12¼	+¾
152	122½	Xerox cv 6s 95	73	147	145½	145½	−½

gust 23, 1971, as reported in the *Wall Street Journal* of August 24, 1971, from which a sample of eight bonds was taken.

The most important difference to remember vis-à-vis stock quotations is the fact that bond quotations are made in percentages of par value, and are expressed in fractions no smaller than one eighth of a percent. For example, the American Telephone and Telegraph 8¾ percent bonds ranged from a high of $1,117.50 to a low of $1,060 for each $1,000 of par value during 1971. We note that sales are given in thousands of dollars, since $1,000 is the most common denomination of a single bond. The format of transaction quotations is precisely the same as in the case of stocks, with high, low, close, and net change listed as before.

The symbols with the individual bonds parallel those discussed earlier. For example, *xw* with American Telephone and Telegraph stands for a bond trading ex-warrant (the bond had been issued with detachable warrants for common stock of American Telephone and Telegraph Company). The symbol *vj* with the New York Central issue indicates the state of bankruptcy of the merged Penn Central railroad and the symbol *f* indicates that the bonds are dealt in "flat," that is, are traded without the payment of current interest due. The symbol *cv* with the Pillsbury and Xerox bonds signals convertibility into common, while the *fn* with the Jamaica issue denotes a foreign bond. We should observe that these two convertible bonds are trading at fairly low yields and high prices relative to the coupon interest rate paid. This is an indication of the boosting effect of convertibility when the value of the shares of common for which they can be traded reaches and exceeds the par value of the bond. Many more symbols are encountered in bond transactions, and all of these are satisfactorily explained at the bottom of the financial pages where they occur.

A slightly different method is used for listing the current quotations for governmental agency bonds and miscellaneous securities which are traded over-the-counter. Again we have taken a selective listing from the *Wall Street Journal* for the trading day of Monday, August 23, 1971, and provided in Figure 7–4 are samples of United States Treasury bonds, United States Treasury notes, Federal Home Loan Bank bonds, World Bank bonds, and some tax-exempt bonds, which are generally issued by municipalities in special tax districts.

As was the case with over-the-counter transactions for stocks,

Figure 7–4

GOVERNMENT, AGENCY, AND
MISCELLANEOUS SECURITIES QUOTATIONS
Monday, August 23, 1971
(over-the-counter)

	Bid	Asked	Bid Change	Yield
Treasury bonds:				
3⅞s, 1971 Nov.	99.25	99.29	−.1	4.24
7s, 1981 Aug.	103.18	104.20	−.24	6.44
4⅛s, 1989–94 May	75.24	76.24	−.22	6.01
3½s, 1998 Nov.	74.24	75.24	−.26	5.17

U.S. Treasury notes:					
Rate	*Mat*				
1½	10–71	99.10	99.18	. . .	5.82
8	2–77	107.20	107.18	. . .	6.35

Federal Home Loan Bank:					
Rate	*Mat*				
7¾	2–80	104.0	105.0	. . .	6.95

World Bank bonds:					
Rate	*Mat*				
6½	1994	88.0	89.0	. . .	7.52

Tax-exempt bonds:						
Agency	*Coupon*	*Mat*				
Chesapeake B Br&Tun *f*	5¾s	'00	37	40	. . .	
Dallas-FtWorth Airpt	6¾s	'00	99	101	. . .	
Ohio Turnpike	3¼s	'92	92½	94½	−½	

we find a format of bid and asked quotations, which stand for
representative bid and asked prices on the trading day and do
not denote specific transactions. An important difference is the
custom of quoting prices in percentage of par value and fractions of a percent in 32d's of a point. Thus a quote of 99.25 refers to a price of 99$^{25}\!/_{32}$ percent, or $997.81 per $1,000 of par.
Added to the picture in the final column is the yield to maturity,
calculated on the basis of the bid value. As expected, we note
somewhat higher yields for longer maturities and lower yields
for bonds maturing in the short term. For example, 4⅛ percent
Treasury bonds due in May 1994 would currently yield the
prospective purchaser 6.01 percent if he acquired them at the
bid of 75$^{24}\!/_{32}$ or $757.50. The government has the option to re-

deem these bonds any time between May 1989 and May 1994. U.S. Government securities will be affected by the general outlook for interest rates even more than corporate bonds, since the likelihood of default is extremely remote and the purchaser is normally looking for a safe investment with an assured long-term or short-term yield. Quotations for these issues found in the financial pages will again be clarified by a number of symbols, all of which are explained where listed.

It is worth noting that the Chesapeake Bay Bridge and Tunnel bonds carrying a 5¾ percent coupon rate are currently traded "flat," at depressed bid and asked prices of $370 and $400 respectively. The symbol *f* thus denotes the financial difficulties of that particular agency, which has not been able to meet past interest payments.

As we found in the case of the stock market, bond market quotations are supported by a variety of volume reports, bond averages, summaries of advancing and declining issues, highs and lows for the year, and so on. Again, these provide the investor with a general feel for the daily movements of the bond markets. The most commonly used averages are the Dow Jones bond averages (40 bonds: 10 higher grade rails, 10 second-grade rails, 10 public utilities, and 10 industrials). Bond averages are calculated in percentages of par, as were the quotations themselves. On Monday, August 23, 1971, the New York Stock exchange bond volume was $21,680,000 for all issues, with the 40-bond average rising slightly to 70.61 (up 0.02), with 668 issues traded, of which 281 staged advances, 186 declined, and 201 remained unchanged. New highs for the year were achieved by 14 issues, and new lows by 7 issues.

Other Financial Data

Most papers carry, in one form or another, leading business and economic indicators—such as indices of industrial production, freight car loadings, price indices, car output, steel production—both in terms of feature stories and at times in tabular form. When supplemented by individual corporate earnings reports, dividend declarations, news about corporate management, analysis and announcement of new financing, and industry analysis, this information can help develop a broad background for the analyst.

Among the more specialized data obtained in the financial pages are transactions in the *commodity markets.* Commodities include a great variety of basic raw materials, such as cotton, lumber, copper, rubber; and foods, such as coffee, corn, and wheat. The best-known exchange for commodity trading is the Chicago Board of Trade, while more specialized exchanges include the New York Cotton Exchange or international exchanges such as the London Metal Exchange. Commodity trading takes place both on a "spot" (cash) basis for current delivery and on a "futures" basis, for delivery at some specified later date. This market is far too varied to describe here the many bases on which trades are made and quoted, since each commodity has its own particular trading format, such as cents per pound or dollars per bushel. The pattern of information provided usually involves opening and closing transactions, as well as highs and lows for the trading day and the season. Changes from the previous trading day are often listed as well. A variety of indices are available, such as the Dow-Jones Spot Index, the Dow-Jones Futures Index, or the Reuter's United Kingdom Index. A company whose operations depend to a large extent on raw materials traded in a spot or futures market can be severely influenced by the fluctuations of these prices. The use of hedging under these circumstances is common practice, and the organized markets for commodity trading allow one to achieve a form of price insurance by buying and selling at the same time with different delivery dates. References are provided at the end of the chapter for more detail on these aspects.

Foreign Exchange

Key aspects are quoted in most newspapers by a listing of the major currencies of the world in equivalents of U.S. dollars. Normally, the quotations represent selling prices for bank transfers in the United States for payment abroad, and quotations are given for the current trading day as well as the previous day. Also, prices for foreign bank notes are often quoted in equivalents of U.S. dollars, both on a buying and selling basis.

PERIODIC FINANCIAL INFORMATION

Apart from the financial data contained in the daily newspapers, a wealth of information is provided by the various periodicals published in the fields of finance, economics, and business. Furthermore, there are readily available reference works which contain periodic listings and analyses of financial information oriented toward the investor and financial analyst. The advent of the computer has made possible the rapid collection and analysis of periodic company and economic data, and collective information is now attainable very quickly after the normal closing dates for company, industry, and government financial and statistical reports and series. We shall now discuss briefly the most important sources of periodic financial and business information.

Magazines

Major Weekly Periodicals. For a general business coverage, *Business Week* remains one of the most useful and widely read publications, which covers the current developments of interest in business and economics, both national and international. It contains analyses of major events as well as reports on individual companies, the stock markets, labor, business education, etc., and a selective listing of economic indicators as well as a special index of business activity. For a more detailed coverage of stock quotations, security offerings, banking developments, financial, industrial, and commodity trends, the *Commercial and Financial Chronicle* is the most comprehensive source available. The *Wall Street Transcript* contains a great variety of security analyses of individual companies, both on a financial and economic basis and on the technical basis of stock market charts. It further contains major corporate presentations to security analysts about past performance and future plans, and round-table discussions on industry groups by security analysts. *Barron's* covers business trends by individual companies as well as major industries, and provides a great deal of information about corporate securities. The section "The Stock Market at a Glance" is a very useful and detailed picture of the securities markets. *Forbes,* a semimonthly magazine, takes the investor's viewpoint in very detailed and searching analyses of individual companies and their managements. The annual January issue reviewing the performance of major U.S. industries is an excellent documentation of industry trends and provides a ranking of companies by a series of criteria. For an international outlook, the English magazine *The Economist* surveys international and United Kingdom developments in politics, economics, and business.

Major Monthly Periodicals. Economic and business trends are covered in considerable detail by the publications of major commercial banks, such as the *National City Bank Monthly Letter* and the *New England Letter* of the First National Bank of Boston. The various Federal Reserve banks issue bulletins and regional bulletins which contain regional economic data of interest. *Fortune* magazine comments on national economic trends and sketches profiles of major U.S. and international executives, in addition to detailed research articles on industry, company, or socioeconomic topics. The *Harvard Business Review* is a highly regarded forum for management concepts and tools, including financial insights, presented by practitioners and academicians to an extensive worldwide readership of business executives. *Dun's Review* presents trade indices, failure data, and key financial ratios in addition to articles about industry and commerce. *Nation's Business,* a publication of the United States Chamber of Commerce, presents articles on general business subjects. Statistical information of great depth is provided by the *Federal Reserve Bulletin,* which contains statistical data on business and government finances, both domestic and international, and by the *Survey of Current Business,* which covers business statistics in detail. Detailed stock exchange quotations and data about many unlisted securities, foreign exchange, and money rates are contained in the *Bank and Quotation Record.* The *Journal of Finance,* a quarterly publication, presents articles on finance, investments, economics, money and credit, and international aspects of these topics.

Other Periodicals. Many specialized periodicals are published by trade associations and banking, commercial, and trading groups too numerous to mention individually. Also useful are the great variety of United States government surveys and publications, statistical papers by the United Nations and its major agencies, and the various analyses and reviews in journals of the academic community. At the end of this chapter we have provided references to several books on business information sources where the interested reader can obtain detailed guidelines for and descriptions of the type of information available.

Shown below is a brief selection of major periodicals which deal directly with, or relate to, the area of corporate finance. Some of these are specialized and oriented towards a specific community of interest, such as banking, consumer finance, or financial analysts. Others deal with financial conditions in foreign countries or the securities markets within the United States. This listing is provided only as a sample to provide some additional guidelines to the reader, and the titles are largely self-explanatory:

Banking
Credit and Financial Management
Journal of Commerce
Corporate Financing
Finance
Financial Analysts Journal
Financial Executive
Financial World
Investment Dealers Digest
National Tax Journal
World Financial Markets

Financial Manuals and Services

The most popular and best-known set of manuals and services is provided by Moody's, with Standard and Poor's a close second. Moody's manuals appear in five volumes: *Industrials; Banks, Insurance, Real Estate and Investment Funds; Public Utilities; Railroads;* and *Government and Municipals.* These annual manuals contain up-to-date key historical data, financial statements, security price ranges, and dividend records of a very large number of companies, including practically all of the publicly held corporations. Helpful summary statistics and industry data are found in the centers of the manuals, the "blue sections." Moody's manuals are updated through semiweekly supplements, with detailed cross-references.

Moody's publishes a *Quarterly Handbook* in which major publicly held corporations are listed, giving one-page summaries of key financial and operating data. Furthermore, weekly stock and bond surveys are published which analyze market and industry conditions. Moody's also provides the semiweekly *Dividend Record,* and a semimonthly *Bond Record* which contains current prices, earnings, and ratings of most important bonds traded in the country.

Standard and Poor's publications include the *Standard Corporation Records,* loose-leaf financial information about a large number of companies, which is updated through daily supplements. A very useful publication is the *Analysts Handbook,* industry surveys which are compilations of key financial data on individual companies and some industries. Other services by Standard and Poor's include weekly forecasts of the security markets, securities statistics, several information services on the bond market, and a monthly earnings and stock rating guide.

Other financial services similar to Moody's and Standard and Poor's are provided by *Fitch's Corporation Manuals,* and by more specialized manuals such as *Walker's Manual* of Pacific Coast securities. An almost overwhelming flow of information, judgments, and analyses of individual companies from an investor's standpoint is provided by the major brokerage houses and their research departments. Furthermore, services available to individuals on a subscription basis provide up-to-date financial analyses of individual companies and their securities. The most important among these services are *The Value Line, United Business Service, Babson's,* and the new *Investor's Management Sciences.* The Value Line investment survey particularly provides ratings and reports on companies, with selections and opinions for the investor; while Investor's Management Sciences concentrates on providing a great deal of standardized statistical information as the basis on which analytical judgments can be formed.

BACKGROUND COMPANY AND BUSINESS INFORMATION

Annual Reports. The most commonly used reference source about the current affairs of publicly held corporations is the annual report furnished to stockholders. The formats used by individual corporations vary widely: from detailed coverage of facilities, products, and services, and detailed financial and operating statistics, and even discussion of current corporate, industry, and national issues, on the one hand, to a bare minimum disclosure of financial results on the other. Nevertheless, the annual report is generally an important direct source of financial information. Since the disclosure requirements of the Securities and Exchange Commission, the recommendations of the accounting profession, and state laws have become more and more demanding over time, the analyst can usually count on a fairly consistent set of data for analysis in annual reports.

Government Data. More specific details about company operations can often be found in the annual statements which corporations must file with the Securities and Exchange Commission in Washington, D.C., on the so-called Form 10K, which is available upon request for public inspection. Furthermore, when a corporation issues new securities in significant amounts or alters its capital structure in a major way, the detailed proposal required by the SEC, the *prospectus,* is generally a more detailed source of company background data than the normal annual report. It will cover the history of the company, the ownership patterns, directors and top management, financial and operating data, products, facilities, and information regarding the intended use of the new funds.

If a company is closely held, or too small to be listed in the key financial services, information about its financial operations can often be obtained at the corporation records departments of those state governments which require the filing of financial statements from companies doing business in the state. Again, these reports are open to the public for inspection.

Trade Associations.   Trade associations are a prime source of information about their respective industries. A great deal of statistical information is made available in annual and even more frequent form, covering products, services, finances, and performance criteria applicable to the industry or trade group. Often the financial and performance data are grouped by types and sizes of firms, to make overall statistics on the industry somewhat more comparable to the affairs of a particular operation. Trade associations include such organizations as the American Iron and Steel Institute, the American Paper Institute, and the National Lumber Manufacturers Association, to name but a few. Sources for listings and addresses of these associations and their publications can be found in the references at the end of the chapter.

Econometric Services.   A relatively recent development of interest to the financial analyst is the increasing acceptance and usefulness of the so-called econometric models, which have been built by a variety of academic institutions and economic advisory services. These computerized models of the U.S. economy, and more recently of economies of other countries as well, can provide valuable clues regarding the likely movement of the country's economy within which financial conditions must be viewed. Among the developers of such models whose forecasts are widely quoted and used, are the Wharton School at the University of Pennsylvania, Data Resources Inc., and Chase Econometric Associates. Many corporations subscribe to these forecasting services and make use of the projections in their operational and financial planning. Increasingly, corporate and academic economists are testing their own assumptions about economic trends with the help of these models.

While the discussion in this chapter merely touches upon the major sources of specific or general information on financial business affairs, the reader is encouraged to make use of these hints as well as the references provided at the end of this chapter. He should not overlook the availability of a great variety of business libraries in corporations, colleges, and universities, and cities and counties. The problem facing today's student, analyst, or financial manager is not a lack of data; rather, he is faced with the problem of selection from among the many sources to find what is truly relevant for his analytical need. This selective chapter has provided a start in this direction for the interested reader.

SELECTED REFERENCES

Background Information

ALLEN, DAVID E. JR. *A Reader's Library of Management; Guide and Checklist*. Stanford, Calif.: International Center for the Advancement of Management Education, Graduate School of Business, Stanford University, 1969.

COMAN, EDWIN T. JR. *Sources of Business Information*. Rev. ed.; Berkeley: University of California Press, 1964.

DONALDSON, GORDON, and STUBBS, CAROLYN. *Corporate and Business Finance, A Classified Bibliography of Recent Literature*. Boston, Mass.: Baker Library, Harvard Graduate School of Business Administration, 1964.

GRAHAM, BENJAMIN; DODD, DAVID L.; and COTTLE, SIDNEY. *Security Analysis, Principles and Techniques*, Part I. 4th ed.; New York: McGraw-Hill Book Co., 1962.

MANLEY, MARIAN C. *Business Information, How to Find and Use It*. New York: Harper & Bros., 1955.

RUDER, WILLIAM, and NATHAN, RAYMOND. *The Businessman's Guide to Washington*. Englewood Cliffs, N.J.: Prentice-Hall, Inc., 1964.

SPECIAL LIBRARIES ASSOCIATION. *Directory of Business and Financial Services*. New York, 1963.

WASSERMAN, PAUL (ed.). *Encyclopedia of Business Information Sources.* Detroit: Gale Research Co., 1970.

Financial Markets and Institutions

EITEMAN, WILFORD J.; DICE, CHARLES A.; and EITEMAN, DAVID K. *The Stock Market.* 4th ed.; New York: McGraw-Hill Book Co., 1966.

FARWELL, LORING C. (ed.); GANE, FRANK H.; JACOBS, DONALD P.; JONES, SIDNEY L.; and ROBINSON, ROLAND I. *Financial Institutions.* 4th ed.; Homewood, Ill.: Richard D. Irwin, Inc., 1966.

FRIEND, I.; HOFFMAN, C. W.: and WINN, W. J. *The Over-the-Counter Securities Markets.* New York: McGraw-Hill Book Co., 1958.

LEFFLER, GEORGE L. *The Stock Market.* 3d ed. (rev. by Loring C. Farwell); New York: Ronald Press Co., 1963.

LOLL, LEO M. JR.; and BUCKLEY, JULIAN G. *The Over-the-Counter Security Markets, A Review Guide.* 2d ed.; Englewood Cliffs, N.J.: Prentice-Hall, Inc., 1967.

LUDTKE, JAMES B. *The American Financial System.* Boston: Allyn & Bacon, Inc., 1967.

ROBBINS, SIDNEY. *The Securities Markets, Operations and Issues.* New York: The Free Press, 1966.

Readings in Finance

FRIEDLAND, SEYMOUR. *The Economics of Corporate Finance.* Englewood Cliffs, N.J.: Prentice-Hall, Inc., 1966.

GORDON, MYRON J. *The Investment, Financing, and Valuation of the Corporation.* Homewood, Ill.: Richard D. Irwin, Inc., 1962.

VANCIL, RICHARD F. (ed.). *Financial Executive's Handbook.* Homewood, Ill.: Dow Jones-Irwin, Inc., 1970.

VAN HORNE, JAMES C. (ed.). *Foundations For Financial Management.* Homewood, Ill.: Richard D. Irwin, Inc., 1966.

Special Topics

MERRILL, LYNCH, PIERCE, FENNER, AND SMITH, INC. "How to Hedge Commodities"; also, "How to Buy and Sell Commodities." Rev. ed., 1958.

STANDARD AND POOR. Method of computation of stock price indices shown in "Security Price Index Record." Orange, N.J., 1962 edition.

THE WALL STREET JOURNAL. "Basis of Calculation of Dow-Jones Averages." New York, 1960.

INDEX

239